"Unfailingly interesting.... Candid, unpretentious, searching."

Publishers Weekly

"A book of uncommon lucidity on a subject of importance to a great many people, physicians and patients alike."

New York Times Book Review

"Between the subject and author, it can't miss."

Kirkus

"Clear, dispassionate, well-balanced, and scientific approach."

National Observer

"He writes with a great sympathy for the healers as well as compassion for their victims.... *HEALING* must be urged on everyone who has a family member or friend who will not have an operation or who is about to turn to faith healers."

Boston Sunday Herald Advertiser

"With a surgeon's keen perception, Dr. Nolen has written an engrossing book."

Jackson Daily Sun

WILLIAM A. NOLEN, M.D.

HEALING

A DOCTOR IN SEARCH OF A MIRACLE

FAWCETT CREST • NEW YORK

Author's Note

I have changed the names and identifying
characteristics of all the patients
and most of the other people in this book.

To my mother
with love

CONTENTS

I

THE SEARCH BEGINS

1

I don't want to die. Ever. As a minister friend of mine says, "Heaven is my home, but I'm not homesick."

As far as I've been able to determine, after twenty years as a surgeon, no one else wants to die either. I've had patients with strokes so severe they can't speak or eat. Saliva drools in a steady stream out of the corners of their mouths. They urinate and defecate in bed if I don't insert catheters in their bladders and order enemas for them every other day. I can't see why in the world they want to go on living. But they do.

And so do the patients with terminal cancer. Watching them grow emaciated and jaundiced, develop bedsores, suffer from increasing pain, I ask myself why they insist on hanging on, why they don't ask me to please put them out of their misery, but they don't. They cling to life until they can't cling any longer. No one—with the obvious exception of those who commit suicide—seeks death. (It's also true, in my experience, that the great majority of those who fail at a suicide attempt are, later, very happy that their attempt failed. For most people the desire to end their life is a very fleeting one.)

Some patients, admittedly, lose that impossible-to-define but very real spirit we call "the will to live." These patients, usually very sick, elderly people, don't actually seek death, but they refuse to cooperate in the fight to save their lives. They won't eat, won't move about, won't take medicine, unless they are forced to do so. Sometimes, if we give them intravenous feedings, lift them into chairs and inject them full of antibiotics, they will improve despite themselves; and when they're feeling better, the will to live returns. Often, however, without their cooperation we fight a losing battle and they die.

Every doctor dreads the patient who quits. They are difficult patients to help.

It's my job as a surgeon to keep people alive and well as long as I can. It's a gratifying profession. I open up someone who has a perforated ulcer, close the hole in the stomach and he's well. Or I take a torn spleen out of a little boy who is dying from hemorrhage and save his life. Or I remove from a seventy-year-old woman a piece of bowel with cancer in it, and cured, she lives another ten years, happy and healthy. The patients I cure, and their families, are very grateful and I get a great sense of accomplishment from my work.

But sometimes I'm not so lucky. The man with the perforated ulcer has extensive peritonitis and dies on the operating table. The boy with the ruptured spleen never comes out of shock. When I open the abdomen of the patient with cancer I find that the tumor has already spread to the liver or wrapped itself around essential blood vessels and I can't get it out. Then people or their families aren't so happy. They're despondent.

There are two sides to a surgeon's life.

Sometimes—often—a doctor has to decide when to quit. If his patient's cancer has spread all over his body and the man is lying in a hospital bed dying by inches, almost invariably there comes a time when the doctor must decide whether to try to keep the patient going or let him die. Assume this dying man develops pneumonia—should I give him penicillin and keep him alive an extra two or three days? What if he stops eating; should I feed him intravenously so he can lie in bed and suffer another week? Most of the time when the situation is obviously hopeless, doctors

4

don't take steps to prolong life; they don't do anything to hasten death but they do let the patient die with dignity.

In cases of extensive cancer or total brain damage, it's relatively easy to decide when to quit. Often members of the family will even make the suggestion. "Don't do anything special to keep him alive, Dr. Nolen," they'll say. "he's suffered enough." (You don't have to have an M.D. degree to spot the dying patient.)

Conflicts don't arise—decisions aren't too difficult to make—in these obviously terminal patients. It's when the fatal nature of the disease isn't apparent that we doctors have trouble persuading patients, and their families, that the situation is hopeless.

Take, for example, the case of Harold Dendroth. Harold was thirty-eight years old when he came to see me. "I'm not really sick, Doc," he said, "it's just that an odd thing happened this morning. When I went to the bathroom my urine was a funny red color. Thought I'd better have you check it out."

I did. There was blood in the urine. Subsequent X-rays showed that Harold had a malignant tumor of the kidney that had already spread to both lungs—beyond the help of surgery, drugs, X-ray treatment or anything else a doctor could offer him.

Harold had six children ranging in age from two to fourteen. His law practice had just started to boom, and he and his wife, Mary, had all sorts of exciting plans for the future. Can you imagine what it was like for me to tell Harold—a man who didn't have a single pain in his body, who felt just wonderful—that he was doomed? It was one hell of an hour for me, and a far, far worse one for him. That kind of news is difficult to accept.

And yet things like this happen in the medical world every day. Men, women and children come in with what they think are minor complaints and we doctors have to tell them there is nothing we can do. "That headache of yours . . . I'm sorry, Mrs. Stevens, but it's a brain tumor—a kind we can't cure"; "That little wart I took off your back, Mr. Herbert, is malignant. And tests show that it's already in your liver. I'm sorry. There's nothing more we can do"; "That hard lump you noticed in little Sheila's abdomen, Mrs. Reilly . . . I hate to tell you this, but it's a cancer. We can't get it out." Dear God, what heartbreak!

It isn't just the death sentences that are hell for us to pass and for patients to accept; there are other tragedies which some might consider worse than death.

"Mr. Rossen, when Mike fell out of that tree he snapped the spinal cord right in half. He'll never be able to move any muscle below his neck again. It's a rotten shame—sixteen years old and such a fine athlete."

"I hate to tell you this, Mrs. Fisher, but we've finally decided that the trouble you've been having with your vision is due to multiple sclerosis. There's not very much we can do for you. I'm sorry."

"It's sad, Mr. Brown, but your wife's heart disease is beyond surgical help. I don't know how long she has left, but I'm afraid she'll be confined to her bed from now on."

These aren't death sentences, but in some ways they're worse.

There's still another group of patients—a very large group—which makes us doctors throw up our hands in despair: patients with chronic problems for which there are, as yet, no cures. We can offer them help, comfort, sometimes improvement, but we can't restore them to perfect health. The list of diseases that falls into this category is a long one; it includes, among other things, diabetes, arthritis, asthma, angina pectoris, epilepsy and a wide variety of psychiatric disorders. The longer a doctor practices medicine, the more aware he becomes of the limitations of his profession. It's gratifying to find the occasional problem, like pneumonia or appendicitis, which you can actually cure. It reminds you that at least you're not completely impotent.

How do patients respond when the doctor tells them that

6

there is little or nothing he can do for them? Most of them, like Harold Dendroth with his kidney tumor, are stunned, of course, but eventually accept what the doctor tells them is inevitable. Harold got his affairs in order as best he could and tried to enjoy life with Mary and his six children for the time he had left. He died—unfortunately a slow, lingering death—eleven months after he first walked into my office complaining of bloody urine.

Mike Rossen is in a wheelchair now, and has been for three years. He's a fine boy—never complains—but I damn near cry every time I see him.

Mrs. Fisher is doing reasonably well. Multiple sclerosis is a cyclic disease (symptoms come and go) and at the moment, except for the fact that she drags one foot when she walks, there's not much evidence of the disease. Next year, who knows?)

Some patients, however, won't accept the diagnoses we doctors lay on them. Like the rest of us they don't want to die and they refuse to believe that nothing can be done for them. If the medical profession can't help them, then somewhere, somehow, they'll find someone who will. They won't quit.

What kind of patient will refuse to accept a doctor's word that his case is hopeless? Any kind. Poor, rich, stupid, brilliant—men and women from each and every social class go looking for salvation elsewhere when a medical doctor admits he can't help.

I have seen this kind of odyssey many times. Not long after I went into private practice I was called to the hospital one afternoon to see a twenty-eight-year-old man, Ray Stark, who had been involved in a tractor accident. He had gotten off the tractor to clean some brush from the undercarriage. As he leaned under the tractor the man who was working with him, not realizing where Ray was, backed up. The rear wheels went across the middle of Ray's back.

When I saw Ray at the hospital it was obvious that his

spinal cord had been badly damaged. He was paralyzed and insensitive from the waist down. X-rays showed the fractured vertebrae. I called in a neurosurgeon and we operated, but there was nothing we could do. The spinal cord was crushed beyond repair.

Ray, who had worked on a farm all his life, couldn't accept the news. "When are these damn legs of mine going to start working, Doc?" he'd say. "I still can't move them."

I had to tell him that his legs would not get better; the only promise I could hold out for him was that we would soon fix him up with braces and that eventually he'd be able to get around on canes. I didn't put it that bluntly, of course, any more than I broke the news to Harold Dendroth as briefly as I've recorded it here, but that was the message I tried to get across—just as I had tried to deliver it to him a dozen other times.

Ray refused to accept my verdict. He wasn't particularly wealthy but he managed to scrape up enough money to fly to a chiropractic clinic in Denver that advertises cures for all sorts of things the medical profession can't cure. They took all Ray's money but they left him in his wheelchair. I still see him around town once in a while. He still believes that someday he'll find someone who will make him walk.

So the search for cures and perfect health goes on. There's a long list of those who profess the ability to do for patients the things we doctors can't do, and patients flock to them. It's sad but understandable.

How do members of the medical profession react to these "healers"? I guess I'd better answer this for myself—not presuming to be a spokesman, though I think my attitude is probably typical. All through my professional life I have reacted negatively. It's as if someone throws a switch at the moment the dean hands you an M.D. degree, and branded onto your subconscious mind is the admonition, "Now you, as a member of the medical profession, know all that there is to know of the healing arts. Outside your profession, no one knows anything. Never forget this!" We don't.

It wasn't until 1971, after eleven years of surgical practice, that my faith in the monopolistic position the medical profession takes toward medical knowledge was shaken. It happened when James Reston of the *New York Times* reported on his experience with acupuncture in China. Reston's credentials are impeccable; it's possible to disagree with his politics, but certainly it's not reasonably possible to call him a dunce or a fake. He has earned a reputation both as an intelligent man and as a knowledgeable, conscientious reporter. If Reston was convinced that there was something valid in acupuncture, then I had to believe he might be right. If so, why hadn't the medical profession looked into it and adopted whatever was efficacious for our own practices? Acupuncture has, after all, been around for thousands of years. That is ample time for even the most cautious investigator to check it out.

But the medical profession hadn't. All we had done was to disparage the practice as if it were a joke—just a crude, unscientific conglomeration of nonsense. It wasn't until Reston, a layman, spoke up, unafraid of looking ridiculous—Hey, look at what the Chinese doctors are doing! They're on to something here—that we doctors finally had to acknowledge that the practice existed. We reluctantly took the first slow steps to investigate acupuncture. Without saying it in so many words, we finally had to admit that someone outside our Western medical profession might know something about the healing arts. Something we hadn't known.

This, I confess, unnerved me. I got my M.D. in 1953 and I've worked at my profession ever since. I've realized for a long time that doctors aren't perfect, that we're as subject to human frailties as anyone else, but on one score I thought we were invariably right. I sincerely believed we did have a monopoly on the knowledge it took to heal people. I had never questioned this. A few doctors had, and they had eventually been labeled "quacks" by their confreres. A doctor gets onto dangerous ground when he dares to question his own profession.

I also believed that if we doctors didn't know how to cure someone, we could at least be certain that no one else did. I'd often used that presumption to console patients when I told them their cases were hopeless. "I'm sorry, Mrs. Radson," I'd say, "but there's nothing I can do." Then I'd add, "And there's nothing anyone else can do either." I believed it; now it appeared that there was at least a possibility I might sometimes have been wrong. Maybe—sometime, somewhere—I'd had a patient beyond my help, but not beyond the help of a Chinese practitioner or of someone else. I didn't intend to let the "discovery" of acupuncture turn me into a gullible person, but I did resolve that I would no longer have a closed mind.

After acupuncture became a "hot" subject I decided the next time I heard of some practitioner outside of our Western tradition I'd listen, look and evaluate before I condemned, as I was still certain I eventually would. I'd try, hopefully, to at least open my mind a crack. It wouldn't be easy—but I'd really try.

2

In November 1972 I went to Detroit to promote my book *A Surgeon's World*. Whenever I met anyone on one of these promotional tours, whether it be a radio interviewer, television talk-show host or newspaper reporter, there was at least a 50-50 chance that before our interview ended, I'd hear something about the medical history of either the interviewer, his family or a friend. There is hardly a person in the world who won't question a doctor on medical matters if the opportunity presents itself.

I understand why this happens. One of the biggest complaints lay people have about doctors is that the doctors don't give them enough time. The doctor tells the patient what disease he has, writes a prescription and ushers him out of the examining room before the patient can blink. He never gets to ask any questions—and he's frustrated.

So I was used to personal inquiries and I didn't mind them. I'd listened to the stories of supposed malpractice victims, women with blood-pressure problems, husbands who wondered if their wives had really needed that hysterectomy. I gave advice whenever I could, but mostly my help consisted of just listening to and reassuring the questioner.

My interviewer on a Sunday morning in Detroit was no exception. After we'd taped a ten-minute question-answer session dealing with the contents of *A Surgeon's World,* he asked me if I'd like a cup of coffee and I said yes. We walked over to a corner of the studio and sat down, and it didn't take him long to get to what was bothering him. "Dr. Nolen," the interviewer—I'll call him Frank—asked, "have you ever heard of psychic surgery?"

"Just vaguely," I replied. "Aren't there some people in the Philippines who are supposed to be able to operate without using instruments?"

"Right. Do you know anything more about them?"

"Not really. I assume they're a bunch of crackpots."

"Are you sure?"

"No," I admitted, "I guess I'm not. Why?"

"Because a friend of mine, a very intelligent guy, recently took his little daughter there for treatment. He's back now and last week I heard him lecture at our church. The story he tells about his experience sounds unbelievable, but he has pictures to back him up. Even without the pictures, this fellow—his name is Manny Hofman—is obviously sold on the whole thing and he's very convincing. He believes these psychic surgeons can cure people that you doctors can't help. I mentioned the story to my doctor and he just made fun of it. But I really think it's something some M.D. ought to look into. If you're at all interested, I can put you in touch with Manny. I'm sure he'd be willing to talk to you."

My immediate reaction was to tell Frank to forget it, that this was obviously another hoax, that it would be a waste of my time to investigate it. Then I thought, "What the hell, suppose it *is* a farce—so what? I sounds interesting, and if I'm ever going to start having an open mind, why not now?" So instead of putting Frank off, I said, "I'm going to be pretty busy for the next couple of months, but after that—yes, damn it, give me your friend's number if you will. It won't do me any harm to talk to him."

The conversation drifted onto other matters while we finished our coffee. Then I went off to the West Coast on my promotional tour.

It wasn't until three months later, in February of 1973, that I got around to calling Manny Hofman. After talking to him for ten minutes over the phone, I decided his story was worth a return trip to Detroit. In March I flew there for a meeting with Manny.

He's a very convincing man. Now, before I begin to relate his story, let me reassure you about Manny. He is not a kook. When we met he was wearing a dark business suit, a blue shirt and a tie. He was dressed conservatively and he looked as if he belonged in his conservative clothes. He and his father-in-law run a $30 million construction business. He is a responsible, intelligent man.

Manny doesn't smoke marijuana, doesn't drop acid, doesn't take drugs of any kind. In the three hours we spent together he drank half of one Scotch highball. It is obvious to me as a physician, or as obvious as it could be, that Manny has never been strung out on drugs. He is—and I hope this won't offend him—almost classifiable as a square.

Manny is Jewish. "I didn't work hard at it," he told me, "but we went to the synagogue with our kids on the holy days. I suppose I've always believed there was probably some sort of guiding force outside our human world, but I never worried too much about it. I was busy with other things." Manny "believed," in other words, about the way most of us "believe," vaguely and without much dedication. The reason for making a point of Manny's religious views will be apparent later.

After we had introduced ourselves I fixed us both a drink and Manny went right to his story.

"My wife, Helen, and I have been married nine years. We've got two little girls—Charlotte, almost six, and May, four. We spoil them rotten I suppose, and so does Helen's father. He and I are in business together. Our kids have always been perfectly healthy—Helen took them for yearly check-ups and all that—until March of 1972. Then, suddenly—I remember it was on a Saturday afternoon because we'd gone to the synagogue that morning—I noticed that Charlotte, who was four and a half at the time, had a weakness at the corner of her mouth; it sort of sagged.

13

I figured it was a nervous tic and when Helen saw it she agreed, so we decided to ignore it. But over the weekend it become more pronounced and on Monday morning I suggested that Helen take Charlotte to our pediatrician. We knew him personally, so even though we didn't think or say that it was an emergency, Helen was able to get an appointment for that afternoon.

"Dr. Saul is, I think, a very good pediatrician. He teaches at the medical school and practices at the best hospitals in the city. Much to our surprise, after he'd examined Charlotte he told Helen he'd like to put her in the hospital. 'Probably nothing to get alarmed about,' he said, 'but I'd like Dr. Lawrence, the chief of neurosurgery at Children's Memorial, to take a look at her. I'm not quite sure what's going on.'

"Well, to summarize very briefly what seemed like an endless, hellish period in our lives, over the next four days Charlotte became almost completely paralyzed on her right side. She could hardly move her arm or leg and her speech became very slurred. She kept losing her balance when she tried to walk and the corner of her mouth continued to sag. The doctors at Children's Memorial did all sorts of blood and X-rays studies and then told us she had a brain tumor; and because she was going bad so quickly, they felt they had to operate at once. We were devastated, but of course we agreed.

"On Monday, less than a week after we'd brought her to the hospital, Dr. Lawrence operated on Charlotte. It took about two hours and we could tell from the way he looked at us afterward that the news was bad. 'I'm sorry. It's a glioma—a tumor. If it were located in some other part of the brain I could take it out, but in Charlotte's case it's inoperable by virture of its location; I didn't even dare to biopsy it. It's in the brain stem—the lower part of the brain just above the spinal cord. We can't take out brain-stem tumors. They're too close to the vital centers, the parts of the brain that control breathing and circulation. We'd kill

Charlotte if we removed her tumor. We can give her X-ray treatment, though, and it will help for a while, but I'm afraid I can't promise you a cure. Charlotte may live two, three or even four years, but that's all I can promise. Unless, of course, some new treatment is discovered; we can hope for that.'

"How we got through the next six weeks I'll never know. I moved into a hotel near the hospital so I could be near Charlotte. One of us was with her all the time. The radiation made her sick to her stomach, and she lot the little hair they hadn't shaved off. She looked awful, but gradually the X-rays began to have some effect. At the end of the six weeks she could walk, though she stumbled a little.

"All our friends were very kind. They knew the sort of hell we were going through. There's so little you can say to console anyone in a situation like ours. We just had to resign ourselves to the inevitable and decide how to live with Charlotte for the time she had left."

Then one day, shortly after Charlotte had left the hospital, Manny got a call from a friend, Louis Stein, who had something remarkable to tell him. Lou's wife, Marsha, had had such a severe heart condition that she was confined to a wheelchair most of the time; at the least exertion she would gasp for air. In desperation, toward the end of 1971 Lou took her to the Philippines for treatment by the psychic surgeons, with such an astonishing result that Lou insisted that Manny come over that night to see for himself; as further proof, Lou had movies he had taken of the psychic surgeons at work.

That evening Manny got his first shock when he saw Marsha—the former invalid looked great and she even told him that she had taken up golf again. The movies were even more amazing: a surgeon operating on patients with bare hands, taking out whatever was diseased, and then, the wound healing over without leaving a scar.

"I was impressed, and as you can imagine, hopeful," Manny went on, "but I knew that I was a prime candidate

15

for a sucker trap, I was so worried about Charlotte, and I decided to look into the matter more thoroughly before I packed up and took my daughter on a ten-thousand-mile trip. First I called Dr. Saul, our pediatrician; to say he was skeptical would be an understatement, but I give him credit—he said he'd look into it. The next day he called me back and said, 'Manny, forget it. I checked with the A.M.A. and they told me it's a bunch of nonsense. They're sending me some literature.' This news discouraged me but didn't put me off completely. I figured the American Medical Association might not be completely open-minded on a matter like this one.

"I asked Lou if he knew anyone else who had been to the Philippines and he put me in touch with a woman, Laura Wise. Her story was as amazing as Marsha's. Laura is a beautiful woman, a socialite, in her mid-thirties. 'A year ago I started having trouble with my left eye,' she told me. 'My vision was blurred. It got so bad that I had to keep my left eye shut when I was reading. I went to not one but three different ophthalmologists. They all told me the same thing: I had a tumor in the back of my eye, and the eye would have to come out.

"'Maybe it was vanity, I don't know, but I couldn't accept the idea of losing my eye. I heard about these Philippine doctors and went to them. They operated on me, left my eye in, and now my vision is fine. I've been back to see one of the ophthalmologists here who had told me I had to lose my eye. He examined the eye and admitted the tumor was gone. "It was a one-in-five-million thing," he said. "You had a regressive tumor." He refuses to give the Philippine surgeon any credit, but I do. He cured me.'

"I was impressed with Laura's story. She seemed to be an intelligent, reasonable, not at all hysterical person. But the A.M.A.'s repudiation of the Philippine group still gave me reservations. Maybe because Laura, Lou and Marsha were laymen, they could be duped when a doctor couldn't.

"Then, two days after I'd talked to Laura, Dr. Saul called

16

me back. 'Manny,' he said, 'I got that literature from the A.M.A. I'm sorry to say it isn't authoritative at all—just a bunch of hearsay refutations printed in newspapers around the country. Apparently the A.M.A. has never looked into this group. I still can't buy it, but I have to admit I haven't got any real evidence that they're fakes.'

"I was elated. I wasn't completely sold yet, but both my father-in-law and I agreed it was time we looked into it ourselves. I couldn't get away just then, so he decided to make the trip. About two weeks after Charlotte's radiation treatment ended he flew to the Philippines.

"As soon as he arrived he called Tony Agpaoa, who is the best-known of the psychic surgeons, and was invited out to watch him work. The next day he called me and said, 'Manny, it's for real. This man performs miracles. Bring Charlotte at once.' Two days later we were packed and ready to leave when he called back. 'Forget it,—Tony's not for real. Just before he started operating yesterday I caught him palming a piece of cotton soaked in something red. I'm sure he just squeezed it to make it look like blood.'

"'What about the cures you've seen?' I asked him.

"'I don't know about those, Manny, but I do know this guy palmed the cotton. Forget it.'

"I thought about it for a minute and then told him, 'Real or not, I'm coming. I've got to see for myself. We haven't got anything to lose.'

"The next day Charlotte, Helen and I left for the Philippines."

3

Manny described how one of the psychic surgeons had "operated" on Charlotte's brain four times, removing pieces of the tumor at each operation; another psychic surgeon spent a number of weeks caring for her "spiritual needs." At the time, Manny had great hopes that these Philippine healers would cure his daughter, but I got the impression that his faith in them was wavering now. At any rate, his story provoked my interest to the extent that I felt the psychic surgeons were well worth investigating, and a few weeks later, with the encouragement of my editor, I decided to take time off from my practice, continue my investigation and write a book.

I have to confess that I undertook the assignment with fear and trepidation. I know that by looking into and writing about psychic surgery I ran a serious risk of being labeled a "kook," a label that might destroy my reputation as a legitimate medical writer. I didn't want that to happen.

Nor did I want my career as a surgeon to suffer. The A.M.A. has a policy of discouraging physicians from ever associating in public with members of the "lunatic fringe." They're afraid, I suppose—and it's an understandable fear—that by being seen with a quack a medical doctor lends him, the quack, credibility. I had ignored this ban on one previous occasion—I had gone to Chicago to appear on a television show and argue with a chiropractor, when the host of the show couldn't find a Chicago doctor who would take the assignment—and I had gotten away with it. But I was afraid that this book could bring the wrath of the medical hierarchy down on my head. Since I love my work as a surgeon I didn't want that to happen.

On the other hand, I didn't agree with the A.M.A.'s policy. It seemed to me that ignoring the lunatic fringe, hoping they would just go away, was unrealistic. Remaining silent while quacks went out and sold their ideas, unopposed, just wouldn't work, particularly in the 1970s when patients were, justifiably, demanding more and more information from those of us who were providing health care. I felt that organized medicine's "silent" treatment just wasn't good enough.

I have to back-track just a moment; where I use the words "quack" or "lunatic fringe" to refer to those practitioners outside the medical profession, I'm doing so as a matter of convenience. I know those are harsh labels, but they're the labels which organized medicine uses. I want to emphasize that at this point in my investigation I was making a very sincere effort not to prejudge the merits of the psychic surgeons whom I was about to investigate. If I had already been persuaded they were charlatons, I would never have undertaken the assignment.

One evening when I talked the project over with my wife, Joan, this was one of the things we discussed. Joan felt strongly, from what I had told her of Manny and his experiences, that the psychic surgeons did have "powers," for lack of a better term, about which I should learn more. "I can tell you this," she said, after reading the first five chapters I had written, "if a doctor told me tomorrow that I had a fatal disease and he couldn't help me, I'd be on the next plane to Manila."

"I agree," I said. "It sounds as if there's something to it, but even if there is not, even if these surgeons turn out to be nothing but charlatans, that's important, too. If patients are being misled—if they're running halfway around the world only to be fleeced—then someone ought to say so, loudly and clearly, to spare them all that anguish."

"But I don't *want* them to be fakes," Joan said.

"Neither do I," I admitted. "I'd like to find that psychic surgeons can cure those patients we can't help. But before I can believe, I've got to have more evidence than I have right now. And I'm going to either find that evidence or prove to my satisfaction that it doesn't exist."

"There's one other point," Joan added. "If you discover that these psychic surgeons are fakes, if you write a book and say it, you're still not going to convince everyone. People are going to continue to go looking for miracles."

"I know that," I replied, "but at least I'll have tried."

As we went up to bed I said, "Anyway, let's hope I don't have to try to talk people out of visiting the Philippines. Let's hope I can refer patients to the psychic surgeons for cures I can't offer them, or better still, learn their techniques and use them myself. That would make a much happier ending for the book. And I like happy endings."

As soon as I had decided to go ahead with the book, I had written to the A.M.A. asking for whatever information they had on the psychic surgeons. The last week in March, I got my reply.

The letter was cordial, helpful and depressing. All their information related to Tony Agpaoa, and it was obvious that the A.M.A. considered him to be less than trustworthy. According to the A.M.A. he had separated hundreds of patients from their life savings and had cured no one. At one time he had been indicted in Detroit, Michigan, on wire fraud charges, which somehow related to a trip that 110 persons from the Detroit area made to the Philippines in 1967. Tony had jumped bail in Detroit and returned to the Philippines. It wasn't clear from the A.M.A. letter what he had been doing in Detroit.

The essence of the A.M.A.'s letter lay in these two paragraphs:

In our responses to lay persons who inquire about

Agpaoa, we point out that it is the person's own choice whether they want to undertake a long, expensive trip to the Philippines for "psychic surgery." Our file information demonstrates the fakery connected with it in the instance of Agpaoa, who was a magician before becoming a "psychic surgeon." We think that persons should receive reliable information before making such a journey, and we supply photocopies such as we are sending you.

We also suggest that they may want to check with other sources, such as the American Embassy in the Philippines, before placing their reliance on Tony's "psychic surgery." Our concern, as you are aware, is not only that they will waste money on worthless "psychic surgery," but far more important, that they may delay proper treatment during the time they are relying on such a procedure.

As I say, the letter depressed me. At first glance it seemed like an irrefutable indictment of Tony Agpaoa, but on a second reading it became apparent that no doctor from the A.M.A. had ever made a personal, thorough investigation of Tony Agpaoa. Nor had anyone ever investigated, even superficially, any of the other psychic surgeons; Manny's friends David Oligani and Joe Mercado, the healers who had treated Charlotte, weren't mentioned in either the letter or the news clippings which the A.M.A. enclosed. Organized medicine had assumed—and expected that I would assume—that psychic surgery had to be a farce. But once I refused to make that assumption, then the letter and the clippings from the A.M.A. became, instead of evidence, simply a harangue against Tony Agpaoa and, by association, all other psychic surgeons. A well-motivated harangue (I'm sure that the A.M.A. sincerely meant it when they said: "Our concern . . . is not only that [patients] will waste money on worthless 'psychic surgery,' but . . . that

21

they may delay proper treatment . . ."), but a harangue nonetheless.

After a careful reappraisal of the letter I felt better; there was definitely a need for an investigation of psychic surgery by a qualified, experienced Western surgeon. I knew I had those credentials and I decided I was going to do the job.

I had a speaking engagement in Detroit scheduled for early April so I had written a letter to Manny asking if he could meet me at that time to talk some more about the Philippines. I was tentatively planning to go there in May and needed, among other things, a letter of introduction to David Oligani. I also asked Manny if he could put me in touch with the other Detroit people he knew who had been to psychic surgeons and, hopefully, make arrangements for me to see films of the psychic surgeons at work.

In his reply, Manny mentioned that a book on the psychic surgeons was forthcoming: *The Psychic Surgeons of the Philippines,* by Tom Valentine. The book was scheduled for publication in June 1973, but through my agent I managed to get an advance copy.

Much to my chagrin—since I'd hoped to be "the first one to write on psychic surgery—Tom Valentine's book wasn't bad ("wasn't bad" is high praise, coming from a competing author). Tom had spent several weeks in the Philippines, had talked to a lot of people who had investigated, more or less, Tony Agpaoa, and had personally observed hundreds of "operations." Although he was impressed by what he had seen and convinced that psychic surgery was real, he too had some reservations. While in the Philippines, he had seen some flagrant examples of fakery and in his book he gave almost as much prominence to the fakes as to the triumphs.

A classic example involved a patient who had undergone a hip operation by a surgeon in the United States, presumably to fix a fracture. The woman had several screws and a metal plate in her hip, and these metallic objects, she believed, were causing her pain. Tony Agpaoa operated on her, removed the hardware and showed it to her. As soon as the operation was over, she was free of pain.

Amazing! Wonderful! Miraculous—right? Sounds that way, certainly.

Unfortunately for Tony Agpaoa, metallic objects show up quite clearly on X-rays, and several months later, when her doctor in the United States took repeat X-rays, it was obvious that all the screws and the metal plate were still in her hip. The patient's pain relief had been psychogenic.

On the other hand, there were dozens of cases in Valentine's book which seemed to him truly miraculous. One involved a woman from San Francisco who was so crippled with arthritis that she had to be carried into Tony's presence on a stretcher. Three days after Tony's ministrations she was walking without a limp and even did a series of deep knee bends to demonstrate her "cure." From her case and many others, Valentine deduced that the psychic surgeons in general, and Agpaoa in particular, did have miraculous healing powers.

But how to explain the obvious fakery involved in operations like the "removal" of the metal in the hip? Valentine offered the theory that although Agpaoa did have miraculous powers, they sometimes failed him. When working before an audience, he felt it imperative, for the sake of his ministry, not to fail. (Tony Agpaoa is a minister in the Philippine Church of Science and Revelation—a church he founded.) And so, when necessary (fortunately, not often) he would resort to trickery. Not the most convincing argument in the world, but if you could manage to retain your objectivity, not a completely implausible defense either.

When I'd finished reading Tom Valentine's book I was still a skeptic, but wasn't ready to discount it all either. I still had an open mind. Since Tom Valentine lived in Chicago, I decided to call him and see if we could get together during my stopover. He agreed to meet me, and so at noon, on

April 5, 1973, we had lunch together at the Ambassador East Hotel.

He wasn't at all reluctant to talk about the psychic surgeons. "Very impressive," he told me, "but really something you have to see to believe. I spent three weeks there and not a day went by but that I saw something that can really be termed 'miraculous.' These people are really on to something."

"How did you get interested in all this?" I asked him.

"Oh, this is nothing new for me," he said. "I've been writing about the occult for years. There are a lot of things going on in this world that no one understands. I look into things and then report on them."

"Where do you publish your articles?" I asked.

"In *The Tattler*," he answered. "It's sort of like *Midnight* and the *National Enquirer*. I know those papers don't have much of a reputation, but unfortunately they're the only ones that are willing to publish articles dealing with the psychic or the occult. If you'll take a look at *The Tattler* someday, you'll find it's really a pretty good paper."

Frankly, the copies I'd seen of *Midnight* and the *National Enquirer* fell, in my opinion, into a category which could be neatly and accurately labeled "crap," but since we were having a pleasant lunch together, I refrained from making this comment.

"In your book, Tom, you admit that there are some cases of obvious fraud—that case, for example, where the screws were supposed to have been removed from a hip but X-rays later showed they hadn't been. Doesn't that sort of thing rather shake you?"

"Sure," he said, "I don't like it. I wish every piece of this puzzle fit together perfectly. But just because it doesn't, I don't intend to throw the whole thing out. You've got fakers in the medical profession, you know, but that doesn't stop you from believing in scientific medicine. Why should one shabby trick by a psychic surgeon completely disillusion me?"

He had a point.

We were just finishing our coffee when Tom threw in a new bit of information. "I think you ought to go to the Philippines, certainly," he said, "but before you do, let me suggest that you make a trip to Houston. There's a healer there, a man who calls himself Norbu Chen. He learned his art in Tibet and he's every bit as effective as the psychic surgeons. Not as flashy—he doesn't open up bodies with his bare hands—but the cures he produces are simply amazing. Edgar Mitchell, the astronaut, is one of Norbu Chen's big promoters, and incidentally, one of the colleges in Texas is currently arranging to test his healing powers in the laboratory. They're trying to keep it all hush-hush for fear they'll get a reputation as a screwball institution. That happens, you know, if you even dare to investigate the occult. Anyway, this fellow is a good friend of mine, very cooperative, and I'm sure he'd be happy to talk to you and test his healing powers in any way you see fit. You can call on me to help you make arrangements if you decide to look into him."

"I might take you up on that," I answered.

"Fine," Tom said, and he gave me Norbu Chen's phone number before we said good-bye.

4

That afternoon I flew to Detroit and I met Manny at the home of his friend, Louis Stein, who had taken his wife to the Philippines, where Tony Agpaoa had operated on her, apparently curing her heart disease. Besides movies of the operation, Lou also had films of an operation Tony had performed on his knees.

The Steins, like Manny, are obviously intelligent, stable people. Lou Stein runs a chain of restaurants; Marsha Stein is active in civic affairs. She is also an avid golfer. When I met the Steins they both appeared, to my critical eye, to be in excellent health, except for mild cases of obesity (which in our society is essentially normal). After introductions and a brief verbal résumé of their trip, Lou showed his films.

They opened with a shot of Tony Agpaoa, about thirty-five, five feet seven, black hair, smiling—as congenial-looking a man as you could hope to see. He was wearing slacks and a colorful short-sleeved sport shirt open at the collar. He looked more like a man who ought to be running a souvenir stand than a surgeon.

Then there was a quick shot of his "operating room," a term I'm using loosely, since, except for a narrow wooden table in the center, it looked like the living room in a beach cottage. Like most amateur moviemakers, Lou didn't give enough time to any one scene. I'd guess that no more than twenty seconds were devoted to these preliminaries.

When Tony got down to business, as he apparently quickly did, things really started to move. Apparently

Marsha had, along with her heart disease, a case of diverticulitis of the colon. Diverticuli are little sacs that sometimes develop in the large intestine. When they become infected and inflamed they cause pain in the lower abdomen, and constipation.

Tony attacked this disease first. The film first showed Marsha stretched out on the "operating table" with her blouse pulled up and her slacks pulled down just far enough to expose the abdomen. Then we could see Tony pushing his hands into the abdomen, using a motion much like that used in kneading dough. In a matter of seconds a red liquid that resembled blood welled up between his fingers, and immediately thereafter he seemed to be pulling out of the abdomen what appeared to me to be globs of fatty tissue. About thirty seconds after he had begun, the operation was completed. He pulled his hands away and there wasn't a mark on the abdomen except for a thin film of this red liquid which he quickly mopped up.

The film was silent but Marsha narrated as we watched. "There's no question in my mind," she said; "his hands were inside me. It wasn't at all painful (psychic surgeons don't use any anesthetics), just a strange feeling. But I'm sure I can tell the difference between someone pushing on my abdomen and someone actually sticking his hands inside me." This seemed reasonable.

The next sequence showed Tony and an assistant operating on Lou's knees. Lou had been bothered with arthritis for years and Tony had said he could cure him. This procedure, except for the area involved, was much like the first: the kneading motion, the "blood," the yellowish brown tissue being plucked from the joints. "It was painless," Lou said, "and a rather unusual feeling. I can't really find the proper words to describe it."

After watching a third operation—this one supposedly on the tissue around Marsha's heart, but in all essentials identical to the others—the lights went on and we all sat down to coffee and cake and éclairs and jelly rolls. I remember thinking that anyone who ate like this regularly would need not only a good surgeon but a heart specialist as well.

I can summarize the situation at this point very easily: all seven lay people at the table—four other friends of the Steins had joined us before the films began—were convinced that they had seen real surgery. I was skeptical, and if I'd had to make a bet I'd have given about ten to one that the whole business was faked. I don't say this to knock the Steins or Manny or any of their friends. They are, as I've said before, level-headed people who certainly didn't build their successful businesses being gulled by every charlatan that came down the road. But the fact remains that they are laymen, and when it comes to surgery, laymen, with very few exceptions, don't know anything.

I know from experience, for example, that a surgeon can show a patient's family an appendix he's removed and no matter what he says about it the family will believe him. "That's one of the longest appendices I've ever seen" is a line surgeons use time and again. The patient and the family get a thrill out of thinking his appendix was so uniquely long. Or, "That appendix was just about to burst," a surgeon will say, holding up a dripping appendix for the family to see. Maybe so, maybe not; "about to burst" is a matter of judgment. But the point is that the family has no way of judging the surgeon's comments. They have to take his word because in all probability none of them has ever seen an appendix before—certainly not more than one.

Chiropractors use this approach all the time when they're trying to sell a series of manipulations to a patient. The chiropractor will hang his X-ray of the patient's spine on a view box and point out abnormalities. "See this shadow here," he'll say, "that's where your fifth lumbar vertebra is out of line. And see this crack—that's the result of an old injury. That explains the pain you're having in your back. Ten good treatments and we'll have you fixed up."

The patient might just as well be looking at a map of

China as at the X-ray of his spine. Spine X-rays are all lines and shadows, and it takes a lot of study to interpret them properly. Sometimes the chiropractor doesn't know any more than the patient about what he's looking at, but if the chiropractor talks authoritatively—and they all do—he can persuade the patient there is indeed something wrong and sign him up for ten treatments at $20 a crack. Fortunately, most back pains will go away in two or three weeks as long as no one does any further injury. The disappearance of the pain will coincide with the last of the ten treatments and the chiropractor will get credit for another cure.

None of the people sitting at the table with me had ever seen the large intestine, or the inside of the knee, or a beating heart. I had, hundreds of times. I knew that an inflamed intestine isn't cured by removing blobs of fat from the abdomen; that arthritic deposits in the knee aren't the size and shape of the things Tony had pulled out; that heart trouble can't be cured by yanking some nondescript material out of the chest. I had to admit that I couldn't say definitely, "No, his hands weren't inside the patient"; the films were clear, but not clear. I could say that whatever operations Tony had performed were like none I'd ever seen before.

So I said as much—and it didn't upset anyone. "You'll just have to go and watch him, that's all there is to it," Lou told me. "Once you've seen him work you'll be convinced. Maybe his operations aren't like yours, but they work. My knees have never been better and Marsha can eat anything she wants now. Never has any bowel trouble—to say nothing of her heart; she couldn't walk upstairs without pain before Tony treated her. Last summer she played eighteen holes of golf, without a cart and never had a bit of pain. Tony's no fake."

What could I say? They'd been to the Philippines, I hadn't. I sat back, relaxed and ate my éclair.

Before returning to Minnesota, I decided to stop off at A.M.A. headquarters in Chicago and see what, if anything they knew about the psychic surgeons and/or Norbu Chen of Houston. I called William Monaghan at the Department of Investigation, and he invited me to come to his office. He assured me he'd be glad to help in any way he could.

The A.M.A. has a bad reputation in this country. Most of the people I know rather like the individual doctors who provide their health care, but it's very difficult to find a layman who has anything kind to say about the A.M.A. To the general public the A.M.A. is an uptight, conservative organization which wages war against all health legislation that is in any way progressive. The A.M.A. has been accused of holding down the numbers of doctors to create a shortage. It has even been said that the A.M.A. suppresses cures of cancer, among other diseases, so that doctors will have plenty of work to do. The A.M.A., as far as the layman is concerned, exists only to protect the high income that most doctors enjoy.

Some of this criticism is deserved. The A.M.A. has—mistakenly, in my opinion—fought legislation such as Medicare, which, by and large, has been good for our country. There was also a time during the Depression when, it has been said, the A.M.A. tried to limit the number of doctors, advocating what came to be known as "professional birth control." This accusation may or may not be true, but for the last thirty years at least, the A.M.A. has supported responsible expansion of medical schools.

On the other hand, it is not true that the A.M.A. has ever done anything to suppress cures for cancer or any other disease. Why in the world should they? Doctors and their families die of cancer too. I know I live in as much dread of "the big C" as anyone I know. The A.M.A. fosters and coordinates a wide variety of programs aimed at reducing the number of cancer deaths that occur every year.

What the A.M.A.—and its Department of Investigation in particular—does is to try to suppress, control and eliminate cancer "cures" that aren't really cures at all. Drugs like Krebiozen and Leifcort, which have never been shown to be effective in treating cancer, are extremely dangerous. Patients with treatable, curable diseases believe the deceptive publicity given these drugs by unscrupulous or ignorant doctors and healers. Then, instead of seeking treatment which might, if administered promptly, cure them, they diddle around for two or three months with worthless, expensive treatment by charlatans. By the time they come to their senses—by the time they admit to themselves they aren't getting any better—it's too late for orthodox treatment to help them.

I'll never forget one patient I had who went this route. I'll call her Mary. She was thirty-five, married, with three children, and taught a class for retarded children. When I first saw her in my office she said, "It's probably nothing, Dr. Nolen, but I want to make certain. I've been spotting a little between my periods for the last couple of months and my husband, Lee, is concerned. He insisted I see you."

I did a pelvic examination on Mary and it looked very much as if she had an early cancer of the cervix. I snipped a small piece of tissue from the neck of the uterus, and after she had dressed, I talked with her. "We'll have a report in a couple of days, Mary, but right now, if I had to make a guess, I'd say you have a very early cancer of the uterus. When we get a positive diagnosis I'll talk with you about treatment."

Two days later, the diagnosis confirmed, she was back in my office. "I'm sorry, Mary, but it is what I expected, a cancer. Fortunately, though, it's early and curable. We can treat it either with radiation or surgery. The results are good either way."

Mary was distressed, of course—who wouldn't be?—but she didn't break down as I've known some patients to do. Instead she asked me the usual questions: "How long will I be in the hospital?" . . . "When will I be able to get back to work?" . . . "What will the treatment cost?" I answered her questions and when she left she said, "I'll call you in a day or two to let you know what I decide. I have to talk things over with Lee."

31

A week later, when I still hadn't heard from Mary, I called her home and asked what she had decided. She was very evasive, didn't seem to want to give me a straight answer, but finally told me, "I'm going away for a couple of weeks, Doctor. I have some things I have to do. I'll probably be in touch with you when I come back." There wasn't anything I could do; a doctor can't grab a patient by the neck and say, "Get into that hospital, you need treatment and you need it now." I did warn her not to wait too long before deciding on therapy, and then hung up.

I didn't see Mary for six months and when she did come back, it was difficult to believe it was the same person. Six months earlier she had been handsome, vivacious, healthy-looking; now her eyes were sunken, she was pale, thin and apprehensive, obviously a very sick woman. "I'm back," she said trying to smile. "I'll take that treatment now—surgery or X-ray, whatever you say. I need help." Unfortunately, when I reexamined Mary, it was quickly apparent that there was no help I could offer her. She now had what we call a "frozen pelvis"—the cancer of the cervix had grown out to the walls of the pelvis on both sides and had infiltrated both the bladder in front and the rectum behind. The tumor was beyond the aid of either surgery or radiation. A month later, Mary was dead.

What had happened in the six months between visits? I got the story later from her husband.

"When Mary first came home from your office and told me she had cancer, I told her to get back to you as quickly as possible. I called my mother right away and she agreed to come out and help with the kids for a couple of months. Everything was set to go.

"Then Mary talked to a friend of hers who had, supposedly, had the same thing Mary had—cancer of the cervix. She had gone to Mexico for treatment, to a clinic just below the Texas border where they use something called Laetrile [the basic ingredient is made from apricot pits] to treat cancer. According to Mary's friend this cleared everything right up, without radiation or surgery or anything else.

"Mary insisted she wanted to try this first. She was a sensible woman, but the idea of either surgery or X-ray to her uterus bothered her—more, I guess, than I ever expected it would. I argued with her every way I knew how, but it didn't do any good. 'Just let me try it,' she said. 'If they don't cure me, I can always have an operation.' Finally I had to let her go.

"For a while, after she got back from Mexico, it did seem that she was getting better. The spotting stopped, but it never had been very heavy. We spent three thousand dollars on medicines over a three-month period, and I guess we both wanted to believe she was cured. It wasn't till six months had gone by, and she was bleeding every day and losing strength fast, that I could convince her the damn Laetrile wasn't worth anything. Finally, she came back to you; but as we both know, it was too late."

Sad. Mary died a needless death, the victim of a cancer quack. It's patients like Mary that the A.M.A. tries to protect.

Bill Monaghan and I met in his office on the fifth floor of the A.M.A. building. After we'd exchanged the usual greetings he brought in two cups of coffee and we got down to business. "I've heard a lot recently about psychic surgeons in the Philippines," I told him. "I wonder what you know about them?"

"We haven't heard much about them for quite a while," he said. "Back around 1968 they were very active. In fact, at one time there was a chartered planeload of patients that flew to the Philippines from Chicago for treatment. We got upset and complained to the Philippine Medical Association. Dr. Wilfrid Marcos—the brother of the President of the Philippines—is head of the government department of health. He claimed he'd never heard of any psychic surgeons. We got the impression they didn't want to hear of them. I think organized medicine just lets them alone. It wasn't our responsibility to protect Philippine people from the psychic surgeons, but we did feel an obligation to protect people in this country. After we'd registered our protest, their activity slowed down and I didn't know they were back in business till you wrote to me."

"Has anyone—any reputable doctor—investigated them? Has anyone gone out there to see what these people are doing?"

"Not officially," he said. "It's a matter of money; if we ran around investigating every crackpot healer we hear of, our budget for the year would be gone in three months. We have to limit the number of investigations we conduct. There have, however, been a few doctors who have looked into the matter unofficially. I just got a letter from one of them—Stanley Dean, a psychiatrist—last week. I wrote to him after I heard from you. I wanted to find out what, if anything, had happened to Tony Agpaoa. He's the 'healer' with the biggest practice, as you probably know. Dean tells me that contrary to what we thought, Agpaoa's not in jail. In fact, he's building a big hotel to accommodate all the patients that fly in to see him."

Bill Monaghan showed me Dr. Dean's letter. I asked Bill about a film to which Dean referred. "Oh, that," Bill replied, "I have to admit it's a problem. Dean has a film of Agpaoa in action that he claims is very impressive. He wants to show it at one of our A.M.A. conventions, but so far we haven't been able to accommodate him. We don't have any meeting where a film on psychic surgery would fit into the format."

This seemed rather strange to me—I'd have guessed that the A.M.A. could have stuck a film on psychic surgery into a side room at almost any meeting, and I'm sure it would have drawn a huge audience—but I decided not to comment on the A.M.A.'s policy. I was sure Monaghan, or more likely, someone further up in the hierarchy who made these

34

decisions, felt they were doing what was best for the country by not letting Dean show his film.

"Have you seen any films of the psychic surgeons at work?" I asked.

"Yes," he said, "dozens. There are people all over Chicago who have films of Tony Agpaoa at work, and for a while, a few years ago, it seems to me that I was looking at one or another of them almost every night."

"What did you think of them?"

"I'd better preface my answer to that by emphasizing that I'm not a doctor, let alone a surgeon. I'm not really the best judge of what looks like a real operation and what doesn't. But, answering as a layman, I'd say that most of the films looked like fakes—as if Agpaoa were palming things. On the other hand, I'll have to admit that some of the films were very impressive. To me it looked as if Agpaoa really had his hands inside the body."

"You mention Agpaoa all the time," I said, "never any of the other psychic surgeons. I understand that there are several others operating in the Philippines."

"That's true, but Agpaoa is the one who gets all the publicity. He's the big operator in more ways than one."

"How would the A.M.A. react if I were to look into this Philippine thing?"

"We'd be delighted," Monaghan said. "You're free to look through all the data we've got on Agpaoa. In fact, I'll send everything that's pertinent. We'd love to have someone expose these people as fakes. I'm very dismayed to hear that they're apparently active again. I thought all that had blown over."

"I may investigate these Philippines surgeons," I said, "but I'm certainly not committing myself to exposing them as fakes. If I go there, I go with an open mind. If I didn't think they might have something to offer, I wouldn't go at all."

"No offense meant," Bill Monaghan said. "By all

means, go with an open mind. I don't want any prejudices, or the A.M.A.'s, to rub off on you.

"I don't think there's much chance of that happening," he added, smiling. "Some of the things you've already written have given us fits at times. And as you well know, we've opposed you before. But that doesn't mean we can't still be friends, does it?"

"Of course not," I said. "And I'll certainly be grateful for any information you can send me, though I may not believe it all."

I looked through my pad for the notes I'd taken during my luncheon meeting with Tom Valentine. "One last thing before I leave," I said. "Have you heard anything about a guy who calls himself Norbu Chen? He's supposed to be some sort of wonder healer who works in Houston."

"Never heard of him," Monaghan said, "but that doesn't mean much. There's a new 'healer' showing up in one place or another almost every day. If I do hear anything about him, I'll let you know."

"Thanks," I said. "You've been most cooperative. I'll keep you posted on what I'm doing—if anything." We shook hands and I left. That afternoon I flew back to Minnesota and my surgical practice.

II

KATHRYN KUHLMAN

5

Manny and I had by now decided to go to the Philippines during the first week in June. Manny felt that on his first trip he had been so emotionally involved that a second look at the entire phenomenon was called for. Although he considered himself a shrewd and skeptical businessman, as a father it had been difficult for him to be objective, and as a physician I could help to interpret what he had seen. After the trip to the Philippines I planned to head for Pittsburgh, home of the Kathryn Kuhlman Foundation. I felt that in any study of miraculous healing Miss Kuhlman's "miracle" services, which regularly pack huge auditoriums all over the United States, ought to be included. Reportedly she healed hundreds—sometimes thousands—at each service. And according to *Time* magazine (September 14, 1970, pp. 62 ff.), at least some of these cures had been medically documented.

Then something happened which, if I were a "true believer," I'd be inclined to attribute to divine intervention. One Friday night I came home after playing tennis and Joan said, "Bill, you had a call from a Mrs. Ryan in Minneapolis. She'd like to have you call her back."

Because I write a monthly medical column for *McCall's* magazine I occasionally get calls from women I don't know personally who have medical problems and are looking for advice; since I'd never heard of a Mrs. Ryan, I assumed that this was one of those calls. When I returned the call Mrs. Ryan said, "Dr. Nolen, you don't know me, but my husband, Ralph, is a lawyer in St. Paul and a good friend of your friend Justin Oudal [he runs a rare- and used-book store in Minneapolis, specializing in the occult]. Ralph was talking to Justin yesterday and Justin told him you might be interested in knowing that Kathryn Kuhlman is returning to Minneapolis. My husband and I went to Miss Kuhlman's service last November and we're both very impressed by her. In fact, we're doing volunteer work to help organize her visit. One of my jobs is to recruit ushers for the wheelchair division. We have more volunteers than we need, but if you're interested, we'd certainly like to have you with us. Reverend Kronholtz is in charge of the local preparations and he thinks it would be nice to have one or two doctors or nurses in the auditorium in case anyone should faint."

"I'd be very happy to work as an usher at Miss Kuhlman's service," I said. "Thanks very much for asking me."

Then Mrs. Ryan put the topping on the sundae. "Ralph has another idea, Dr. Nolen. He's wondering if you'd find it useful if he had a couple of legal secretaries take down the names and addresses of the people at the service who say they are healed by Miss Kuhlman? He thinks it would be great if someone could check on some of these patients after the service to see if they really have been healed. He's very impressed by Miss Kuhlman, but he's a lawyer, you know, and he likes to be certain that no one is fooling him."

"Mrs. Ryan," I said, "you can't imagine how happy I'd be to have all those names and addresses. There are few things I'd like more."

Over the next two weeks I brought my passport up to date, read two books on the Philippines and, again with the help of Mrs. Ryan, arranged to interview Miss Kuhlman after her healing service ended. On the Friday night prior to the Sunday healing service, Joan and I drove to the First Covenant Church in Minneapolis, where I was scheduled to attend a 7 P.M. ushers information meeting.

This is probably as appropriate a place as any to briefly sketch my religious background. Religion is a personal matter, but since religious beliefs must inevitably influence to some extent one's interpretation of a phenomenon such as spiritual healing, it seems to me only fair to let the reader know how I stand.

I was born and raised a Catholic. I'm a graduate of Holy Cross, a college run by the Jesuits. Joan and I and our children all belong to St. Philip's Catholic Church in Litchfield, Minnesota, where we live.

Am I religious? Not very, I'm afraid. Despite Catholic education I can't claim to be a "good" Catholic. Not if you define a "good Catholic" as one who observes all the Church rituals, and that, generally, is the way a "good Catholic" is defined. (Or used to be, anyway.)

I do believe in God and I also believe that after physical death, we continue in existence in some other form. If someone should ask me if I believe that "when we die we go to heaven," I guess, all things considered and realizing heaven is a nebulous term, I'd answer yes.

Frankly, and I don't want to get into an argument over this because my knowledge of theology is not deep, I find it difficult to comprehend how anyone cannot believe in God; it seems to me you have to be almost irrational to be an atheist.

But let's return to the ushers meeting at the First Covenant Church. This was the first time Joan and I had ever been in a church where everyone seemed to take their religion very, very seriously, as if it were the most important thing in the world. Most of the ushers—there were about three hundred of us—greeted each other with enthusiastic waves and/or embraces, and salutations such as "Hallelujah, Brother Mike!" or "Praise the Lord, Brother Jeffrey!" At least one third of the men and women carried Bibles, and these Bibles looked worn—as though they'd actually been read. In fact, as Joan and I sat in a pew and looked around us, we could see many of the people reading passages to

41

each other and apparently discussing the meaning of the words. It was, to us, a strange sight indeed.

I don't want to give the impression that these people looked physically different from us; they didn't. They were to all appearances just like everyone else in Minneapolis. There were kids with long hair, wearing jeans; men in suits and ties; women in dresses of various lengths. The only difference between us and all the others was that these people were very religious and I'm afraid we are not. It showed.

The contrast became even more apparent when everyone started singing hymns. In a Catholic church—at least all the ones I've been to—it's like pulling teeth to get anyone in the congregation to sing. Not here. Without so much as an announcement, without a hymn book anywhere in sight, the pastor, Tim Kronholtz, opened the meeting shortly after seven by stepping to the microphone and singing. Instantly everyone in the room, except Joan and me, joined in. In fact, since the words were simple, I managed to join in the last three choruses. It was sort of pleasant.

Next the pastor asked one of the ushers—a Brother Herman, I think it was—to offer a prayer. Unfortunately Brother Herman had a tendency to mutter, so since Joan and I were sitting about twenty rows back, we couldn't understand him. However, we nudged each other simultaneously when we saw people all over the church hall raising their hands over their heads, eyes shut, smiling as if in ecstasy, saying things like "Amen, Lord," "Praise the Lord" and "Hallelujah, Lord." I guess this sort of thing goes on with some frequency in the so-called fundamentalist churches, but it was all brand-new to Joan and me. It reminded us both, when we talked about it later, of Burt Lancaster in *Elmer Gantry*.

After the hymns and prayers, the meeting got down to its real purpose: the orientation and instruction of the ushers.

As you'd probably guess, Kathryn Kuhlman doesn't just fly into town on Friday, hire a hall on Saturday and hold a "miracle" meeting on Sunday. Not when twelve or fifteen or twenty thousand people—the only limit being the size of the hall or stadium, since she almost invariably draws a capacity crowd—are involved. It takes a great deal of organization (particularly when most of the audience are sick) to make certain that the meetings go smoothly. For weeks before her arrival in Minneapolis Rev. Kronholtz and, under his general direction, a team of volunteers had been working very hard. The success of the miracle service depended, ultimately, on Miss Kuhlman, but as she told me when I eventually met her, "All these wonderful people—they work so hard for me. Dear God, it's such a terrible responsibility."

After the prayer the first speaker was the head usher, a man I'll call Raymond.

Joan and I spotted Raymond up on the stage when we first came in. He looked like what used to be called a "smoothie." Dark hair, dark-blue suit, white shirt and tie, trim, handsome, in his early thirties (I guessed); he looked too good to be true. "There's a guy I certainly wouldn't buy a used car from," I whispered to Joan. "He looks like a real phony." She nodded in agreement.

When Raymond started talking I decided that my snap judgment had been wrong. He came across as very sincere, dedicated and above all efficient. It had been his job to organize the ushers and he had done it well.

He talked for about a half-hour—counting hands, pointing out chiefs, assigning geographically designated meeting places. Altogether there were fifteen groups; a group to handle the busloads of people that would be coming in from cities and towns all over Minnesota (one busload even made the trip from a town in Canada, nearly three hundred miles away); a group to guide dignitaries, clergymen and guests of the ushers to their special reserved section; a group for each of the subdivided seating areas on the main floor and in the balcony of the auditorium; and, of course, Group 15— the wheelchair group—to which I had been assigned. This, it turned out, was the biggest of them all. Wally Hanson was our chief.

By the time Raymond finally finished his assignments, the room was very noisy, what with everyone asking everyone else questions such as "What group are you in?" . . . "Where did he say group twelve meets?" . . . "What's the name of our group captain?" Anyone who has ever had the misfortune of being involved in a group undertaking will know exactly the sort of hubbub I mean. The meeting was on the verge of falling into disarray.

Rev. Kronholtz promptly corrected the situation. He stood up, walked to the lectern, and without so much as an introductory word broke into song. In seconds all conversation ceased. Everyone joined in the singing. Once again the hymn was a simple one and I was able to join in the refrain.

"Now," said Rev. Kronholtz, the hymn ended and silence restored to our hall, "it is my great pleasure to introduce Mr. William Rice. Mr. Rice, as some of you may know, is Miss Kuhlman's aide and the director of organization for Miss Kuhlman's miracle meetings. He is going to give you a brief rundown on the Sunday schedule."

Applause, mild to moderate, welcomed Mr. Rice as he stepped to the lectern. (I think perhaps the applause would have been more vigorous except that there always seems to be some doubt in one's mind about the propriety of applauding in church.) "Let me tell you first," said Mr. Rice, a short gray-haired man in a dark suit and, like Raymond, wearing a white shirt and tie, "Miss Kuhlman has arrived in Minneapolis and has gone to her hotel room to rest."

At this announcement, church or no church, there was wild applause.

"She has had a long day," Mr. Rice continued. "There was a miracle service at dawn in Pittsburgh, and let me assure you it was"—pause—"absolutely fantastic.

"As usual," Mr. Rice added with a smile (there were chuckles and light applause).

"Now," he said, "to business. How many of you have ever been to a Kathryn Kuhlman service? Let's have a show of hands." About one third of the crowd had been to previous meetings. "Do you think it would be helpful if I went over the general format?" We all nodded yes.

"All right. First, I have to warn you that Miss Kuhlman is unpredictable. She acts as the Spirit [capital S] moves her. So what I'll tell you should be considered only a rough outline.

"The service is scheduled to begin at one, but it may begin at twelve-fifteen, one-fifteen or any time in between. The doors will open at twelve and I expect that there will be a huge crowd waiting to get in—there always is—so the hall may fill up immediately. If it does, Miss Kuhlman may begin the services at once. Otherwise, she'll wait."

The choir would start to sing at twelve, and continue singing until Miss Kuhlman came out on the stage. After some talk and praying by Miss Kuhlman, interspersed with hymn singing by Jimmy MacDonald and piano playing by Dino, it would be time for the offertory hymn, and the offertory.

"Now, you have to understand—this is a very difficult time for Miss Kuhlman. She doesn't like to think or talk about money—sometimes she even forgets about the offertory. [Author's note: *Time* magazine said the same thing.] But it costs money to run these miracle services, so, though we don't like it, the offertory must be collected.

"While the offertory hymn is being sung, the ushers in each section will pass the offertory baskets. We'll tell you where to bring the baskets and we want to be sure to count them before and after the offertory. We don't want to lose one. [There was no smile, no attempt at levity, here. Mr. Rice was very serious indeed.]

"One other thing; don't pass the offertory basket to the choir while they're singing. It disrupts the hymns. Wait till after they've finished singing. [Again, no levity. Not even a smile.]

"After the offertory, Miss Kuhlman will give a sermon. This is the most unpredictable segment of the service—she may talk five minutes, she may talk forty-five minutes. So you ushers have to be prepared. At any moment she may feel that someone is being healed and ask him or her to come to the front of the auditorium. Soon there may be people from all over the auditorium crowding the aisles to get to the stage. You have to keep them under control.

"Those of you who are in the wheelchair section have a big job. No one is supposed to go to the stage unless they have been healed so there won't be any wheelchairs out in the aisles. But if someone does leave a wheelchair to go to the stage, we want an usher to carry the wheelchair to the stage too. That way Miss Kuhlman can show proof that someone has been healed.

"A few general points. First, no tape recorders, no cameras. It isn't that Miss Kuhlman objects to having her picture taken or her sermons taped—it's just that the clicking noise disturbs people. You can't take cameras or tape recorders away from people, but if they bring them, ask them not to use them.

"Second, keep babies in the back of the hall. Miss Kuhlman, of course, loves children, but if they start crying it can disturb the service. It's best if they're in the back so their mothers can take them out if they get too noisy.

"Third, try to keep people from roaming around too much, particularly at times when things really should be quiet. We don't expect everyone to sit without moving for five hours. In fact, the one question you ushers will most often be asked, and to which you'd better know the answer, is 'Where are the rest rooms?' But there are times . . . during a prayer, for example, when too much moving around is disturbing. Try to keep people quiet at those times.

"Finally, try to keep young people, particularly those wearing wild clothes, out of the first three rows. Miss Kuhlman has no objection to young people and she doesn't dislike hippies, but sometimes they do make trouble; it's best, and safest, if the people in the first few rows look and act conservatively.

"As far as what you ushers ought to wear [the temperature in the church hall was about ninety and most of us were in short sleeves], when I'm asked about that I always reply, 'You're going to a religious service; you'll be in the presence of the Lord—wear what you think is appropriate.'" Which led me—and, I assume, everyone else—to the conclusion that we were expected to dress like Mr. Rice. It was going to be a hot Sunday.

When Mr. Rice had finished, Rev. Kronholtz once again led us all in a hymn; then, after another muttered prayer punctuated by "Amens," "Praise the Lords" and more hand waving, we were dismissed.

I joined Wally Hanson and twenty of my confreres in the wheelchair division in the southeast corner of the hall. Wally turned out to be a cheerful man in his early thirties. He climbed up on a chair so we could all see him, gave us a brief rundown on our Sunday assignment and then asked, "Now, are there any doctors or nurses in this group?"

I hated this moment (I have to admit that it made me feel like a kook; after all, a doctor at a faith-healing meeting?) but, however reluctantly, I raised my hand. As did a chubby woman in her mid-forties.

"Great," Wally said. "Would you identify yourselves?"

"I'm Sonia Waters," said the nurse. "I'm Bill Nolen," I whispered. Everyone was looking at me; at least I felt as if everyone was looking at me.

"Will you both stand on chairs so we can get a good look at you?" Wally asked. Feeling more like an ass than ever, I climbed up on a chair.

"There's a first-aid station just outside the entrance you'll be using to bring wheelchairs into the auditorium" Wally said. "If anyone should faint, or complain of feeling ill, just bring them there. Then we'll find either Ms. Waters or Dr. Nolen to help them."

I stepped down from the chair, and then went and joined Joan in the car. "What do you think of it?" I asked her.

"It was certainly different," she said. "These people just aren't like anyone we know."

"I agree," I said. "They seem like nice people, and are probably 'nicer'—no drinking, no smoking, no fooling around, you know what I mean—than most of the people we see. But I'm afraid it's too late for us to be like them. In fact, I'm not sure I'd even want to be like them. Sunday should be interesting."

"I'm glad you're going and not me," Joan said.

6

Every usher was allowed to bring one guest to the miracle service and I decided to invite George Dougherty.

George, a Boston Irishman who emigrated to the Midwest in 1950, is a good friend of mine. Four years ago, when he was fifty years old, George had a heart attack, a bad one. He was in the intensive care unit at the hospital for three weeks and in a regular hospital room for another month. When he went home Dr. Michael Murphy, an internist who was working with our Litchfield Clinic group at the time, said, "George, you take it easy for another month. Then we'll see about letting you go back to work on a part-time basis."

The day after George went home his wife, Betty, heard a strange noise in the basement. She went down to see what was going on and there was George, jogging in place, perspiring, gasping for breath. "What in the world are you trying to do, George," Betty asked, "kill yourself?"

George stopped jogging. When he got his breath back he said, "I just thought, 'To hell with it—I'm going to see if I'm going to live or die.' I don't want to stay alive if it means I've got to sit on my ass for the rest of my life." That's the kind of guy George is.

Two years later, early in 1972, George had another heart attack. The first one had been bad; this was far worse. Twice during the first week his heart stopped and he had to have electric shock to get it restarted. It seemed to all of us who had anything to do with the case that the odds on George surviving were ten to one, against.

He made it. Ten weeks after his heart attck Michael sent him home on a Tuesday. The next evening at seven o'clock I was sitting in the golf club, when George walked in. Wednesday night is "Men's Night" and George had come out for a little action. He got into a poker game that wound up, at four o'clock in the morning, at the home of one of the players. George won $1,800. This apparently, was George's idea of "taking it easy." Michael heard about it—nothing is secret for long in a small town—but this time he just shrugged his shoulders and said, "What can I do about it? If George Dougherty wants to kill himself, there's nothing I can do to stop him."

Since his doctor had given up on him six months earlier, I decided that George could really use Kathryn Kuhlman's help.

As you'd probably guess from his name, George is a Catholic and not a believer in Kathryn Kuhlman. When I explained what the service would be like and asked George to come with me, he said, "I'd love to go. It ought to be interesting. But I sure as hell don't believe she's going to make me any better."

"No problem," I said. "Kathryn Kuhlman says in her book [*I Believe in Miracles*] that faith in her doesn't seem to matter. Skeptics come to her miracle service and go home cured; believers come and she doesn't help them. There's no way she can predict who will be helped. So you're as much of a candidate for a cure as anyone else."

On Saturday, George came over to the Clinic and we ran an electrocardiogram as a "control." It showed all the changes one expects to see in the EKG of a patient who has had two severe heart attacks.

Sunday morning George and I drove to Minneapolis, arriving shortly before eleven. Even at that time, two hours before the service was scheduled to begin, there were long lines outside every entrance. At the wheelchair entrance, through which we entered, I'd estimate that there were at least one hundred people waiting.

George found a seat in the section near the stage, the section reserved for the clergy and guests of the ushers. I was surprised to see among the former several nuns and two priests. Ecumenism is, indeed, a reality.

I went off to meet my fellow ushers. Wally Hanson, our leader, quickly divided us into three groups: one to bring the wheelchair patients and their attendants, if any, to the elevator; a second group, to which I was assigned, whose job was to guide the wheelchairs from the elevator to the auditorium entrance; and a third group, which would finally arrange the wheelchairs in their reserved section of the auditorium. It was also the job of those in the third group to tie matching identifying tags to the wheelchair and on the patient who was sitting in it.

I have seen some sad sights in my life, but few that could match the one that greeted me when the doors opened and our first charges arrived. The freight elevator they were on was jammed with about thirty wheelchair patients and their attendants. Some of the afflicted were elderly men and women, drooling from a corner of their mouth, an arm lying loosely and uselessly on a paralyzed leg. There were the "stroke" victims—and they were numerous.

Others were children, six, eight or ten years of age, crippled by birth defects. The head of one little boy was nearly as large as his body, and it rolled from side to side, his neck too weak to support its weight. He obviously had hydrocephalus (water on the brain) with severe mental retardation. Another child, a girl about fifteen, kept flapping her arms in uncontrollable jerks. I hadn't seen a case in years but it looked to me like Sydenham's chorea, a disease that causes loss of muscle control and possible idiocy. A third child, a boy about eight, seemed to be intelligent and aware, but there was a bag containing urine in his lap, connected to a catheter in his bladder, and his legs were withered and paralyzed. I guessed he probably had had a meningocele (a defect in the spinal cord) that had left him paralyzed below the waist.

There were men and women of middle age as well. Some had the pale, wasted appearance that a doctor learns through experience is often associated with widespread cancer; others had paralysis or disfiguring defects—withered arms or legs—that could have been either congenital or the result of injury. Every patient I saw, except of course those who were retarded, had the desperate look of those who have all but given up—who are nearly, but not quite, resigned to their fate.

I offered to help a man of about forty whose son sat, eyes vacant, collapsed in his wheelchair. "Let me push this for you," I said. "I'll take you to the wheelchair entrance."

"Thanks," he said wearily, "I'm kind of tired."

"Do you mind telling me what's wrong with your son?" I asked as we started down the corridor.

"Not at all," he said. "Jimmy had measles when he was seven. It affected his brain. Before that he was a strong, bright kid. Now he can't do anything for himself; can't even talk. Doctors tell us there's nothing they can do, that we ought to put him in an institution. But me and the wife just can't do it; we keep remembering him as he was, even though that was eight years ago.

"Friend of ours told us about Kathryn Kuhlman. Our friend had arthritis in her knees and she claims Kathryn Kuhlman cured her. So when we heard Miss Kuhlman was going to be in Minneapolis we decided to drive up here from Des Moines. It's a four-hundred-and-fifty-mile drive and it took us most of the night. My wife is exhausted; she's with some friends of ours now, sleeping. But I came right over so I'd be sure to get Jimmy in. Kathryn Kuhlman, I guess, is our last hope."

By now we'd reached the entrance to the hall, so I turned the wheelchair over to one of the other ushers, wished the father well and went back to the elevator. I felt like crying.

In the next crowd that got off the elevator was one man,

in his middle sixties, who didn't have a wheelchair. Somehow he'd gotten lost downstairs and had wandered onto the freight elevator by mistake. As he walked off the elevator I could see him wincing with pain. He was limping badly, so I offered to help him to the auditorium.

"I'd appreciate that," he said. "My back and hips hurt like the devil. I've got cancer of the kidney. Had it operated on two years ago and I've been taking pills ever since. Now the doctors tell me it's in my spine and in my hipbones. They give me pain medicine to take, but it doesn't do me much good. I'm hoping Kathryn Kuhlman will cure me."

"Did you tell your doctor you were coming here?" I asked him as he shuffled along.

"I mentioned it to him. He said that was my business. He didn't recommend her, didn't knock her either. Said it was entirely up to me."

During the course of the afternoon I asked this question of many patients; their answers were essentially the same. None of their doctors had advised them to go to the service; none made any attempt to dissuade them from attending. Apparently, even if the doctors weren't believers, they weren't anti-Kathryn Kuhlman either. Before I left this man with his kidney cancer, I found a wheelchair for him so he wouldn't have to walk back to the elevator when the service ended.

The first-aid station—a small room containing a cot, a few Band-Aids and several stretchers—was adjacent to the wheelchair entrance to the auditorium. I was the only M.D. in the usher group—I was probably the only M.D. in the auditorium—and though Mr. Rice had assured me that no one ever became ill at a Kathryn Kuhlman service, I was called to see my first patient before the service had even begun. It wasn't a serious problem—an elderly woman had fainted, probably a result of the heat—but she didn't come around as quickly as I would have liked; and when I checked her blood pressure and found it at 80 over 60 (average is 120/80), I decided she'd better go to the hospital. Someone called an ambulance and she departed.

Soon after—again before the service began—I had to go out into the auditorium to see a very heavy black woman whom I had noticed when she came in because she was wearing a hockey helmet; a rather unusual sight, I expect you'll admit. This woman had fallen and now complained of pain in the knee. I examined the knee and could only say that it might be either a fracture of the patella (the kneecap) or a bruise. We'd need an X-ray to be certain. "Would you like me to call an ambulance?" I asked her.

"Not if I don't have to go," she said. "Can I wait till the service is over and see how it feels?"

"Sure," I told her. "If it's broken, you may need a cast or an operation, but a four-hour delay won't affect the treatment. If you're not having too much pain, you can stay."

"The pain's not bad," she said. "I'm used to falling—that's why I wear this hockey helmet. I've got epilepsy and I take a lot of medicine to control it—you can see how sleepy I am—but I still have a lot of seizures. Sometimes I fall from the seizures, sometimes just from the medicine. I'm tired of it and I want to see if Kathryn Kuhlman can help me."

The third patient I had to go and see was a young black man who was sitting slumped down in his wheelchair. "What's the matter?" I asked him.

"Just weak," he said. "I'm not used to sitting very long. Do you think I could lie down?"

"Sure," I said. "I'll get a stretcher." With a couple of the other ushers I loaded him onto a stretcher, and by shifting a few wheelchairs around, we were able to find a space for him on the auditorium floor.

"Thank you," he said. "That's much better."

"What's your problem?" I asked him.

"I've got cancer of the liver," he told me. "My belly keeps swelling up." I put a hand on his abdomen and easily

54

confirmed the diagnosis. He was as swollen as a woman in the ninth month of pregnancy. And in the upper half of his abdomen I could feel stony-hard lumps, deposits of cancer in his liver. He was obviously in the terminal stages of his disease.

"You take it easy now," I told him. "If you decide you want to leave, just let us know."

"I don't want to leave," he said, "not if I can help it. I want to be cured."

As I was walking away, a young girl who had been standing nearby came up to me. "Sir," she said, "are you a doctor?"

"Yes, I am," I told her.

"I'm Mrs. Whalen. That's my husband you just saw," she said. "We've been married a year. Six months ago Richard got sick, and like he told you, the doctors say he's got cancer in his liver. They keep sticking needles into him to take away the fluid, and they give him medicines to take that make him vomit and feel awful sick. He don't know it but they told me that he can't live very long—they can't cure him. What do you think?"

"It's hard to say without knowing what the doctors' tests showed," I answered, "but I'll have to agree, it doesn't look very good. He's an awfully sick boy."

"But he's only twenty-one, Doctor"—she was almost in tears—"how can that be? Isn't cancer something that kills old people?"

"Not always, I'm afraid," I said. "It can strike anyone. Sometimes we can operate and remove it; sometimes we can cure cancer with medicine. But when it starts in the liver there's usually nothing we can do. I'm afraid that's the kind your husband has."

"Oh God," she said, "I hope Kathryn Kuhlman can help us."

7

At twelve o'clock the choir volunteers from churches all over the Minneapolis area began to sing. To my untrained ear it sounded fine, lots of melody sung with feeling. The singing kept everyone entertained until Kathryn Kuhlman appeared onstage.

Which she did at one o'clock. She wore a flowing white robe and came out waving her hands and smiling. Kathryn Kuhlman is about five feet eight, thin, with brown hair. She is not particularly beautiful but she has that indefinable quality known as "presence." When Kathryn Kuhlman appeared onstage every eye in the auditorium was quickly on her.

It was apparent from the very beginning that she is a superb actress. I'm not saying this disparagingly; anyone who gets things done, and I include physicians, has to be an actor. Some of us are better actors than others. Kathryn Kuhlman is an expert.

"It's so beautiful to see you all here," she said. "I just know the Holy Spirit is going to work many miracles. Wouldn't it be wonderful if every single one of you were healed today?" Everyone applauded wildly.

Then Kathryn Kuhlman played a little trick on the audience. "This is a huge auditorium," she said, "and I know that some of you way up high may not be able to hear me. If you can't hear me, will you shout 'Amen!'" There was a chorus of "Amens" from the balcony, followed, as soon as everyone realized what they'd done, by generalized laughter which Miss Kuhlman joined in.

"Now," she said, "let's try it once more. Those of you who can't hear me, shout 'Amen!'" This time there was absolute silence. "That," said Kathryn Kuhlman, "is what I call a large-scale miracle." Gales of laughter, again; it was sort of cute.

So the meeting went. Dino, dressed in tails, played the piano. Jimmy MacDonald, also in tails, sang hymns in a strong, full baritone. Both, as far as I could tell, were capable performers, Kathryn gave them both rousing introductions, and informed the audience that their albums were available for sale in the corridors of the auditorium.

Between their performances Kathryn talked to us all. She didn't preach; she talked. She told us how wonderful the Lord is and how grateful she is for the works the Holy Spirit performs. And often she commented on the burden she feels in being His instrument.

"The responsibility—the responsibility!" she cried. "You see me up here and you think 'how glamorous'—but it isn't. I cry for those that don't get out of their wheelchairs, for those who won't be cured today. I ask, 'Am I at fault?' Oh, the burden of it all. Sometimes it seems like more than I can bear." At this point she buried her face in her hands, sobbing momentarily while we all sat there, almost embarrassed to be watching her.

But then she recovered. "Is it worth it, O Lord? Yes, it is! It's worth the price when you see one cancer healed . . . one child made better . . . one woman get out of a wheelchair. Those moments more than repay me for the anguish of the awesome responsibility I feel."

It's hopeless for me to try to convey in words the charisma of the woman. You have to be there to see her stride across the stage; watch her gesture and pose with arms outstretched; listen to the emotion in her voice as she cries and prays; watch her face light up in rapture; and above all see her smile. You have to be there to fully understand how she captures and holds her audience. Like all great evangelists, Kathryn Kuhlman is, first and foremost, a wonderful performer.

This happened to be one of those days when she did not forget the offertory. After the piano playing, the singing and some praying, she said, "Now we're going to take up the offertory—the money we need so we can come to you people and help the sick and needy everywhere.

"I want twenty people out there to write out checks for one hundred dollars. I want fifty people to write checks for fifty dollars. I want one hundred people to write checks for twenty-five dollars. We need that money.

"But if you can't give a hundred dollars, or fifty dollars, or twenty-five, we're not going to forget you. Just give whatever you can give. I'm not going to ask for a show of hands; I'm just going to pray." And at that point the ushers hustled the wastebaskets into the crowd, the choir broke into the offertory hymn, and Kathryn Kuhlman prayed.

The offertory hymn took about ten minutes. When it was over and baskets were being passed to members of the choir, Kathryn Kuhlman gave her sermon. She talked mostly of the wonders of the Lord and the Holy Spirit—nothing really different from the sort of conversation she'd been carrying on all through the meeting, though she began to talk more about healing. "I don't heal anyone," she said more than once. "I'm a nobody. I have no power. But the Holy Spirit heals. I am only His instrument."

Suddenly she paused, eyes shut, one leg thrust forward. It was a tense moment, a dramatic moment, and the audience was silent.

"The Holy Spirit is healing someone right now," she said. "It's a woman. A woman down here on the ground floor. About halfway back. She had a cancer—a cancer of the lungs. And now . . . and now . . . she is being healed! You know who you are. You can feel the Holy Spirit working in you. Stand up and come forward and claim your healing."

When no one came forward immediately, Kathryn suddenly pivoted and pointed toward the balcony. "There's another healing. Oh, praise the Lord, there's another healing. There's a man in the balcony who has had bursitis in his shoulder. He's had it for some time. Now it's gone. He can wave his arm. Stand up and wave your arm. You've been healed." There was a note of frenzy in her voice. And up jumped a man, waving his arm. The audience gasped.

Then, magically, healings began to take place all over the auditorium. "Don't come to the stage unless you've been healed," Kathryn said. "But if you have been healed, come up and give praise to the Holy Spirit."

"There's a woman with a bronchial condition in the chorus. That bronchial condition is now gone."

"There's a man down front with a heart condition. I rebuke that heart condition."

"There's a child with diabetes. The sugar is gone from his body."

"There's a young girl with a skin rash over here on the left side of the auditorium. In three days that rash will be gone."

"There is someone in the audience who has a tumor. The tumor is in the lower half of the body. They are supposed to have an operation in a week. Now the tumor is gone. They'll never need that operation. Praise the Holy Spirit."

Kathryn has an assistant and companion, a woman named Maggie about whom I could find out nothing. "Nobody knows anything about her," one usher told me, "except that she's very devoted to Kathryn." Maggie appears to be in her late fifties. Apparently one of Maggie's jobs is to start the cured patients flowing to the stage; at least she was the one who got them going on the Sunday I was there.

First she spotted a woman who had looked around bewildered when Kathryn mentioned lung cancer. Maggie went over to her, spoke for a few seconds, and she finally got up, and with Maggie holding her by the elbow, walked toward the stage. Next a man cured of bursitis was found, again by Maggie, and started on his way. A few seconds later the cured heart condition was making his way to the front.

Once the first few started forward, dozens of others quickly followed. Soon there were lines of people on both sides of the auditorium waiting to get up on the stage and tell Kathryn Kuhlman their stories and give praise to the Lord. When they reached the stage, the patients were guided by Dino or Jimmy or another of Kathryn's assistants. One at a time they were led to Kathryn.

"And you," Kathryn said to a woman who was claiming a cure, "what did you have?"

"Lung cancer," the woman answered.

"O good Lord, we thank you," Kathryn said, looking toward the ceiling. "Now," she said to the woman, "take a deep breath."

The woman did.

"Did that hurt?"

"No, it didn't."

"Do you see her?" Kathryn cried into the microphone. "Lung cancer. And now she can breathe without pain. The Holy Spirit is surely working here today."

Then she put her hands on either side of the woman's face, after Dino had positioned himself behind the woman, who collapsed. The power of the Holy Spirit had knocked her right over.

Every few minutes Miss Kuhlman would pause between "cures," turn as if she had heard a voice and point out into the audience. "Back there," she said on one occasion, "way back on the right. There's a man with cancer in his hip. You're cured. Your pain is gone. Come down and claim your cure." Someone back in the hall struggled to his feet and slowly worked his way down the aisle as the crowds applauded. Behind him came one of the ushers, carrying his wheelchair. When the man got closer to the stage I could see that he was the fellow I had talked to earlier, the man with cancer of the kidney.

60

When he was up on the stage, his wheelchair behind him, Kathryn Kuhlman said, "Is that *your* wheelchair?"

"Yes, it is," said the man, bewildered.

"And now you're walking. Isn't that wonderful? Praise the Lord. What do you think of that?" Kathryn asked, turning to the audience. Enthusiastic applause.

"You've had cancer in the hip and now your pain is gone; is that right?" she asked.

"Yes," he answered.

"Bend over so everyone can see."

He bent over.

"Walk around."

He walked around.

"Isn't the Holy Spirit wonderful!" she sighed, and Dino helped the man off the stage.

Fifteen or twenty times, scenes like this were repeated. Patient and wheelchair delivered to the stage, patient put through running, bending or breathing paces, depending on the nature of the cure. Applause for each performance. Patient and wheelchair returned to the aisle. Asthmatics, arthritics and multiple-sclerosis patients all ran through their new tricks.

Occasionally Miss Kuhlman would turn and say, "Someone with a brace . . . a brace on your leg . . . you don't need that brace any more. Take it off, come to the stage, and claim your cure."

The first time she called for a brace there was a delay in the proceedings. No one came forth. The audience began to grow restive; you could sense that they all felt this was most embarrassing for Miss Kuhlman. Finally, after what was probably a minute but seemed an hour, a very pretty young girl limped up to the stage. She waved her leg brace in the air and stood, with her pelvis tilted badly, on one good leg and one short, withered leg. Kathryn Kuhlman questioned her.

"How old are you?"

"Twenty."

"How long have you worn the brace?"

"Thirteen years. Since I had polio at seven."

"And now you've taken it off."

"Yes," she said, "I believe so much in the Lord. I've prayed and he's curing me."

Everyone applauded. The girl cried.

This scene was, to my mind, utterly revolting. This young girl had a withered leg, the result of polio. It was just as withered now as it had been ten minutes earlier, before Kathryn Kuhlman called for someone to remove her brace. Now she stood in front of ten thousand people giving praise to the Lord—and indirectly to Kathryn Kuhlman—for a cure that hadn't occurred and wasn't going to occur. I could imagine how she'd feel the next morning, or even an hour later, when the hysteria of the moment had left her and she'd have to again put on the brace that had been her constant companion for thirteen years and would be with her the rest of her life. She was emotionally high right now; soon she'd be emotionally low, possibly despondent.

This case shook severely what little hope I had left that Kathryn Kuhlman was, truly, a "miracle worker."

I had accepted as a misunderstanding the deception that went with "Not yours surely?"—referring to the wheel-chair—even though I knew the man hadn't been in a wheelchair until that afternoon; I had chalked it up to innocent error when the ability to take a deep breath was passed off as evidence of a lung-cancer cure (even though I knew most patients with lung cancer can breathe deeply); I had assumed that it was simple overenthusiasm that enabled Kathryn Kuhlman to call a multiple-sclerosis patient "cured," even though she obviously still walked with the multiple-sclerosis gait; but this episode involving the girl with the brace was pure, unadulterated, flagrant nonsense. For Kathryn Kuhlman to really believe that the Holy Spirit had worked a miracle with this girl, it seemed to me that Kathryn Kuhlman would have had to be either blind or incredibly stupid, and she was obviously neither. Was she, then, a hypocrite or a hysteric? I didn't know, but I had begun to seriously question her credibility and that of her organization.

Not once, in the hour and a half that Kathryn Kuhlman spent healing, did I see a patient with an obvious organic disease healed (i.e., a disease in which there is a structural alteration). At one point the young man with liver cancer staggered down the aisle in a vain attempt to claim a "cure." He was turned away, gently, by Maggie. When he collapsed into a chair I could see his bulging abdomen—as tumor-laden as it had been earlier.

One desperate mother managed to work her child's wheelchair down to the front of the auditorium. The little girl in the chair, about five years old, glassy-eyed, hydrocephalic, could barely sit upright. The mother, weeping, lifted her daughter out of the chair and attempted to get her to walk to the stage. The child, with the mother holding her, made two pitiful attempts to walk, both times nearly collapsing on the floor before the mother could catch her. Finally, weeping, the mother put her imbecilic child back in the wheelchair and pushed her away down the aisle.

The stage was getting so flooded with people waving their arms to demonstrate bursitis cures, and touching their toes to show off healed backs, that Kathryn Kuhlman and her crew could barely control them all. Fortunately, at that point, a mass miracle occurred. Miss Kuhlman turned to the audience and said, "All of you with bad backs, stand up." Three or four hundred people stood.

"Go into the aisles," she commanded.

They went.

"Now bend forward . . . bend to the side . . . touch your toes . . . do all the things you haven't been able to do." Three hundred people ran through calisthenics. "Oh, God is so good," said Miss Kuhlman, eyes raised heavenward.

The audience applauded.

Finally it was over. There were still long lines of people

waiting to get onto the stage and claim their cures, but at five o'clock, with a hymn and final blessing, the show ended. Miss Kuhlman left the stage and the audience left the auditorium.

Before going back to talk to Miss Kuhlman I spent a few minutes watching the wheelchair patients leave. All the desperately ill patients who had been in wheelchairs were still in wheelchairs. In fact, the man with the kidney cancer in his spine and hip, the man whom I had helped to the auditorium and who had his borrowed wheelchair brought to the stage and shown to the audience when he had claimed a cure, was now back in the wheelchair. His "cure," even if only a hysterical one, had been extremely short-lived.

As I stood in the corridor watching the hopeless cases leave, seeing the tears of the parents as they pushed their crippled children to the elevators, I wished Miss Kuhlman had been with me. She had complained a couple of times during the service of "the responsibility, the enormous responsibility," and of how her "heart aches for those that weren't cured," but I wondered how often she had really looked at them. I wondered whether she sincerely felt that the joy of those "cured" of bursitis and arthritis compensated for the anguish of those left with their withered legs, their imbecilic children, their cancers of the liver.

I wondered if she really knew what damage she was doing. I couldn't believe that she did.

I waited in the corridor for about ten minutes, until the flow of patients slowed to a trickle, and then went back to Miss Kuhlman's dressing room. I found her standing outside the room, sobbing loudly. Dino had his arms around her, doing his best to comfort her. When he spotted me he waved me back into the corridor. Then, a couple of minutes later, having led Miss Kuhlman into her room, he came out and spoke to me.

"Wait about five minutes and then go on in," he told me.

"I wonder if I should. I hate to bother her when she's so distraught."

"Don't worry," Dino assured me, "she'll recover. She's always this way after a service, but she bounces back fast. She's expecting you."

"If you say so," I said. "I really appreciate it."

When she let me into her dressing room five minutes later, Miss Kuhlman had indeed recovered. She was, in fact, buoyant—smiling, laughing, talkative, on an emotional "high." I apologized for bothering her.

"Not at all," she said. "I'm delighted to talk to you. I feel just wonderful. I have enormous energy. Thanks to the Lord."

"I'd like to ask you some questions," I began.

"Ask me anything at all. I love to talk. Sit right there," she said, pointing to a chair a few feet from her dressing table. Then she sat on the edge of the table, smiling radiantly. (I'm not going to mention that smile again; simply assume that when Miss Kuhlman is not crying, she is smiling. Radiantly.)

"To save some time, Miss Kuhlman, is it safe to assume that Allen Spraggett's biography of you is accurate?"

"Yes," she said, "except, of course, for one thing—my age. He asked me how old I was and I gave him a figure; a joke, of course, but he used it. Aside from that, everything else is correct." (I subsequently rechecked Spraggett's book, *The Unexplained*, in which he had made a facetious reference to Kathryn Kuhlman as being eighty-four years old. Some readers took it seriously. I'm not much of an age guesser, so let's just say, as they do in a popular song, that Kathryn Kuhlman is "somewhere between 'forty and death.'")

"I'll skip the biographical stuff, then, and ask some medical questions. As a doctor, that's the particular aspect of your ministry in which I'm interested. How do you get along with the medical profession?"

"Wonderfully well," she replied. "I have a great many doctor friends. You see, I have nothing against doctors, and I hope they have nothing against me. I don't cure people; as

65

you know the Holy Spirit, happily, cures through me. Doctors cure people, too. I think doctors are wonderful. I'm on their side."

"Do you think any of the patients you cure are simply hysterical people?"

"Of course," she answered, laughing. "Aren't any of the patients you treat hysterical?"

I admitted they were.

"But many of our cures are documented," she continued. "All those patients we show on television, for example. [Miss Kuhlman has a one-hour syndicated show on television every week, which is shown in Minneapolis on Sunday morning.] They are documented cases. And I always tell people who say they've been cured to go back and check with their doctors. I have nothing to hide."

"What about organic diseases—things like gallstones, for example? Do you cure these too?"

"Oh, certainly, Gallstones, cancer, arthritis, everything. But don't say I cure them; I cure no one. The Holy Spirit cures them."

"Have you any idea why the Lord chooses to work miracles through you?"

"I don't know why I've been chosen," she said. "In fact, I always worry that one day I'll go out on the stage at a healing service and find that the Holy Spirit has decided not to use me at his instrument any longer. But I do know why miraculous healings are occurring. The explanation is in the Bible."

"I'm afraid I don't know the Bible as well as I should," I apologized.

She laughed and picked up her Bible, which was literally falling apart; it was apparent she'd been through it thousands of times. "Let me give you a little lesson," she said.

"In the Bible, Christ says, 'If you won't believe me, believe my miracles.' We are now approaching the millennium—the time when the Holy Spirit will leave us and the Church, the elect, will be taken up. All the signs point to this. For example, read Ezekiel 37, 38, 39. It says, 'The ten greatest nations will reform like the Roman Empire.' And you see what's happening in Europe? The Common Market? The loss of prestige of the United States? And in the Bible they speak of 'the spoil'; that's the oil in the Middle East. Make no mistake—the Second Coming is near.

"Miracles—miraculous healings—are Christ's way of telling us to prepare for Him. There are more miraculous healings now, in the 1970s, than there have been at any other time since the days of the early Church. Even in Bolivia, where miracle healings never occurred before, there is a boy in his early twenties who is curing people by the thousands. And I'm proud to say that he received the gift of healing at one of our services at the Shrine in Los Angeles. You know, don't you, that once a month we hold a healing service at the Shrine and it is always packed? We even have a V.I.P. section. People like Robert Young and Merle Oberon often come to our services. Not because of me, of course; because of the Holy Spirit."

It took Miss Kuhlman about twenty minutes to review the Biblical explanation of miracles for me. She thumbed through her Bible as she spoke and I kept busy taking notes, though I admit the explanation didn't seem very clear to me then. Probably it was my fault, but when I tried to check out these references, I was unable to find any of them in the Bible.

Now, in the entranceway, just outside the dressing room, I could see Dino pacing back and forth. He didn't signal me to leave but the message was clear, and justified. After all, the entire troupe had been working hard for five hours and they were probably hungry. So I stood up, shook hands with Miss Kuhlman and thanked her for her time and for the Bible lesson.

"You're perfectly welcome," she said. "The Bible is a wonderful book. You should really look into it." I promised I would.

Even if I hadn't felt obligated to leave, I don't think I

would have found much more to ask Miss Kuhlman. It seemed obvious to me that she was a sincere, honest woman who felt that she had been chosen to perform a mission for Christ and that she was honored to have been so chosen. She believed without a doubt that she was helping the sick and the maimed as Christ wished her to help them. Not personally, as she had pointed out endless times, but simply as His instrument.

As I was about to leave her dressing room she stopped me. "Let me give you my private address," she said. "Just write to me if there's anything more I can do to help you. I'm always happy to cooperate."

I put down the address in my notebook, and a few weeks later, when I wrote to her, I found, as I'd expected, that her offer to help me in my investigation was a sincere one.

Kathryn Kuhlman believes, as she told me, that she has "nothing to hide."

8

During the healing service, as patients who had "claimed a cure" came down off the stage, two legal secretaries wrote down the names, addresses, phone numbers and diagnoses of all those who said they would help in a follow-up study. (These girls had been recruited by Mrs. Ryan, as she had promised when she suggested that I participate as an usher, and Kathryn Kuhlman had raised no objection to our study.)

As it turned out, almost every patient who was approached expressed a willingness to cooperate. We got eighty-two names. The only reason we didn't get more was that the flow of cured patients was so heavy that the secretaries simply couldn't get to them all.

I had mixed emotions about the follow-up study. On the one hand I felt that Kathryn Kuhlman was a sincere, devout, dedicated woman who believed fervently that she was doing the Lord's will. I didn't want to hurt her. On the other hand, I wasn't sure that whatever good Miss Kuhlman was doing wasn't outweighed, far outweighed, by the pain she was causing. I couldn't get those crippled idiot children and their weeping, broken-hearted parents out of my mind. I decided to go ahead with the investigation.

First, George and me—he with his heart problem, me with my bursitis. Both of us had been caught up in the magic of Miss Kuhlman's performance. Seeing her out on the stage in her flowing white robes, listening to Dino play his marvelous music, hearing Jimmy MacDonald and the choir singing their inspirational hymns, and above all, listening to Kathryn Kuhlman call, loudly, clearly, emotionally, on the power of the Holy Spirit—all these things created a mood that was almost impossible to resist. You wanted to believe so badly you could hardly stand it. You didn't want to reason; you wanted to accept.

"I tell you," George said, "I was damn near ready to go up on that stage myself. It's funny, but whenever she said 'Someone is being cured of a heart condition,' I'd get a sort of burning sensation in my chest. If no one else had gotten up to claim a heart cure, I think I'd have claimed one. But someone else always did, so I stayed in my seat."

I'd had the same sort of experience. At the time of the meeting I had a moderately severe case of tennis elbow, a torm of bursitis. When Kathryn Kuhlman said, as she did several times during the service, "Someone is being cured of bursitis," I'd find myself moving my elbow back and forth trying to see if the pain was gone. A couple of times, for a few seconds, I thought it was. Then I'd exercise it a bit vigorously and find the soreness still there.

Remember—these were the reactions of a skeptic (George) and an M.D. (me). We hadn't come to the service hoping to be cured, praying to be cured, crying to be cured. We had come as cool, dispassionate observers. After watching Miss Kuhlman in action it was easy for me to understand how, when I reacted as I did, those afflicted who had come seeking help would become believers. After five hours at the service the wonder to me was that everyone in the audience didn't claim a cure.

But at least one answer to that was apparent; the spastic idiot child, the man with the paralyzed arm and leg, the young man with the gigantic swollen abdomen—they could hardly claim cures. The evidence—their appearance—precluded such claims. If you were suffering from an ailment or a deformity that was self-evident, then you could hardly climb onto the stage and give testimony to the Holy Spirit and Miss Kuhlman. When you did, as in the case of the girl who stood there with a withered leg waving her brace, the situation became extremely embarrassing.

The day after the meeting George came to the Clinic and we ran an electrocardiogram. Skeptical as we both were, we hoped, and perhaps even sligtly expected, that there would be an improvement. I know George was disappointed, as I was, when we found his EKG unchanged. The scars, the result of his two heart attacks, were still there.

The second patient followed up was me. I have hypertension—not bad, but not good either. I have no symptoms and I lead a very active life, but I have to take pills every day to keep my blood pressure at respectable levels. Even with medication my pressure runs above normal.

Before the miracle service I'd had my blood pressure taken; it was 155 over 90. The day after the service I had it taken again: 160/95. Not enough of an increase to be of any significance, but certainly evidence that the service hadn't helped me. (I might add here that neither George nor I derived any delayed benefits from the service. As this book goes to press, eighteen months after the service, George's heart is still scarred and my blood pressure remains elevated.)

Since neither George nor I had "claimed" a healing, we weren't really a fair test of Miss Kuhlman's results However, a few weeks after the service we sent letters to all those on our list who had claimed healings, inviting them to come to Minneapolis on Sunday, July 15, and tell us about their experience (when I would be back from the Philippines). Twenty-three people showed up and I interviewed them all. I'm not going to give all their case histories, though I have them on file. There were many cases alike in almost every detail but the name.

Nor am I going to use the real names of these patients, thought most of those who attended the meeting signed releases allowing me to do so. I am wary of the mail that some of these case histories might attract. In the past I've received hate mail, and I have little doubt that I'll receive more in the near future, but that is one of the prices you pay for writing about controversial, emotionally charged subjects. It's a punishment which I think should not be inflicted on patients.

The following five cases are typical of the patients who were willing to reaffirm their cure.

Case # 1. Marilyn Rogers is eighteen years old. She is a tall, pretty girl with long black hair, blue eyes and a dark complexion. She is intelligent and told her story fluently.

Marilyn graduated from high school in 1972. She wanted to go to college, hoping to get a degree in special education so that she could work with retarded children. Unfortunately, her parents weren't able to pay for her education, so she went to work as a sales clerk. She had expected to earn enough money so that she could start school in the fall of 1973.

Shortly after going to work, eight months before the Kathryn Kuhlman meeting, Marilyn had an acute attack of dizziness and vomiting. At first she attributed the episode to something she had eaten, but when the attack persisted for three days she went to her family doctor, who referred her to a neurologist. The neurologist admitted Marilyn to the hospital and kept her there for two weeks while he ran a series of blood tests. He then started her on cortisone. Her symptons subsided and she went home and back to work. At the time of her discharge the neurologist told Marilyn she had "inflammation of the blood vessels of the brain."

Two weeks after returning to work Marilyn suddenly developed numbness in her left arm and leg. She went back to the hospital and this time the neurologist told her that his initial diagnosis had been wrong. Marilyn did not have "inflammation of the blood vessels of the brain"; she had multiple sclerosis. He transferred her to a hospital associated with a medical school where there were specialists doing research in this disease.

Marilyn spent the next six weeks at the university hospital. She was treated with massive doses of cortisone and with a new drug, anti-lymphocytic globulin. (Anti-lymphocytic globulin—or A.L.G., as it is called—is obtained from the tissues of animals. In Marilyn's case it came from goats. A.L.G. has proved very helpful in preventing rejection after organ transplants. Since there is a resemblance between the disease process in multiple sclerosis and a rejection reaction, some research doctors are hopeful that A.L.G. may be effective in controlling multiple sclerosis). Marilyn received sixteen bottles over a period of thirty-eight days.

Shortly after Marilyn entered the hospital, her weakness and numbness progressed to the point where she lost the use of both legs. For a while she was confined to a wheelchair, but gradually, as treatment progressed, she was able to get around, first with a walker, later with a cane.

Multiple sclerosis is a terrifying disease. No one knows what causes it; no one knows how to cure it. Hundreds of drugs, alone or in combinations, have been used to treat this disease. None, so far, have been consistently helpful.

In the short run, however, almost any treatment will seem to work. There are two reasons for this. First, the disease is cyclic; that is, its symptoms may come and go. One day a patient may be blind in his left eye; the next day his vision may be normal. He may lose bladder control for three months, then regain it; have perfect control for a year, and then lose control again. He may develop paralysis in his legs, which becomes so bad that he can get around only in a wheelchair; then, gradually, his strength may return so that he can walk unaided.

It is only by studying large groups of patients over a long period of time that an investigator can tell whether improvement in a patient with multiple sclerosis has been produced by the medicine under investigation or is just another remission for some unfathomable reason. So far, in

73

all the studies that have been done, no one has found firm evidence that any medicine will cure multiple sclerosis.

The second reason why, in the short run, any treatment may help such a patient, is that multiple sclerosis is one of those diseases in which the psyche plays a major role. During the healing service when Kathryn Kuhlman said, "Go into the aisle, you people with spine injury, but don't come up on the stage till you know you've been healed," Marilyn felt a burning sensation in her spine. She left her wheelchair and walked to the stage. An usher brought the wheelchair to the front of the auditorium and passed it up onto the stage.

Kathryn Kuhlman turned to Marilyn and asked, "Whose wheelchair is that? Not yours surely." Marilyn didn't want to go into a complex explanation about how she had borrowed it, so she simply said yes.

"And now you're walking?" Kathryn Kuhlman asked her.

"Yes, I am," Marilyn answered.

"Oh, praise the Holy Spirit," Kathryn Kuhlman said, looking up at the ceiling. The audience applauded vigorously.

Then Kathryn Kuhlman had Marilyn walk back and forth across the stage, demonstrating her "new" ability to walk. Since it was obvious to everyone that Marilyn's gait was not completely normal, Kathryn explained, "Of course, since these muscles haven't been used for a long time, it will take time to get them back to normal. But isn't she doing well . . . isn't God wonderful?" And, of course, there was more applause. Marilyn then walked down the aisle to her wheelchair, which had been returned to its place. All of the audience applauded, and many wept with joy as Marilyn walked by them.

Marilyn wants so badly to get better that she will interpret anything that happens to her as evidence that she is improving, that she is being cured. She may even function better physically if it is suggested to her that she can do so.

Sometimes, when Marilyn is tired and not really trying, her muscle weakness and her waddle are severe and easily apparent. But put Marilyn up on the stage, with ten thousand people watching her, have a woman in flowing robes and a close relationship with the Holy Spirit say to her, "Walk, Marilyn, walk. I rebuke your multiple sclerosis"—and Marilyn will walk. Not perfectly, but better, perhaps, than she has walked in months. And Marilyn's heart will leap with joy and she'll say to herself, "I'm cured," and she'll give praise to Kathryn Kuhlman.

One final note, before we move on. Multiple sclerosis is a diagnosis no one wants to make. The first time Marilyn went to the hospital with "weakness" she says her doctor made a diagnosis of "inflammation of the blood vessels of the brain." The chances are excellent that even then, the doctor suspected that Marilyn had multiple sclerosis; "inflammation of the blood vessels of the brain" is almost an unheard-of diagnosis. But it's an unspoken, regularly observed rule in medicine not to make a diagnosis of multiple sclerosis unless it's unavoidable; most doctors try not to make it until the patient has had a second, possibly third attack of suggestive symptoms. The reasoning is: Why make a diagnosis which will only depress the patient when, after you've made the diagnosis, there is very little you can do, anyway?

You will find, however, that because multiple-sclerosis patients are always, understandably, looking for miracles, and because it is a cyclic disease and responsive to suggestion, it is one of the diseases charlatans most like to treat. No matter what nonsense the faker preaches or practices, he invariably finds it easy to persuade his desperate victim he has been helped.

In the two months since the meeting Marilyn felt that her gait had improved steadily and that her headaches had decreased in frequency and intensity. She was sure Kathryn Kuhlman had cured her and that it would only be a matter of time until she was perfectly normal. True, her doctors at the university hospital had been unable to find and measure any real change in her muscle strength, but they agreed that she walked very well and had no explanation for the improvement in her headaches. They were very happy for her.

I thanked Marilyn for telling me about her case, wished her well and and watched her leave my office. She walked with the wide-based waddle to which victims of multiple sclerosis often resort. To my eye, there was no discernible improvement in Marilyn's gait. But I was glad her spirits were so high.

Case # 2. Arthur Holmberg is twenty-two years old. He is quiet, reserved and pleasant. He is a graduate student working on his master's degree in education. He is very religious and belongs to a Pentecostal church. He was one of the volunteers who sang in the choir at Kathryn Kuhlman's miracle service.

Arthur had been troubled with migraine headaches since the age of eighteen. Nervous tension—worry over an impending examination, for example—would trigger them. Sometimes he had to lie down for several hours before they would go away, and occasionally he had to miss school and the examination.

At the Kathryn Kuhlman service, while she was healing, Arthur "felt a migraine coming on." Just as he noticed the first early symptoms—a feeling of tightness in his head—Kathryn Kuhlman turned toward the choir and said, "Someone back there is being cured of a migraine." Arthur was surprised to feel tingling and heat in the back of his neck. He found it difficult to believe that it was actually he who was being healed of his headaches. Even when an usher came back into the choir and asked, "Someone here being healed of a migraine?," Arthur was reluctant to stand up. But after he had waited a few seconds and no one else from the choir stood up, he decided that it must really be he who had been cured. So he stood, went forward with the usher and claimed his cure.

You will find, as we go along in this book, that I'm going to say with disturbing frequency, "We doctors don't know the cause of this disease"—as in the case of migraine headaches. Physicians do know some superficial things about them—that they are produced by spasm—tightening —of the blood bessels in the head, followed by complete relaxation, almost a paralysis, of the same vessels. Unfortunately, we don't know what it is that causes this blood-vessel spasm-relaxation to occur. Some people never have migraines, some have them on rare occasions, some have them frequently.

Migraines, as in Arthur's case, are often precipitated by tension. A wife can get a migraine from fighting with her husband, or even more likely, by not fighting with her husband when she wants to fight with him. If she doesn't shout and scream and get it out of her system, the unrelieved tension may surface as a migraine. A man may get a migraine when he first learns his son is smoking marijuana. In susceptible patients almost any emotional upset can cause a migraine, and reassurance and relaxation may abort an attack.

Arthur had a typical migraine personality: compulsive, tense, inclined to keep things to himself. He may or may not have been about to have a migraine when Kathryn Kuhlman turned to the choir and said, "Someone back there is being cured of a migraine," but for one reason or another, he didn't have one then. There is no doubt that reassurance from Miss Kuhlman or any other authority figure may abort a migraine attack in a patient who will believe.

About a week after the miracle service Arthur had a migraine. He had been canoeing, however, and his muscles were overtired. And he hadn't eaten. So he ate, rested for a few hours, and the migraine went away.

He has had migraines off and on since that time, but he doesn't think that they are as frequent or as severe as they were before the miracle service. The reassurance he received from Kathryn Kuhlman may help him avoid severe migraines.

That will be very nice, but it will hardly be a miracle.

Case # 3. Sister Marian is a Roman Catholic nun who teaches sixth grade in a parochial school in a small town in Wisconsin. She is fifty-three years old and has been a nun for twenty-five years. She had heard of Kathryn Kuhlman from a friend, Ralph Hutchins, who lived in the same town as Sister Marian. Ralph had been to an earlier Kathryn Kuhlman service where he claimed a cure for cancer. Unfortunately, Ralph was wrong; he died of cancer six months after the healing service.

This had not shaken Sister Marian's faith in Kathryn Kuhlman. After all, she knew Kathryn Kuhlman never promised anyone a cure. What persuaded Sister Marian that Kathryn Kuhlman was an authentic "healer" was the fact that she never took any glory for herself. She always gave full credit for cures to God. And Sister Marian assured me, "Pope Paul agrees; he gave Kathryn Kuhlman a commendation."

Sister Marian went to the service more to observe than to seek a healing; after all, she wasn't really very sick. Her only problem was pain, off and on, in her left shoulder—"a sort of bursitis," the doctor called it.

She was sitting about halfway back on the ground floor when Kathryn Kuhlman said to the audience, "All those having trouble with an arm, stand up." Sister Marian really didn't want to stand—she felt conspicuous in her nun's habit—but when Kathryn Kuhlman said "Stand up!" for the third time, Sister Marian felt obliged to stand.

Then Kathryn Kuhlman said to those who were standing, "Wave your arms, wave your arms. Wave them like you haven't waved them in a long, long time. See if the Holy Spirit hasn't cured you." Sister Marian just had to wave her arm. As she did so she felt no pain, just a tingling, hot feeling. For the first time she thought she actally might be one of those cured.

Still, when Kathryn Kuhlman directed those who had been cured to come to the stage, she was reluctant to go. But when the usher asked her, "Have you been cured?" she felt as if she had to nod "yes." And when he said, "Go up and claim your cure," she really couldn't hang back. However, she couldn't bring herself to say a definite "Yes" when Kathryn Kuhlman asked, "Sister, have you been cured?" Instead, she waved her arm in the air. This, of course, was (as I remembered well) enough to elicit a loud ovation from the crowd.

The cure of Sister Marian's bursitis isn't of much consequence. Anyone who has had bursitis, and certainly anyone who has ever treated it, knows that it is an off-again, on-again thing. Bursitis is an inflammation in the bursa of a joint. The bursa is a tough, smooth sac that lines every joint and allows the bones that meet in the joint to move easily against one another. Usually there is a small amount of fluid in a bursa. When the joint is used excessively or in some unusual way the fluid in the bursa increases and the bursa becomes swollen and inflamed. For example, a man who is not used to manual labor and spends a weekend painting his house is very apt to develop bursitis in his shoulder. Resting the joint is usually all that is required to effect a cure, though sometimes cortisone injections into the joint (cortisone is an anti-inflammatory drug) will help.

What is most interesting about Sister Marian's case is that even though she was reluctant to go up on the stage and claim a cure, she did so. When the usher said, "Go up and claim your cure," she couldn't refuse. Nor could she turn back once she had started down the aisle. Nor, even though she was doubtful, could she say "No" or even "Maybe" when Kathryn Kuhlman asked her if she was cured. She couldn't quite say "Yes," because she wasn't certain and didn't want to lie; instead she equivocated by waving her arm in front of the audience, saying in effect, "You be the judges."

Sister Marian's reaction was typical of many in the audience: no one wanted to let Kathryn Kuhlman down, no one wanted to embarrass her. The girl that took off her brace and stood on her withered leg did so, she admitted later, because when Kathryn Kuhlman said, "Someone who is wearing a brace . . . you don't need that brace any more," she looked around and failed to see anyone taking off a brace. The delay was embarrassing. So she said to herself, "Kathryn Kuhlman must mean me," and she went down to the stage.

Consider the situation yourself. You are in the audience. You have a painful back. Kathryn Kuhlman says, as she did at this service, "All you with bad backs, stand up. Go into the aisles." You go into the aisle. Now Kathryn Kuhlman says, "Bend forward . . . bend to the side . . . touch your toes . . . do all the things you haven't been able to do. Oh, God is so good!"

Ten thousand people are watching you. When Kathryn Kuhlman says "Bend," are you going to stand there, rigid, like some sort of ninny? You are not. You're going to bend, damn it, if it kills you. And maybe it won't hurt as much as you anticipated; backs are like that. So you go into the Kuhlman ledger as another "bad back—cured." Miraculous.

The whole scene—the religious fervor, the wheelchairs on the stage, the lines forming to claim cures—casts a spell over the audience. As with Sister Marian it becomes almost more difficult not to claim a cure than it does to claim one.

Sister Marian still has trouble with her shoulder but not as often as before the healing. When she has an attack of pain she says to herself, "Jesus Christ died for me," and often the symptoms go away.

Sister Marian remembers Kathryn Kuhlman saying to those with painful arms, "I rebuke that pain in the name of Jesus Christ." Sister Marian thinks her pains may recur off and on until a deeper, spiritual healing occurs. She believes Kathryn Kuhlman has started her on her way to that spiritual healing.

Case # 4. Rita Swanson is twenty-three years old. She is a senior student in a small Baptist college, and in her spare time she works for an interdenominational religious organization called Child Evangelism Fellowship. The purpose of Child Evangelism Fellowship is, as Rita put it, "to make Christians out of children." Specifically, it is Rita's job to teach the children hymns and games that will, in a subtle way, teach them what is in the Bible.

Rita is a very pleasant girl; I'm almost tempted to call her "sweet," but I don't like the word and I did like Rita. I would have been happy to have her teach the Bible to my children.

Rita went to Kathryn Kuhlman's service both to watch Miss Kuhlman—Rita has been a fan of hers for several years—and because she, Rita, suffered from a skin problem. She hoped Kathryn Kuhlman would cure her.

The skin problem was apparent. Rita had blemishes all over her face, the sort of pocked, scarred skin that is a common consequence of severe adolescent acne. She had been treated by dermatologists off and on for years. Her latest therapy had consisted of vitamins and antibiotics.

At the service Miss Kuhlman pointed in her direction and said, "Someone there—someone in Section Six—is suffering from a skin problem. I rebuke that problem. In three days that skin problem will be cured." Rita looked around, saw no one else in her section with an obvious skin problem, and knew then that she would be cured.

Three days later, her face was very much improved. Since that time, even though she wasn't taking any antibiotics or vitamins, her skin hadn't gotten any worse. Even her dermatologist agreed that her skin was better, though he wouldn't go so far as to say she was "cured."

Rita knew she owed her improved skin to the Holy Spirit, working through Kathryn Kuhlman.

Rita's case is a lot like that of Marilyn, the girl with multiple sclerosis. Rita wants very badly to have a nice complexion. She has worked very hard at it—witness the constant stream of dermatologists that she has seen in the last five years. A bad complexion is a tough cross for a young girl to bear.

Her desire to be cured makes her highly susceptible to suggestion. If someone tells her her skin will be better in three days, when she looks in a mirror three days later, she will look for evidence that her skin has improved, and the chances are excellent that she will find it. "Is that scar a little less prominent? Yes, I think it is. And is that red spot fading? Thank the Lord, yes." After all, judging the appearance of skin is highly subjective. You look in the mirror, and unless things are too shockingly obvious, you will see, at least in part, what you want.

There are two other points worth mentioning here, both having to do with skin diseases.

The first is that Kathryn Kuhlman did not say, and as far as I've been able to determine, never says, "Someone with a skin disease has just been cured." At her services there are instant cures of cancer, bursitis, hearing loss—all ailments that no one can see—but skin defects, which are obvious, take three days or more to cure. Kathryn Kuhlman wouldn't want Rita or anyone else coming up on the stage to claim a cure of a skin disease when it would be perfectly obvious to everyone that it was still there. It wouldn't be honest—and Kathryn Kuhlman is, at least in her own mind, honest—to plant in the audience someone with an unblemished face and have her come up on the stage and claim a cure. Besides, all those sitting next to that person would know the claim was false. Much better to promise skin cures for three days later, when the audience is dispersed and Kathryn Kuhlman is many miles away.

The second point is that it is perfectly possible that, three days after Kathryn Kuhlman leaves, someone with a skin disease who was at the miracle service will find all manifestations of the disease gone. Not a girl like Rita, unfortunately (Rita's skin disease is at least in part organic, as opposed to functional or psychogenic, terms we'll discuss later), but someone with a skin disease which falls into that category known as neurodermatitis. This means, literally, an inflammation of the skin caused by nerves. How? We don't know exactly (there's that confession again), but doctors encounter it frequently. The nerves to the skin and/or the glands of the skin get into some sort of imbalance, and rashes or other skin blemishes develop.

A simple example of nerves working on the skin is blushing. Some people blush when they're embarrassed; nerves cause the blood vessels of the skin to fill with blood and the cheeks get red. These nerves to the blood vessels are part of the autonomic nervous system, i.e., they are nerves that are not under voluntary control.

Another example of a neurodermatitis is warts. Warts are, in part, due to infection with a virus; but no one will deny that psychological and nervous factors may play a role in the genesis and cure of warts. For example, one way that some doctors treat warts is to give the patient gentian violet, an innocuous purple dye, and say, "Paint those warts with this solution every day for three weeks, and your warts will go away." Sometimes this works—just as burying a frog at midnight, or some such routine, worked for Huck Finn or Tom Sawyer. In these cases what is really at work is neither the frog nor the dye but simply the power of suggestion, a sort of low-grade hypnosis. And for the more severe neurodermatitises—a rash over the entire body, for example, or a terribly itchy rash—deeper hypnosis, by a physician trained in the technique, is often effective.

Many of the techniques that Kathryn Kuhlman uses are hypnotic. It would be odd if occasionally a neurodermatitis, or one of the many other diseases susceptible to hypnosis did not respond to her miracle service.

Miss Kuhlman's miracle services may produce an improvement in Rita's acne; it will not eliminate the scars, an organic manifestation of the disease.

Case #5. Lois Robinson is thirty-six years old and a Roman Catholic. She is married, and even though she has seven children, she has managed to keep a trim, athletic figure. She also has an attractive face.

Lois has had trouble with varicose veins for many years. After the birth of her third child she had an operation on her veins. they recurred, and after the birth of her fifth child she underwent another operation. This time she had twenty-four incisions in the left leg and twelve incisions in the right. Six weeks later she had some residual veins injected.

Her seventh child was born just two months before the Kathryn Kuhlman meeting. During her pregnancy Lois developed more varicose veins, which she described as "very obvious."

On the morning of the Kathryn Kuhlman service in Minneapolois, Lois turned on her television set at eight-thirty and watched Miss Kuhlman's syndicated show. After it was over, Lois said to her daughter, "I'm going to that miracle service this afternoon. I'm going to be cured." Lois knew, just as certainly as if Christ Himself had told her, that Kathryn Kuhlman would cure her.

At the service Lois couldn't find a seat on the ground floor, so she went up to the balcony. During the healing period Miss Kuhlman pointed to the balcony and said, "Someone way up high doesn't like where she's sitting. Her varicose veins have been cured." At that moment Lois "felt the power of the Lord go through me," and she knew her varicose veins had been healed. Lois' girl friend, who had come to the service with her, urged her to go up on the stage and claim her cure, which she did. (I remembered her very well, not only because she was quite attractive but because she was wearing a pants suit when she claimed the healing of her varicose veins. She, of course, made no attempt to show us her legs; there was really no way she could have done so without disrobing on the stage and that would, admittedly, have been highly inappropriate. As a result, however, the audience had to take Lois' word for the cure.)

While I was interviewing her I asked her about this; how, wearing pantyhose and a pants suit, she could have known, at the service, that her varicose veins had been cured.

Lois became irate. "I knew," she said, "because I felt the power of the Lord go through me."

Then she turned on me. "Have you been reborn?" she asked. When I replied that I didn't know what she meant, she said, "Reborn in Christ, of course. If you haven't, then how can you possibly understand how He works?"

I told her I was doing my best to learn more about all of this and apologized for upsetting her, after which we got along reasonably well.

Before she showed me her legs. She had scars of at least thirty incisions on the right and twenty or more on the left, the result of her two operations. There were a few small veins still visible, but no large veins.

When I talked to her doctor later, he said, "Yes, she developed a couple of varicose veins during her pregnancy. They went away, as they usually do, after delivery."

Lois hadn't told him about Kathryn Kuhlman.

Lois' case demonstrates two points, and the first concerns the religious fervor that is typical of believers. Lois became furious with me when I started probing, trying to piece together her story in order to learn whether she had been cured or not. Lois thought this was presumptuous of me, and that I should accept her word and the power of Kathryn Kuhlman. In short, she demanded that I have blind faith.

This wasn't the only time I was to encounter resentment. I learned, over and over again, that people who believe, the "True Believers," as Eric Hoffer calls them, don't want anyone asking questions to find out how things really are. They want to hang on to their beliefs, and they fear and resent anyone whose inquiries might shake them. Sometimes these "believers" become so irate that they're belligerent; you can practically taste the hostility. Occasionally, during the course of my investigation, this hostility frightened me. I wanted to get at the root of the "healing" scene, but preferably without sustaining serious injury.

Once in a while this led me, I'm sorry to confess, to dissemble. Even when there were apparent misinterpretations of evidence or flagrant deceptions, I didn't always point them out at the time; I went along as if I were a believer myself. To do otherwise could only have antagonized people to the point where they would cut me off from information I wanted and needed. I didn't like myself for behaving deceptively, but I couldn't then and still can't see any workable alternative.

The second point that Lois' case makes has to do with misinterpretation of evidence. Lois had a few varicose veins which developed during her preganancy. This, as most women know, happens frequently. There are two reasons why women who are pregnant develop varicose veins: one is the direct effect of the female sex hormone estrogen on blood vessels; the other simply the bulk of the enlarged uterus containing the baby. The uterus fills the pelvis, pressing on the iliac veins and impeding the flow of blood from the veins in the legs. The back pressure on the veins causes them to balloon. Once the baby is delivered, the estrogen level drops to normal, the uterus shrinks, flow in the iliac veins becomes unrestricted and the veins in the legs go back to their normal size. Though sometimes, if they've been stretched too badly, the veins don't collapse to normal size and the woman is left with varicose veins.

Lois may or may not have understood all this. Whichever the case, she chose to attribute the disappearance of her varicose veins to the miraculous intervention of the Holy Spirit, working through Kathryn Kuhlman, rather than to the normal physiological response of the body to relief from a preganancy.

That is Lois' privilege. But it would be very difficult to convince anyone, even a rabid Kathryn Kuhlman devotee, that the decrease in the size of Lois' veins was, indeed, a miracle.

In talking to these patients I tried to be as honest, understanding and objective as possible. The only things I refused to dispense with—couldn't have dispensed with even if I had tried—were my medical knowledge and my common sense. I listened carefully to everything they told me and followed up every lead which might, even remotely, have led to a confirmation of a miracle. When I had done all this I was led to an inescapable conclusion: none of the patients who had returned to Minneapolis to reaffirm the cures they had claimed at the miracle service had, in fact, been miraculously cured of anything, by either Kathryn Kuhlman or the Holy Spirit.

9

Although well over a hundred patients had claimed cures at the miracle service, there were, of course, thousands who had not. How did they react to the service?

All were disappointed, some deeply so; for example, the mothers with retarded, deformed children whom I had seen crying as they left the auditorium. Others tried to be philosophical about their experience—after all, Kathryn Kuhlman hadn't promised them a cure, had she? If they weren't cured, perhaps it was their own fault. Perhaps they weren't spiritually ready to be cured. It was the Holy Spirit's right to decide whom He would and would not cure. No one blamed Kathryn Kuhlman; most blamed themselves.

Many of those who weren't cured were reluctant to talk about the experience at all. From Litchfield, for example, two busloads of patients, about sixty people, had gone to the Kathryn Kuhlman meeting. For two weeks prior to the meeting our local newspaper had run notices telling those who might want to make the trip what numbers they could call to make reservations.

Not only because I was looking into "faith healing," but as a surgeon in practice in Litchfield I was curious to learn if any of the local people (I assumed some of my patients would be in the group) derived any medical benefit from the service. So, a few days before the meeting, I called the number listed in the paper and asked the woman in charge of the trip to help me out.

"I have no desire to infringe on anyone's privacy," I told

her, "but I'm interested in spiritual healing and perhaps you might do me a favor. Just tell those who make the trip that I'd be most grateful if they'd contact me afterward and report on their experience." She agreed to make that announcement.

I never heard from any of those who went to the service from Litchfield. I assume no one was cured. Litchfield being the small town it is, I think that if anyone had been cured (even to the extent that those I've reported on were "cured"), word would have gotten around. I made a few discreet inquiries, with negative results.

I did, however, learn of one repercussion I sustained from even daring to ask about the local trip to see Kathryn Kuhlman. A friend of mine told me at a party one night that there was some resentment toward me in Litchfield because I was "looking into this Kathryn Kuhlman thing." The feeling was that I was a doctor and that Kathryn Kuhlman's work was not medical, not in my field, and that I had no business nosing around locally trying to find out who went to her service. I mention this episode only because it is typical of the attitude, which I've already mentioned, that believers have toward probing. Believers just do not want anyone asking questions; they resent those who do.

Still, in my nosing around, I discovered one thing about those who weren't helped: they frequently rationalized their visit as being something they did "just out of curiosity." One woman, for example, took her seven-year-old son, sick with inoperable bone cancer, to the service. The mother, a very intelligent woman, was embarrassed because she knew that many of us in town were aware that she had taken Michael to the service. "I didn't really take him down there because I thought he'd be cured," she told a friend. "It's just that I was curious to see what the service was like and I couldn't find anybody to stay with Mike so I brought him along."

God knows, she didn't have to explain. No one with any compassion would ever have criticized her or laughed at her. Her son was dying a slow, painful death. It was easy to understand any parent grasping at the straw that the Kathryn Kuhlman service—as advertised and publicized—represented.

But did the Kuhlman service even offer a remote chance that a patient with a malignant disease might be cured? Even though none of those who had claimed a cancer cure at the time of the service returned to Minneapolis to reaffirm their cure, I was anxious to find out what had happened to them. I wrote to everyone on my list who at the time of the meeting had claimed a cure of a malignant disease. I called or visited those who didn't respond. This is what I learned.

Case A—Richard Whalen, the twenty-one year old boy with what appeared to be cancer of the liver. He had tried to claim a cure, but Maggie had prevented him from getting to the stage. The legal secretaries had gotten his address.

Richard had died of his cancer twelve days after Kathryn Kuhlman's visit.

Case B—Leona Flores, the woman who had "claimed a cure" of lung cancer, and who had, on the stage, at Kathryn Kuhlman's suggestion, "proved" her cure by taking deep breaths without any pain.

Leona, it turned out when I contacted her, did not have lung cancer at all. "I have Hodgkin's disease," she said, "and some of the glands in my chest are involved. But since no one else got up when Miss Kuhlman said, 'Someone with lung cancer is being cured,' I figured it had to be me.

"I've been back to my doctor and he says he can't see any change in my X-ray. I think I breathe better than I did before the miracle service, but it's hard to tell, since I never had much trouble with my breathing anyway. I've had Hodgkin's disease for almost four years now. I still take my drugs regularly and my doctor says I'm doing nicely."

Hodgkin's disease is difficult to classify. It may or may not be a type of cancer. One thing is certain—it is a very unpredictable disease. Some patients can be cured by surgery, others by radiation or drugs. Many live comfortably with the ailment under control for ten or fifteen or twenty years or longer. Unlike lung cancer, Hodgkin's disease is certainly not a highly malignant illness.

Leona Flores, who had breathed deeply to a loud ovation at the miracle service, had definitely not been cured of lung cancer, Hodgkin's disease or anything else by Kathryn Kuhlman.

Case C—Peter Warren, the sixty-three-year-old man with kidney cancer which had spread to the bone. He is the man I helped to walk into the auditorium and for whom I found a wheelchair. He went to the stage to claim a cure of bone cancer. The wheelchair I had found for his temporary use was carried to the stage by an usher and put beside him as evidence of his cure. He was one of the many to whom Kathryn Kuhlman addressed the question, "Is that *your* wheelchair?" in a voice full of amazement; and when he answered yes she said, to a rousing ovation, "Praise the Lord."

On the stage Mr. Warren had performed, at Kathryn Kuhlman's suggestion, a number of deep knee bends to demonstrate his cure. I asked Mr. Warren's daughter, when I reached her two months later, about Mr. Warren's subsequent course.

"After the miracle service he felt real good for about three or four days," she said. "Then he began to get weak again and we took him back to the doctor. The doctor took some more X-rays and told us that the tumor had grown some more, and that was making Dad's blood drop. So he gave him a transfusion and changed his medicines around.

"Since then he's had to go back once a week for shots. He's losing weight and he needs pain pills now for his back.

"I guess Dad was wrong when he thought Kathryn Kuhlman had cured him."

* * *

91

Case D—Joseph Virgil, a sixty-seven-year-old man with cancer of the prostate.

Mr. Virgil had been a most impressive witness for Miss Kuhlman. He too had his wheelchair brought to the stage. When Miss Kuhlman asked him to tell everyone what had happened, he said clearly and fervently, "I came here with incurable cancer and now it's gone. I feel perfectly well." When he left he pushed his wheelchair back down the aisle, to loud applause.

When I talked to Mr. Virgil, three months after the service, he said, "I was feeling pretty low when I went to that miracle service. I've always been an active man. Just a few days before Kathryn Kuhlman came to town I had gone to my doctor for a routine physical examination and he discovered a cancer of the prostate. He told me there wasn't any point in operating on it, that the chances of curing it with surgery were very poor. So he just put me on some pills. I didn't feel sick when I went to the doctor, but I sure felt lousy afterward. I figured my number was up.

"When I heard she was coming to Minneapolis I decided I might as well give Miss Kuhlman a try. I was feeling awfully low when I got to the auditorium but after the singing and the praying and seeing all those people going up, cured, I began to think, 'Maybe it can happen to me too.' Then when she pointed in my direction and said, 'Over there, about halfway back, there's someone who is afraid of dying of cancer. He doesn't have to worry. The Holy Spirit is healing him. Stand up and claim your cure.' I just knew it had to be me. Because, boy, was I worrying about dying of cancer.

"I went back to my doctor a few days later just to make sure it had been me. He tells me the cancer is still in my prostate, but this time he also said he didn't think I'll die of it. He says I don't need surgery but if I take those pills which he's giving me I can go on working and hunting and doing everything I've always done. I don't know whether Kathryn Kuhlman cured me or whether I just misunderstood the doctor the first time. Either way, I feel a lot better now. I'm not worrying any more."

Cancer of the prostate gland is, in many instances, a very benign form of cancer. Often the disease causes no symptoms. The doctor finds it, as in Mr. Virgil's case, when he does a routine rectal examination on a patient. The cancer feels like a hard rough spot in the prostate gland.

Some surgeons operate on early cancer of the prostate, but most doctors prefer to treat the disease with stilbestrol, a female hormone which will cause the cancer to shrink. Patients with cancer of the prostate can live comfortably for years simply by taking one stilbestrol pill a day.

Mr. Virgil's doctor made an error that doctors make only too often: he hadn't fully explained Mr. Virgil's problem to him. Once a doctor tells a patient he has cancer, the patient, understandably, panics. Cancer is a disease we all dread. And when the doctor adds, "No operation is necessary," the patient, again understandably, may interpret this statement as meaning, "There's nothing we can do." After being clubbed with that message, it is only natural that a patient responds as Mr. Virgil did, by going into a severe depression.

Mr. Virgil's doctor, because he didn't do his job properly, drove Mr. Virgil to Kathryn Kuhlman. She didn't hurt him—in fact, she helped him by lifting his spirits—but she didn't cure him. Nor did the Holy Spirit, working through her, cure him.

Mr. Virgil still has prostate cancer, but now that his doctor has explained his disease to him, Mr. Virgil is no longer depressed. He may very well live many more years—to die, as the saying goes, "of natural causes."

Case E—Mrs. Helen Sullivan, a fifty-year-old woman with cancer of the stomach which had spread to both her liver and vertebrae in her back.

At the miracle service Mrs. Sullivan had, at Kathryn Kuhlman's suggestion, taken off her back brace and run back and forth across the stage several times. Finally she walked back down the aisle to her wheelchair, waving her brace as she went, while the audience applauded and Kathryn Kuhlman gave thanks to the Lord.

Two months after the miracle I talked to Mrs. Sullivan. At that time she was confined to her bed, which had been moved into the living room of her farm home. Her husband was at work in the fields and Mrs. Sullivan's eighteen-year-old daughter, the youngest of her three children (the other two are married), had just arrived home from school and was busy cleaning the house.

Mrs. Sullivan was not thin; she was emaciated. Her arms weren't much thicker than a broom handle and her cheekbones were barely covered with flesh. Despite this wasting away, when she smiled you could tell that she had once been a pretty woman. Her eyes, though they were sunk far back in her head, still radiated a feeling of warmth. I liked her immediately.

"In September of 1971," she told me, "I began to have trouble with swallowing. Food would stick in my throat. I didn't think much of it, just began to chew my food more, but when I started to lose weight I thought I'd better see a doctor. He took some X-rays and told me I had a growth in my upper stomach and esophagus. They operated on me and found a cancer. They took out the part of the stomach and esophagus where the tumor was, but they couldn't cure me with the operation; the tumor had already spread to the liver.

"After the operation I could swallow pretty well, but I didn't have much appetite and I kept losing weight. The doctor gave me treatment with 5-F.U. [5-fluorouracil, a relatively new anti-cancer drug] and after I got over the nausea that the treatment caused, I felt better for about three months. Then I began to lose weight again. My doctor gave me another course of treatment with 5-F.U., but this time it didn't do any good.

"I knew about Kathryn Kuhlman from watching her television show, and when I read that she was coming to

Minneapolis, I got pretty excited. My husband tried to calm me down—he kept telling me not to get my hopes too high—but when you're awfully sick and someone tells you that you may be cured, it's impossible not to get excited. By the time Kathryn Kuhlman came to the auditorium I was just about sure I was going to get better.

"At the service, as soon as she said, 'Someone with cancer is being cured,' I knew she meant me. I could just feel this burning sensation all over my body and I was convinced the Holy Spirit was at work. I went right up on the stage and when she asked me about the brace I just took it right off, though I hadn't had it off for over four months, I had so much back pain.

"While I was up on that stage, bending over, touching my toes and running up and down as she asked me to, I felt just wonderful. I didn't have a pain anywhere. Even when we were riding back home [Mrs. Sullivan lives 130 miles from Minneapolis] I refused to wear the brace. I was sure I was cured. That night I said a prayer of thanksgiving to the Lord and Kathryn Kuhlman and went to bed, happier than I'd been in a long time.

"At four o'clock the next morning I woke up with a horrible pain in my back. It was so bad that I broke out in a cold sweat. I didn't dare move. I called to Ralph and he got up and brought me some pain pills. They helped, but not enough so I could sleep. In the morning we called the doctor. He took me to the hospital and got some X-rays that showed one of my vertebrae had partially collapsed. He said it was probably from the bending and running I had done. I stayed in the hospital, in traction, for a week. When I went home I was back in my brace.

"Since then, as you can probably guess by looking at me, I've gotten a lot weaker. I can't make it upstairs any more; that's why we've got the bed down here. Sometimes I can sit up to eat, but not often.

"I was awfully depressed for about a month after Kathryn

Kuhlman's visit. I cried a lot. Our minister finally convinced me to forget about her and just put my faith in God.

"I know I'm going to die soon but I've learned to accept the idea of death. I've had a pleasant life . . . nothing out of the ordinary, I suppose, but I've had a loving husband and three children I'm proud of. A lot of women haven't had as much.

"I still pray a lot—not to be cured and not even to be free of pain; just to have less pain, so that I can bear it. And God answers my prayers. He never gives me more pain than I can stand. I'm very grateful to Him."

Mrs. Sullivan died of cancer four months after she had been "cured" at Kathryn Kuhlman's miracle service.

The more I learned of the results of Kathryn Kuhlman's miracle service, the more doubtful I became that any good she was doing could possibly outweigh the misery she was causing. I wrote to her and asked if she'd send me a list of patients she had cured so that I could check on them.

Miss Kuhlman was most cooperative. Almost by return mail I received a letter listing sixteen patients by name, address, telephone number and diagnosis. Her letter was very friendly but the line that interested me most was this: "What I tried to do [referring to the list of patients] was give you a variety, and diseases that could not possibly have been psychosomatic." When I looked at the list I found that two thirds of the patients suffered from diseases such as multiple sclerosis, rheumatoid arthritis, paralysis (no cause listed), loss of sight, and allergies, in all of which the psyche often plays a major and dominant role. It was apparent from her letter that Miss Kuhlman knew very little—next to nothing—about psychosomatic diseases.

Before I return to this matter, let me briefly report on the results I obtained pursuing those patients on Miss Kuhlman's list who had, supposedly, been cured of cancer. In her letter Miss Kuhlman had said: "I am sure they will not mind if you contact them for further information." In this matter, too, I found that Miss Kuhlman was either misinformed or naïve.

I wrote to all the cancer patients on her list—six of them—and only two answered my letters. I phoned the others, only to find that they were not the least bit amenable. Of the two who wrote, one said that he had granted exclusive rights to his story to Miss Kuhlman. I sent a copy of Miss Kuhlman's letter to this man, after which he sent me the name of his doctor so that I could get more information. Unfortunately, the doctor refused to cooperate.

The one patient who offered to help out was a man who claimed he had been cured of prostatic cancer by Miss Kuhlman. He sent me a thorough report of his case. I have already mentioned that prostatic cancer is frequently responsive to hormone therapy; if it spreads, it is also often highly responsive to radiation therapy. This man had had extensive treatment of his disease with surgery, radiation and hormones. He had also been "treated" by Kathryn Kuhlman. He chose to attribute his cure—or a remission, as the case may be; only time will tell—to Miss Kuhlman. That is, of course, his privilege. But anyone who reads his report, layman or doctor, would immediately see that in his case it is impossible to tell what modality of treatment had actually done most to prolong his life. If Miss Kuhlman had to rely on his case to prove that the Holy Spirit "cured" cancer through her, she would be in very desperate straits.

Which brings me back to Kathryn Kuhlman's lack of medical sophistication—a point that is, in her case, critical. I don't believe Miss Kuhlman is a liar; I don't believe she is a charlatan; I don't believe she is, consciously, dishonest. I think (and this is, of course, only my opinion, based on a rather brief acquaintance with her) that she honestly believes the Holy Spirit works through her to perform miraculous cures. I think that she sincerely believes that the thousands of patients who come to her services every year and claim cures are, through her ministrations, being cured of organic diseases. I also think—and my investigations confirm this— that she is wrong.

The problem is, and I'm sorry this has to be so blunt, one of ignorance. Miss Kuhlman doesn't know the difference between psychogenic and organic diseases; she doesn't know anything about hypnotism and the power of suggestion; she doesn't know anything about the autonomic nervous system. If she does know something about any or all of these things, she has certainly learned to hide her knowledge.

There is one other possibility. It may be that Miss Kuhlman doesn't want to learn that her ministry is not as miraculous as it seems. If so, she has trained herself to deny, emotionally and intellectually, anything that might threaten the validity of her ministry.

Personally, I favor this latter hypothesis.

As far as the other people who work with Miss Kuhlman and her foundation are concerned, I reserve judgment. I haven't investigated their organization except from the medical point of view. I find it difficult to believe that all those who surround her are true believers. I know, for example, from talking to people who have attended many services, that one of Maggie's main functions is to find reluctant patients and encourage them to stand, claim cures and start the flow toward the stage—hardly an honest or honorable assignment.

I don't have anything more to say about Kathryn Kuhlman as a person. Having finished my report, I'm inclined to rest my case on the axiom, often used by the prosecutor in malpractice cases when a sponge has been found in an abdomen, that *res ipsa loquitur*—"the thing speaks for itself."

III

NORBU CHEN

10

While on a trip to California, I remembered Tom Valentine's suggestion that I look into Norbu Chen's miraculous-healing practice in Houston, and since I was not far from Los Altos, I decided to stop off at the Institute of Noetic Sciences, which is headed by the former astronaut Captain Edgar D. Mitchell, Sc.D., who is, according to Tom Valentine, "one of Norbu Chen's big promoters." The Institute of Noetic Sciences is a tax-exempt organization headed by Dr. Mitchell. "Noetics" means "the study of consciousness." The purpose of the Institute, according to an article by Mitchell in *Psychic* (July-August 1973), is "to help achieve a new understanding and an expanded consciousness among all people."

Mitchell, who was the sixth man to walk on the moon, dropped out of the space program in 1970. Since then he has devoted much of his time and energy to the promotion of ventures designed to "expand human consciousness." Uri Geller, the man who supposedly can cause objects to move simply by staring at them, is one of those Mitchell has investigated. "Geller can also materialize objects out of nothing," Mitchell told me. "He's really an amazing man."

Mitchell was also sold on he psychic surgeons of the Philippines. "What's the most fundamental form of existence?" he asked me.

"I don't know," I said. "I suppose it's a neutron or a proton or an electron—one of those things that goes to make up an atom." My knowledge of physics is rudimentary.

"No sir," Mitchell said, "it's none of those. Consciousness is the most fundamental form of existence. When those psychic surgeons operate, they use consciousness. They just slip their hands right in between the cells—the matter—that makes up the human body. They use their consciousness in ways that we can't use ours."

I didn't quite follow his explanation, and since I could see we didn't have much common ground for discussing these things, I shifted to Norbu Chen. "I understand that when you were in Houston you observed a healer called Norbu Chen."

"I certainly did," Mitchell replied. "I worked very closely with him. He's a remarkable person."

"I'm limiting my interest in the paranormal, if you'll excuse the phrase, to healing; as you'll probably agree, there are so many fascinating things going on in the paranormal world that it would be impossible for any one man to look, with any depth, into all of them. With my medical background I thought healing would be the natural subject on which to focus my attention. From what I've learned, Norbu Chen is an outstanding healer. Would you agree?"

"No doubt about it," Mitchell replied. "There may be other healers as good—we've got many healers out here in California—but I'd say Norbu is as good as or better than any of them."

"Then you think he'd be a good person for me to study?"

"By all means. But let me warn you, he's a very temperamental guy. I had a hell of a time getting along with him. That's one of the reasons I left him back in Texas when I came out here. I'm still interested in studying him, but I don't want to get too close to him. He's up one minute and down the next. If he gets mad at you, he explodes. He's very volatile. He lived in my home for a while, but I couldn't take it."

"What kind of results does he get?"

102

"He doesn't cure everyone," Mitchell replied, "but he cures most. Up around eighty or ninety percent, I'd guess."

"How about cancer?" I asked. "Do you think he could cure, say, two out of ten?"

"Oh, hell, he'd do a lot better than that," Mitchell answered. "He's really very good. Just be damn careful when you're around him. Don't get him mad at you. Don't trifle with Norbu." I assured Dr. Mitchell I wouldn't.

John White, a man in his mid-twenties I'd guess, serves as Mitchell's assistant at the institute. He said he would approach Norbu Chen for me. Norbu agreed to let me visit him, with the stipulation that Dr. Wilfred J. Hahn, head of the Mind Science Foundation, which has an office in Los Angeles, also agree. The Mind Science Foundation was financing studies on Norbu Chen and he, Norbu, was, so to speak, under contract to them. I called Dr. Hahn and explained my project to him, and he assured me that he had no objection.

So I wrote to Norbu Chen, told him what I wanted to do and asked him to set a convenient date. When two weeks went by and I hadn't received a reply I phoned him. His secretary assured me he had received my letter but hadn't yet gotten around to answering it. I asked her to have him call me, collect, if he could find the time. When, a week later, I still hadn't heard from Norbu Chen, I phoned him again. This time he was in, and he was, to say the least, belligerent. "What do you think—I got nothing to do but hang around letting people study me? The Mind Science Foundation pays for all these studies, then some guy like you wants to come down and find out about it, all for nothing. Bullshit." (Norbu Chen, I found later, uses this expletive frequently. He pronounces it boool—shit. Sort of melodious.)

"Besides," he continued, "Tom Valentine told me about you. Shit, what do you know about healing? You goddamn M.D.s are all the same. You know what I say 'M.D.' stands for? 'Mostly Dumb.'

"And I don't like guys who sneak around trying to get to see me. I like guys who come right to the source—me. I don't like this goddamn sneaking-around stuff."

When he paused I tried to explain my position, how I'd been advised to go through the Mind Science Foundation.

"That's bullshit," he said. "all you guys are full of bullshit.

"All right—you can come down. Not right now though. I'm too goddamn busy. How about a couple of weeks from now? Let me know when you're getting in and I'll have a car meet you."

I wanted to ask him how long I might stay, where I could conveniently live, several other questions, but I didn't. It was enough that he'd said yes. I decided to get off the phone before he changed his mind.

I wasn't looking forward to this visit. I don't like to go where I suspect I'm not welcome, and I certainly suspected I wasn't welcome in Houston. But I had to find out if Norbu Chen could, indeed, "heal" with some strange Tibetan power. So, two weeks later, I flew to Houston.

When I landed at the Houston airport I looked around for someone who might conceivably be looking for me. I had let Norbu Chen know what time I was arriving and he had said someone would meet me. When it was apparent that no one was there to pick me up I phoned Norbu Chen and he snarled, "Get a cab. We're waiting for you."

Idiotically, I had taken only $20 in cash with me. When the meter on the cab reached $8 and we were still on a freeway, I asked the driver how much it would cost me to get to Norbu's home. "Twenty, maybe twenty-one dollars," he said. I then decided it might be less expensive and more convenient if I rented a car. So, having driven me from the International Airport, across Houston, the cabdriver took me to Hobby Airport, Houston's second, smaller airport. There, after my $18 taxi ride, I rented the car I should have rented at International. I'm not always well organized.

Norbu Chen lives southeast of Houston on a short street

104

that ends by making a circle around a small park. The neighborhood looks as if it had once been fashionable but is now on its way down. Norbu's home is set about a hundred yards back from the street. There is a wall in front with a gate through which one enters. At first I didn't realize that the gate was large enough to admit a car and that the walk was actually a driveway, so I pulled off the street, planning to walk to the house. When I saw a sign saying "Beware of the Dog" nailed to a tree just inside the gate, I returned to me car immediately, deciding I could, after all, drive in. When it comes to savage dogs, I am a first-class coward.

Unfortunately, my car was stuck in the mud (it has been raining in Houston almost constantly for three days before I arrived, and it rained almost continually during the four days I was there). One of Norbu's neighbors saw me trying to get my car out of the mud, and succeeding only in sinking it further. He was nice enough to get a chain, and using his station wagon, drag me out. I finally pulled up to Norbu's door at five-thirty on Sunday evening. The dog, I learned later, was away at obedience school. "Learning how to kill," Norbu told me with enthusiasm.

When I stepped out of the car I knew immediately why the neighborhood looked as if it was on the way down. There was a pungent, sickening odor in the air; I learned later that it came from an oil refinery, out of sight but not far away. This was really a shame. Norbu's home is surrounded by eight acres of land, with a bayou down a hill from the back of the house. There are many trees on the property, the house is large and attractive, and there is a guesthouse about thirty yards from the main house. But the odor from that refinery spoils it all. In the four days I spent with Norbu I was always aware of the smell, and my eyes would get red, itchy and irritated minutes after I arrived in his yard. They'd clear up ten minutes after I was out of the driveway. A beautiful setting, but pollution has made the area virtually unlivable, at least for someone who is accustomed to the clean air of rural Minnesota.

Norbu, as his secretary told me later, rarely introduces anyone to anyone else, but some young woman, I think it was probably Norbu's wife, did introduce me to Norbu and two couples who were sitting in the living room eating hamburgers when I arrived. The men were Dr. Howell Cobb, a biologist at Trinity College in San Antonio, Texas, and a man whom I shall call Randy Lewis, a patient of Norbu's who now serves on the board of Norbu Chen's foundation. One of the women was Randy Lewis' wife, the other was Jean, an associate of Dr. Cobb's who was working with him on the scientific investigation of Norbu Chen's healing powers.

Norbu Chen said he was thirty-nine years old, but he looked older. He is not Oriental; I learned later that he had changed his name to "Norbu Chen." He has a weather-beaten face with many wrinkles. His hair is gray and close-cropped, like a monk's. He is about five feet four, stocky, with a slight paunch. When I met him he was wearing brown slacks and a short-sleeved sport shirt. He is muscular and has tattoos on both forearms. The one on the left is about three inches in diameter and has, on the top, the letters "U.S.M.C." which, I presume, stands for United States Marine Corps. I couldn't get a good look at the tattoo on his right forearm.

Norbu also has two scars, one about six inches long running obliquely from under his right ear down to the lower midline of his neck. The other is a shorter, vertical scar in the midline of his neck. It looked to me like a tracheotomy scar, the kind Liz Taylor has, except that Norbu's isn't the work of a plastic surgeon. (I never asked him where the scars came from. As you'll see when I tell you more about him, I had to be very careful what I asked him, or he might have tossed me out. But a friend of Norbu's told me Norbu had attributed the scars to "Korea," without elaborating on the circumstances.)

A few minutes after I arrived, we got down to business. "Dr. Cobb is running the research on me for the Mind

Science Foundation," Norbu said. "Usually I go to San Antonio to work but today he brought the mices [*sic*] here. I'm going to treat them and you can watch."

"Great," I said. "Can you tell me something about the experiment?" I asked Dr. Cobb.

"Happy to," Dr. Cobb replied. "We are studying mice in groups of thirty. We inject all the mice with cancer cells of a type which we know grow very easily in mice. Ordinarily about ninety percent of the injected mice will die of the cancer in two to three weeks.

"After injection, Norbu treats fifteen of the mice; the other fifteen remained untreated. It's a blind study; only Jean, my assistant, knows which of the thirty mice have been treated."

"When do you sacrifice the mice?" I asked.

"We don't," Dr. Cobb answered. "We wait till they die. Then Jean tells uks which were treated by Norbu."

"Have they all died?" I asked.

"So far," Dr. Cobb answered. "But those that had been treated by Dr. Chen have lived significantly longer than those that hadn't been treated."

"And up till now," Norbu Chen interrupted, "they haven't let me get my hands on those mices. [Norbu often has a problem with plurals. Once I heard him tell a patient to "take your shoeses off."] I've had to treat them from about a foot away. Not only that, but I've been treating them in San Antonio in a laboratory where the vibrations aren't good. Tonight I'm going to treat them right here and I'm going to get my hands right on those mices. That's going to make things go even better."

"Shall we get at it?" Dr. Cobb asked.

"Okay with me," Norbu Chen said.

Five of the mice would be put to sleep so that Norbu could get his hands right on them. "Do you want the anesthetized mice first?" Dr. Cobb asked.

"Makes no difference to me," Norbu answered. "Suit yourself."

Dr. Cobb and his assistant went out to the kitchen to prepare the mice and Norbu left the room to prepare for his healing work. In the five minutes Norbu was gone I worked on my notes.

When Norbu reappeared he was wearing a brown robe, like the surplice that Catholic priests wear, and he had a gold pendant on a chain around his neck. "Let's go," he said, beckoning to me. I followed him into the treatment room.

This room was dimly lit by candles. The smell of incense was strong. The walls were hung with dark-red tapestries. In one corner was a small altar on which there were a skull cup and a small Buddha statue. In the center of the room was a table and on the table were three boxes, each about a foot square. Two of the boxes had wire-mesh covers; these boxes each contained five live mice. The third box was open on the top and in it were the five anesthetized mice. Near the table were two chairs. Norbu told me to sit on one; Randy Lewis was assigned the other.

Norbu then turned to the altar with his back toward us. He made a series of waves with his arms outstretched and then started howling like a wolf. After he had howled for about a minute he picked up two small bells that were on the altar and clanged them together over his head. Then he howled some more.

After five minutes of this sort of behavior, Norbu came over to the table and held his hands for a few seconds over each of the two boxes of alert mice. He put his hands on the anesthetized mice. Then he walked back to the altar, looked at it for a few seconds, turned to us and said, "That's all." We followed him from the room. (On April 26, 1974, the Mind Science Foundation reported that Norbu's experiments with mice were as yet inconclusive.)

He went somewhere, presumably to his bedroom, and a few minutes later joined us all in the living room. He had removed his robe and pendant and was wearing his slacks and sport shirt.

"Did that exhaust you, Mr. Chen?" I asked. (Norbu never told me what to call him, so sometimes I called him Mr. Chen, sometimes Dr. Chen, and toward the end of my visit, Norbu. I noticed that others varied their salutation as I did.)

"Of course not," he said. "Why should I? I don't do anything. The power does it." Norbu answered this and all of my subsequent questions with the resigned air of an expert who is forced to explain things to an imbecile.

"What power is that?"

"The power of The Way, of course. The power I learned to use when I was with my lama. It's very simple. It's just one-point concentration. I use sound, one-point concentration and breathing to raise my emotional level to a great height. We say then that I shoot through the golden lotus to another level of being. I focus all the dynamic tensive forces of my body at one point for one instant—and then I hit."

"When you say 'hit,' do you mean you release all that force to heal someone?"

"Of course." Again he answered with a bored, paternalistic sigh. (I won't mention this attitude again. Just assume this was the way Norbu Chen always answered my questions.)

"Can you feel this power leaving you?"

"Yes."

"But it doesn't exhaust you?"

"No."

Norbu could see I was puzzled. "Look," he said, "don't try to understand all this. Goddammit, how could you? All you know is that stupid M.D. bullshit. You want to understand me, you've got to do what I did. You got to learn 'The Way' and that ain't easy.

"I don't mean to be obsequious [sic], but goddamn, you asking me how I work is like me asking you about some stupid tonsil you took out. It's simple for me. It's almost an insult to ask me about it. Why should I waste all my time explaining things to you? Dr. Hahn and the Mind Science

109

Foundation—they're the ones spending money to find out about my power. Then you want to come in and steal all that information. Bullshit."

"I'm not trying to steal anything," I said.

"Oh, I don't mean you personally. I mean all these goddamn people want to learn The Way without working at it. They're all bullshit."

"Maybe we should start at the beginning," I said. "How did you happen to learn The Way?"

Norbu told me. Not fully, not completely and not in one continuous stream of talk, but over the next three days he summarized his life history for me. He refused to be pinned down on names and dates—in fact, when I asked him what his name had been before he assumed the name Norbu Chen sometime in the early sixties, he became very hostile.

"What you want to know that for?" he said.

"I guess I'm just curious," I answered.

"Oh yeah?" he said. "Well, it's none of your goddamn business."

After that one exchange I felt it best not to push Norbu for information, lest I be cut off completely. I simply tried to get him talking, sometimes—usually unsuccessfully— trying to steer the conversation in the direction I thought might be productive. Here is Norbu's story as he told it to me.

In 1956, when he was twenty-two years old, Norbu— under his original name, whatever that may be—said he was working for the Kennedy political organization in Kentucky. He told me a man named Dick Cohn was his boss. Norbu's assignment apparently involved some sort of undertaking, the purpose of which he said was to discredit the incumbent governor and lieutenant governor, "Happy" Chandler and Harry Lee Waterfield. Norbu says that the Kennedy organization wanted Bert Combs elected governor.

According to Norbu, as a result of work for the Kennedy organization the police got after him. He spent some time in

110

jail and in the "nut house" and then, in 1958, was forced to leave the United States and go to Europe.

First he went to Switzerland, sometime later to England. While in London he went to the British Museum and felt drawn to the Tibetan exhibit. He noticed that most of the pieces on display had been donated or lent by Lady Alexandra David-Neel, a woman who had spent many years in Tibet and had written three books on the subject; *Initiation Rites of Tibet, Magic and Mystery in Tibet* and *My Journey to Lhasa.* Norbu felt a compulsion to go and visit Madame David-Neel, who was then living in Switzerland. (It's important for the reader to understand, as I learned later, that Norbu Chen professes to believe in reincarnation. He says that everything we do we do because we must; we are the result of all our previous lives. He went to jail, to Switzerland, because all these things were preordained.)

In Switzerland, Norbu spent some time visiting with Madame David-Neel. When he left, he knew he must eventually go and learn The Way. Madame David-Neel gave him a letter, written in Tibetan, which language, of course, he couldn't read. He took this letter and went to Paris, where he worked to earn money so he could go meet his lama.

In 1960, having now been out of the United States for two years, he left Paris and went to Sikkim, high in the Himalayas. Since the Chinese Communists made Tibet off-limits for foreigners, Sikkim is the only country where one can now learn The Way. Today, the ruler of the 200,000 Sikkims is Maharajah Palden Thondup Namgyal. Sikkim was briefly prominent in the news in 1963, when the Maharajah, then the Crown Prince, married Hope Cooke, a New York debutante.

When Norbu arrived in Gangtok, the capital, he went directly to the marketplace. There he saw a man whom he had never seen before. Norbu felt a compulsion to walk up to that man and give him 500 rupees, all the money he had saved. Norbu also gave the man the letter from Madame

Alexandra David-Neel. The man, who was to be Norbu's lama, said only, "You've been a long time coming." Then he walked away and Norbu followed him.

Norbu spent the next three years learning The Way. He was unable to tell me exactly how this is done ("to understand it you must live it") but he did tell me about some of his experiences.

For the first eleven and a half months Norbu lived in a cave. He wore only a loincloth, although the temperature in Sikkim gets down to twenty degrees below zero in the winter. He neither saw nor spoke to anyone in all that time.

There was a spring at one end of the cave, so he had all the water he needed. "I went to the other end to piss and shit," Norbu said.

Every three days Norbu ate a light meal. The food was passed to him through an S-shaped tunnel, so he never saw the person who brought him his meals. During these eleven and a half months he communed with himself. When he left the cave he had made a start toward learning The Way. The Way, as best I could understand it from Norbu's explanation, is a matter of learning how to put man's mind and body in harmony with the rest of the universe. When we do not have this harmony, we are ill.

Over the next two years Norbu acquired some startling powers. For example, Norbu asked me if I'd ever heard of *rolang*. I hadn't, so he told me about it.

"*Rolang*," Norbu said, "means 'dancing with a corpse.' You lie down on a dead body, a body that's been dead about seven days, and you put your mouth on its mouth. Then the corpse gets up and starts dancing around. You hang on to that corpse while it jumps and dances, and you keep your mouth on its mouth."

I was almost ill with the thought of all this, but I asked, "Why? What's the point?"

"After a while," Norbu said, "the corpse will stick its tongue out. Then you bite it off. The corpse moves around a little longer, then drops to the ground."

"What do you do with the tongue?" I asked.

"Keep it," Norbu said. "It's a power piece."

"Have you done this—have you danced with a corpse?"

"Of course," Norbu answered, "but I'm not going to do it for you. And I've got tongues too, but I'm not going to show them to you. I'm not here to entertain you, goddammit." I had mixed emotions about not seeing Norbu dance with a corpse.

Norbu seemed disgusted with my lack of knowledge of his powers. "I bet you never even heard about 'psychic sports,'" he said accusingly. I admitted I hadn't.

"Hell," he said, "that's what we do in Sikkim, like you play football here. We have contests. Like in the winter, when it's twenty below zero, we break the ice and soak sheets in that water and then wrap them around us and see which of us can dry the most sheets fastest.

"Or sometimes we try *lung-gum;* we see which one of us can float in the air the longest.

"If we feel like it, we do astral projection. Our astral body leaves our material body and travels around the country. If we want, we do *pho wa;* we get into someone else's body."

"Have you done all these things?" I asked.

"Of course; no problem. And I can do other things. You see that picture over there?" Norbu pointed at a tapestry on a far wall. I got up, walked to it and looked at the picture. It was a figure of an ugly half-human beast.

"That's a picture of a being from another order of existence," Norbu said. "I can make that being appear just by staring at the picture."

"You mean you could bring that being into existence, right here in this room, just by staring at that picture?" I asked.

"Goddammit, I just said I could, didn't I? Of course I can. But I'm not going to; I'm not here to put on a show for you."

I went back to my chair and sat down. I'd certainly have

113

liked to see Norbu materialize this creature from another order of being, preferably in a cage, but I was certain I'd never persuade him to do so.

After learning how to do all these strange things (strange to me, at any rate) and having acquired the ability to heal, using The Way, Norbu came back to the United States.

"I didn't want to come," he said, "but my lama told me to come back. I'm here to bring The Way to the Western world. I don't seek anybody out, but some will seek me. I'd rather be back in Sikkim, but for now I've got to stay here."

"Do you still keep in touch with your lama?"

"Of course."

"How?" I asked. "Do you write?"

Norbu's look of disdain was something to behold. "Of course not," he said. "We communicate directly."

"Mental telepathy?"

"I can't explain to you, goddammit. Only those who know The Way can understand."

It was 1965 when Norbu came back to the United States. He was very vague about the next three years, though he mentioned that in 1967 he spent four months in the Philippines watching the psychic surgeons. He said that he tried to heal between 1965 and 1970, but the M.D.s wouldn't let him. "You know what they told me down in Florida? They told me to go stick pins into dolls. All the time they were killing patients I could have cured with The Way. You see why I call them 'Mostly Dumb'?"

Sometime in 1970 or 1971 Norbu met Dr. Edgar Mitchell at an E.S.P. convention in Arkansas. Mitchell was impressed with Norbu Chen's healing powers and persuaded Norbu to come to Houston, where Mitchell had his office at the time.

"I worked on 'motor-mouth,' one of Mitchell's secretaries," Norbu said. "She had bad kidney disease. I cured her. But you know what that dumb broad did? A few weeks later she went out and got drunk and had a recurrence. How dumb can you be?

114

"I worked on Mitchell's mother, too. She had arthritis. I treated that and fixed her eyes too. She used to wear glasses but she doesn't need them any more."

When Mitchell left Houston for San Antonio, Norbu stayed behind. By that time he had started his own organization, the Chakpori-Ling Foundation, and was firmly established as a healer.

"My foundation is nonprofit," Norbu said. "I've got it set up like a church. I support it with the money I earn healing, but I've got people with a lot of money on my board. Doris Duke is on my board, and so is C.V. Wood, Jr., president of the McCulloch Oil Company. They all help me.

"Take Sam Jones, for example. ["Sam Jones" is a fictitious name I am using instead of the actual name Norbu used.] Sam's got four planes, but the foundation uses them when we need them. That's how we flew Dr. Cobb and his assistant out from San Antonio and back. I've got lots of support." [Checking later with the office of the Secretary of State in Austin, I found out that Doris Duke and C.V. Wood, Jr., were listed at the time of registration as trustees of Chakpori-Ling Sangha. Although "Sam Jones" was not included on this list, he might have become a trustee later.]

"Of course, I don't need their money," he continued. "Shit, I can make two phone calls and fart more money than Sam Jones earns with his surgical practice in a year." (Dr. Jones told me, later, that his practice brings him about $200,000 a year. Norbu has an amazing digestive tract.)

"What do you charge for healing?" I asked Norbu.

"The minimum donation is five hundred dollars," he said. "Lots of people donate more, because I get good results. Not like you stupid M.D.s."

"Can you cure patients with one treatment?" I asked.

"That's a dumb question," Norbu said. "It depends. Some patients I cure with one treatment, no problem. Sometimes it takes more than one treatment. And I don't cure all of them. I admit it. But my results are a hell of a lot better than yours. Remember, I'm just treating the ones you guys have screwed up."

"Do you have figures on your results?"

"Not exact. I haven't got time to fool around with that bullshit. But I can give you an idea.

"With kidneys I cure about ninety-five percent, hearts ninety percent, multiple sclerosis only about thirty-two to thirty-eight percent. Some of the M.S. patients I can't help at all; some I improve; some I cure completely."

"How about cancer?" I asked.

"Without metastases [i.e., without spread of the tumor from the organ in which it arose to a distant organ] eighty-seven percent cures."

Later, when I got a cursory look at Norbu's "records," I wondered about the percentages that he rattled off so glibly. Most of his records contained nothing but the name, address and phone number of the patient, and some didn't even have all of these.

"How many patients do you treat in a month?" I asked.

"It depends on how I feel," Norbu answered. "Just like you. You wouldn't go in and operate if you felt lousy, would you?"

"Not if I could help it," I admitted.

"Well, I'm the same way. I could have all the patients I want, but I only work when I'm feeling good. Shit, I've had some patients fly in here to be treated and I didn't feel like healing, so I sent them home. I even paid their way.

"Sometimes, if a patient isn't satisfied with the result I get, I fly him back and treat him again for nothing. That's more than you goddamn M.D.s do."

I had to admit he had a point.

Later I learned from his patient Randy Lewis what Norbu's treatment routine was like.

"Norbu has room here for four patients," Mr. Lewis told me. "He has sleeping accommodations for two women and two men. The patients fly here on the day before treatment. They are supposed to be here by one P.M. They go to bed at three P.M. and are not supposed to get out of bed, except to go to the bathroom, until they receive treatment the next morning. The patient fasts, except for grapefruit juice, from three in the afternoon till the next morning."

"What time does Norbu treat his patients?"

"Whenever he feels like it," Mr. Lewis said. "Sometimes at eight in the morning, sometimes not till ten."

"What's the treatment like?"

"Exactly like the treatment you saw him give the mice. He works in front of his altar for a while, then shoots his power through you."

"Do you feel anything as the power goes through you?"

"No, nothing."

"So the entire treatment, including his work in front of the altar, takes only about five minutes?"

"Right."

"Then the patient goes home."

"Correct," Mr. Lewis said. "Though, as Norbu told you, in some cases it's necessary for him to return for more treatments later."

Norbu never would tell me how many patients he treated in a week or month or year, though he assured me that he could have as many patients as he wanted. However, with facilities at the Chakpori-Ling Foundation (Norbu's home is the foundation) which will accommodate four patients, Norbu says he can earn, whenever he pleases, a minimum of $2,000 a day. That should support Norbu's foundation, and Norbu himself, quite comfortably.

Some of us may have reservations about Norbu's ability to dance with a corpse, but one thing is certain: he sure knows how to make money.

11

Norbu Chen is a difficult man to put on paper. He is pompous, arrogant and vulgar; he is also humorous, warm and clever. He is a master of double-talk, and some of the things he says are prime examples of the "bullshit" to which he so often refers. He contradicts himself constantly and if you question him about these inconsistencies, he looks at you as if you were so ignorant as to be beneath his contempt. After spending four days with him I left liking him very much, but in the way you might like a clever huckster who you know is laughing at himself and the whole human condition. Before long I got the impression Norbu knows this is a dog-eat-dog world—you either eat or get eaten—and goddammit, he is going to be one of the eaters. Perhaps a few excerpts from our random conversations may give you a better idea of what he's like:

Norbu often referred to his lama and the advice the lama gave him. "My lama asked me once, 'What's worse than wanting?' Do you know the answer?" Norbu asked me.

"No," I answered.

"Getting."

Then he explained. "It's like the story of the queen who looked into the magic mirror and said, 'Mirror, Mirror, grant my wish / Make them bigger than a fish,' and all of a sudden she's got tits that stick out to here," Norbu moved his hands to outline for me the queen's new shape.

"So," he continued, "the king sees what happened and

he steps up to the mirror and says, 'Mirror, Mirror, on the door / Make it hang down to the floor.' And all of a sudden the poor son of a bitch hasn't got any legs.''

"You know why I got this big Cadillac and this big house and the Porsche and all this stuff?" Norbu asked. "Because my lama told me to get these things. Over here they're symbols of power, so I have them. Hell, there's nothing to getting money. I can fart Cadillacs all day long."

Ten minutes later Norbu got on the subject of Billy Graham. "He doesn't care for people—no minister does. Shit, if he really cared for people, you think he'd be living in a big house and driving around in a Cadillac? What kind of Christian bullshit is that? Christianity and Mohammedanism are the two biggest curses of mankind."

Once we got into a conversation about other healers. Here are Norbu's comments:

"Kathryn Kuhlman makes me sick. She holds a big rally in Texas and they fly in cancer patients from all over. Thousands of really sick people get jammed into an auditorium, and who gets cured? Fifteen arthritics! I call that 'shotgun therapy.' Kathryn Kuhlman is bullshit. The American people deserve her."

Mister A is a healer publicized in Ruth Montgomery's book *Born to Heal*. He was flown to Alabama to work on Governor Wallace. Norbu says, "Mister A is nothing but a seventy-nine-year-old broken-down mechanic. He couldn't cure a pimple.

"They wanted me to fly to Alabama and work on Wallace, but I refused. I'm afraid of what that man might do if he was well."

Of Olga Worral, another well-known healer, Norbu said, "She's nothing but a mixed-up old lady. Shit, she talks about her astral body flying around in the sky and how the golden cord that connects it to her physical body keeps getting tangled up in the trees. What kind of nutty talk is that?"

On the psychic surgeons of the Philippines, Norbu feels: "Out in the back country there's some real healing going on, but Tony Agpaoa and the rest of those 'famous' healers over there are 'nothing.'"

Every now and then Norbu would talk about the gullibility of people. "A few years ago this 'past-life reading' stuff was popular, so I pretended to do it. Some guy came to me with narcolepsy [a condition in which the patient often drifts off to sleep unwillingly and at any time]. He was six feet four inches tall and two hundred and fifty pounds, and all man. I told him that in one of his past lives he was a hermit and lived in a cave, and some guy used to come in once in a while and suck dick. He didn't want to remember that, so he kept dropping off to sleep.

"An old woman came to me and I told her that in one of her previous lives she was the Queen of Sheba. But she had stuck a corncob up King Solomon's ass and that's why she's white now.

"And can you imagine? They both believed me. How dumb can you get?"

To a female employee of Norbu's who came to work with a scratched-up face and a swollen lip: "You look like someone shot at you and missed, and shit at you and hit."

The employee laughed. Norbu is the sort of person who can say things like that and get away with it.

Finally, an example of Norbu's ambiguity when asked to explain how he works. This is from an interview in the *Cosmic Echo*, Vol. 1, No. 2 (September 1972); the newspaper subsequently folded.

As to my technigue it is a long involved process. Like Truth, unexplainable. For the inadequacy of words do not lend themselves to be understood, if you are placed in the position to define. If you are only to describe, yes, but fortunately no other thing exists like this so therefore, nothing to describe from, only to define. One who works like this knows, they don't have to speak. Like if you know Truth, Truth is communicable with unspoken words between two Truth knowers.

This speaks for itself.

Over the next few months I learned all I could about Norbu Chen. I wanted to know how much of what he had told was fact.

One day while I was in Texas, I had lunch with "Dr. Sam Jones," a well-trained, intelligent surgeon. I asked him how he happened to get involved with Norbu Chen.

"I met him at a racing meeting," he said. "Norbu is a sportscar racer and so am I. We got talking and I found out not only that he was living in a house I own—I had rented it out through a real estate agent—but that he knew quite a lot about acupuncture. I was getting interested in the subject at that time, and I asked him to tell me what he knew. With the acupuncture, the house and racing, we've kept our friendship up."

"Do you know anything about the healing he's doing?" I asked.

"Not really," Dr. Jones said. "I don't see that much of him. I keep busy enough with my practice."

"Someday you ought to talk with Norbu about his healing powers," I said. "You might find it interesting."

"I might do that," Dr. Jones answered.

We got onto other subjects—the politics of surgery in Texas in particular—and I let Norbu drop. I didn't want Norbu to think I was turning Jones against him, and I figured that Sam Jones could easily look into Norbu's activities if he chose to do so. It was up to him.

While Dr. Jones couldn't offer me any leads, through

other contacts—who at their request shall remain nameless—I was able to talk with a number of patients other than those whose names Norbu had given me. Here are the reports of three typical patients.

1. Mr. Baker, who runs a successful office-equipment manufacturing business, had taken Steve, one of his associates, to Norbu Chen. "Steve is thirty-three years old and a very bright fellow; I'd call him brilliant. But he has been badly crippled by multiple sclerosis and when I read that Edgar Mitchell thought Chen was a remarkable healer, I decided I'd fly down to Houston with Steve. After all, Mitchell was an astronaut; he had to be a wise man.

"Steve was skeptical, but he agreed to try Norbu—what did he have to lose? By this time—it was May of 1972—Steve couldn't walk at all, though his arms were still strong and he got around his office in an electric wheelchair.

"I didn't like the idea of leaving him alone, but Chen insisted. Steve told me later that he shared a room with a heart patient and that he drank so much grape juice he thought he might turn purple.

"The next morning when they brought him into the treatment room Chen introduced him to two doctors—chiropractors—who were there to observe Chen at work. Norbu howled for a while in front of an altar and then 'hit' Steve. Steve told me later that after the hit, Chen asked, 'Did you feel tingling or did you feel heat?' Steve answered, 'I felt heat,' and Norbu said, 'That's very good. If you'd felt tingling, it would mean I hadn't got a good hit. Heat means you should do well.' Steve told me later he hadn't felt a damn thing, 'but since I had to choose between tingling and heat, I chose heat.'

"When I picked Steve up the next morning, Norbu told me what he'd done. 'Multiple sclerosis is a nerve disease,' he said, 'so I concentrated all my energy in my brain and then hit Steve's brain. Don't expect anything for three months; then the energy from my brain will make his brain work. Then he will get better and better.' When we were driving to the airport Steve said, 'I think it's all a crock of shit.' "

"How's Steve now?" I asked.

"Worse," Mr. Baker answered. "Six months after his visit to Chen he decided he'd better move to a nursing home; his arms had been getting progressively weaker, and even with the electric wheelchair, he could barely get around. He insisted that his wife divorce him so that she could get remarried while she's still a young woman. Reluctantly, she did.

"I still see Steve two or three times a week—in fact, he still works for us. His brain is as sharp as ever, but his body is failing fast. It's sad."

"How does Steve feel about Norbu Chen?" I asked.

"Just as he did at the time; he thinks the guy is a complete phony. But he's able to laugh at the experience. Steve is a remarkable man."

2. Mrs. Hayes told me of her experience with Chen's treatment of her dying fifteen-year-old son. "We were desperate," she said. "Jimmy had a brain tumor and had gone into a coma. He was being kept alive by artificial methods—respirators, heart stimulators, all those things. Our doctors told us there was nothing that could be done.

"We couldn't accept this. We refused to give up. We're comfortably off, and so for two weeks I called all over the world trying to find someone who could help Jimmy. Finally we reached Norbu Chen. He agreed to fly here and treat Jimmy. The doctors, since they had nothing to offer, agreed to let him try.

"We talked to Mr. Chen before he entered Jimmy's room and told him that the doctors had given up. He told us not to pay any attention to that talk—doctors didn't know what they were doing—that he wouldn't promise but he'd certainly try.

"Then he went into the room and did his thing—you've

seen him. Just as Norbu 'hit'—this is almost funny, if you can forget the circumstances—the machines that made the bleeps and the tracings that recorded Jimmy's heart and breathing rates went sort of crazy. The lights and tracings bounced around all over the place for about a minute.

"Norbu got very excited. I think he was actually shocked and wondered if he had caused these bleeps—wondered if he really did have some strange power. He spent the next half-hour examining the machines. We knew from experience that these bleeps meant nothing; even static electricity could cause them. We'd seen the machines do this dozens of times over the previous two weeks, so we didn't think it was anything to get excited about."

"Did Norbu help your son?" I asked.

"Of course not, Dr. Nolen," Mrs. Hayes said. "You know better than that. Oh, he told us he'd had a good hit, and for a day or two we were hopeful, but nothing really changed and five days later Jimmy died. It's almost two years now, but it still hurts to talk about it. I guess it always will."

3. Mrs. Cheever, forty-seven, had gone to Norbu for treatment of persistent headaches. "I read about him in *The Tattler*," she said. "He sounded wonderful. I'd had trouble with headaches for years and no one had been able to do anything for me. I had a thousand-dollar bond put away—all the money I'd ever managed to save—and I hated to part with it, but it sounded as if it would be worth the investment. Besides, I understood I'd get my money back if he didn't cure me.

"I cashed the bond, bought a ticket, and flew to Houston. When I got to Norbu's home, nobody even talked to me. They stuck me in a bedroom at three in the afternoon and I didn't get out till they came for me at ten the next morning. No one to talk to, nothing to do; I thought I'd go crazy.

"In the morning a woman assistant came and took me to this strange healing room with an altar. Norbu Chen came in and I started to tell him what was troubling me, but he wouldn't listen. 'No need to tell—I know' was all he said. Then he started baying like a wolf in front of the altar and doing a lot of crazy moving around. Finally he pointed at me, blew on my head and left the room. I couldn't believe that was the whole treatment, but it was.

"His woman assistant took me out to the front hall and I gave her my check for five hundred dollars. Then I told her I wanted to talk to Dr. Chen, to find out what was the matter. He came in for about ten seconds, said, 'You will be all better in three weeks,' and left. I wanted to ask questions but they wouldn't let me. 'Your taxi is waiting,' his assistant said, and rushed me out the door.

"If I'd had any sense, I'd have stopped payment on the check right then—but, idiotically, I thought I'd wait the three weeks and see. After all, I had been promised my money back if I didn't get better.

"After three weeks I was no better, but just to be certain I waited another two weeks before writing. There was no answer to my letter. I wrote again after another month and once again two weeks after that. Still no answer. Finally I got ahold of the man who had written the article and complained to him. That got me a note from Norbu's secretary saying they'd never received my letters—odd, because I'd had a return address on the envelopes and they'd certainly received the letter I sent to make the appointment. But, I thought, now at least they'll send me my money. They didn't. I wrote a fourth letter—still no answer—and gave up. I've lost seven hundred dollars—five hundred to Chen and two hundred for transportation—and I've still got my headaches. I feel like an absolute fool. I can't understand how a reporter can write such glowing reports about a man like that."

I'm going to disgress for a moment to raise the point of journalistic responsibility. Many of the patients to whom I spoke had read about Norbu Chen—and the psychic surgeons of the Philippines and Kathryn Kuhlman and Mister A and a host of other miracle workers—in the *National Enquirer, The Tattler* or other tabloids of the same general type.

I know how appealing those tabloids are—I'm just as interested in what's happening to Jackie and Ari as the next guy. The headlines in these sheets are real grabbers, and though the articles usually deliver much less than the captions promise, still lots of people buy them hoping for some sensational revelation. As long as no one takes these papers too seriously, no one gets hurt.

But the sad fact is, a lot of people do take seriously the articles printed in the *Enquirer, The Tattler* and other similar papers. Even then, if the article has to do with some genius who has discovered a pill that turns water into gasoline—or the facts about Glenn Ford's new romance—the reader may be misled, but that's all. However, when the articles deal with miraculous healing, and are read by people who are either afflicted with some serious disease or have a friend or relative afflicted with a serious disease, then these articles are misleading and dangerous. They aften contain half truths, misinformation and stark errors, and they raise false hopes in patients who are, in desperation, looking for miracles. The patients waste their money on charlatans. Even worse, while they are off on a wild chase, they may be postponing medical help that could be life-saving.

This is irresponsible journalism at its worst.

Even writers for *Newsweek*, hardly a "scandal sheet," sometimes publish misleading information. For example, on April 29, 1974, the magazine had an article on psychic healing that reported two alledged triumphs.

The first involved the daughter of a Dr. Robert Owellen, a physician currently working at Johns Hopkins. Dr. Owellen believes that Kathryn Kuhlman cured his daughter's congenital hip dislocation.

I talked to Dr. Owellen. He reports his daughter's case in detail in Kathryn Kuhlman's latest book, *Nothing Is*

Impossible With God, but the essentials are as follows. In 1960, before he had become a physician, he and his wife noted that their baby daughter cried a lot when they picked her up. They took her to their family doctor, who suggested that a congenital hip dislocation might be the problem. He arranged a consultation with an orthopedist.

Kathryn Kuhlman happened to be in the neighborhood at that time, so the Owellens took their child to a healing service. There, Dr. Owellen reports, he noticed that a skin crease in his child's buttock became less apparent. When they took their child to an orthopedist a few days later, he told them that she did not have a dislocated hip.

"Did you have any X-rays taken before you went to the Kathryn Kuhlman service?" I asked Dr. Owellen.

"No," he answered. "But I'm sure she was cured by Kathryn Kuhlman."

Without an X-ray there is no way to be certain an infant has a dislocated hip. All doctors—Dr. Owellen included—know this. If he chooses to believe that Kathryn Kuhlman cured his daughter, that's his privilege. But there is not one iota of evidence to support this claim. When Dr. Owellen sings the praises of Kathryn Kuhlman, as he does with great vigor, his M.D. status gives him a credibility which, concerning this case, he probably does not deserve.

A second statement in the *Newsweek* article says: "Dr. James Bruce, an Alabama surgeon, swears that [Norbu] Chen cleared up his chronic uremia." Perhaps this is the claim that Dr. Bruce made to the *Newsweek* writer, but when I talked to Dr. Bruce he told me that he was still undergoing dialysis, on an artificial kidney, two or three times a week. It was the artificial kidney, not Norbu Chen, that kept Dr. Bruce's uremia from getting out of control.

Why are these misleading reports published? Sometimes, I suspect, it's because a layman is writing the article. The M.D. degree does wrap a certain aura of reliability and respectability about an individual, particularly when that individual speaks of medical subjects. A reporter may feel that without a medical education himself, it would be presumptuous to question a doctor critically.

It may also be true that the reporter doesn't know the proper questions to ask the doctor; how many reporters know that you need an X-ray to make a diagnosis of congenital dislocation of the hip? Probably not many. Medical doctors can pass off as "proven" to laymen material that other doctors would immediately recognize as speculation or supposition. This sort of thing happens too often. In many instances, the doctors, not the reporters, bear the greater responsibility when erroneous medical reports appear in general-circulation magazines.

It is equally unfortunate that physicians—M.D.s—lend credibility to these reports by allowing themselves to be quoted in such a fashion as to endorse the miracle worker. For example, in an article by David Klein in the *Enquirer*, a reputable physician, whose name I will not use here, is quoted as saying: " 'I saw him [Norbu Chen] cure a girl of acute sinusitis in three minutes—just by looking at her from a distance of about 10 feet. I checked the girl afterwards. Her sinusitis was gone.' " From the scientific point of view the doctor's report is so incomplete as to be valueless. He had examined this girl before Norbu's treatment? How thoroughly did he examine her afterward? Did he take X-rays of her sinuses? Did he culture any organisms that were in her nasal passages? How long did he follow this patient to be certain her sinusitis had cleared up? After all, sinusitis is one of those diseases that come and go.

The doctor later told me it was his impression that Norbu Chen relieved the young woman of the symptoms of her ailment; however, he also told me that six weeks later her sinusitis symptoms returned. The doctor did not attempt to document a cure.

The journalists who write this nonsense, the publishers who publish it and the physicians who lend credibility to the reports are responsible for a lot of wasted money and dashed hopes.

* * *

Now back to Norbu. After a bit of nosing around I learned more about Norbu Chen than he wanted me to know.

In fact, one evening in March 1974, two days after I had written to a man who had known Norbu Chen in 1959, Joan and I came home from the movies and found my son Billy sitting at the dining-room table, finishing his homework. "Dad," Billy said, "you had a call about an hour ago from someone who wants you to call back right away. I told him you might not be in till after eleven, but he said to call no matter how late it was. He just called back a few minutes ago to make sure I hadn't forgotten to give you the message. He sure is anxious to talk to you."

I didn't recognize the number when I called but I recognized the voice when he answered—after only one ring; it was Norbu.

"Bill," he said, "how the hell are you?"

"Not bad, Norbu," I answered. "How about you—keeping busy?"

"So busy I can hardly stand it," Norbu said. "Patients, patients all the time. I'm leaving for Costa Rica on a vacation tomorrow." Then he paused. "Bill," he went on, "you almost done with your research for this book of yours?"

"Almost," I said. "Why?"

" 'Cause I hear you been snooping into my background, Bill—that's why. You been writing letters trying to find out about me. I don't like that, Bill. You're a nice guy, but I hope you're about done with this snooping-around shit—you understand?"

"Sure, Norbu, I understand," I said. "Have a nice time in Costa Rica."

"I will, Bill," he said. "Don't worry about me."

And so our conversation ended. I told Joan about my little chat and she asked, "You don't think he's dangerous, do you, Bill?"

"No," I said. "Norbu's all right. Just worried that I'm

129

going to find out too much about him—things he doesn't want dug up. From what I've already learned, I really can't blame him. But he'll be okay. Norbu's tough. He'll survive anything I'll ever say about him."

But, to tell the truth, I had to take a pill to get to sleep that night. I'm not a very courageous guy.

Eventually I learned some more about Norbu. I'm not going to share all my information—it isn't necessary—but I will straighten out the record on a few matters.

First, his name and age. When I checked with the appropriate offices in Harris County, Texas, I learned that on August 22, 1972, Charles Vernon Alexander II had legally changed his name to Norbu Chen. According to the county records, Mr. Alexander had given his birth date as November 13, 1934.

However, I later got a copy of Charles Vernon Alexander II's birth certificate; this document states that he was born in Lexington, Kentucky, on November 13, 1924. Which explains why Norbu Chen, in 1973, looked to me to be an awfully old thirty-nine.

Perhaps he did work indirectly for the Kennedy organization but my brother Jim, who has been a representative in the Massachusetts State Legislature for fourteen years, checked with friends who had worked for the Kennedys from the day John F. Kennedy first went into politics, and none of them had ever seen (I sent Norbu's picture to Jim) or heard of anyone even remotely resembling him.

He has, as he admitted, spent time in jail. He also briefly, was committted to a state hospital, not because he had any mental problem but rather, it seems, as a matter of political convenience. According to a lawyer with whom I spoke, a man well acquainted with Norbu Chen, "They stuck him in this state hospital while they were trying to decide what to do with him. Wherever he was, even in prison, he was nothing but trouble for everyone.

"Finally the 'authorities' decided that the easiest thing they could do was to just let him leave. Somebody supposedly told him that if he just walked away from the hospital, no one would go after him, provided he got the hell out of this state and stayed out.

"Funny, I kind of miss the guy. For a while, he made life around here damned interesting."

For the next ten years—from 1961 to 1971—Norbu moved around quite a lot. He became interested in car racing, an interest he continues to cultivate while living in Houston. Reportedly he lived for a time in North Carolina and Wisconsin.

I can't say for sure whether Norbu Chen ever went to Sikkim. Between 1961, when he walked away from the state hospital, and 1972, when he legally became Norbu Chen, he is said to have used, at one time or another, many different aliases, such as Mike or Michael Alexander. He was a tough man to keep track of.

I do know, however, having read Madame Alexandra David-Neel's books after my visit to Norbu, that he could have acquired all the knowledge he shared with me simply by reading books. Everything he told me about his life in Sikkim—the ordeal in the cave, the psychic sports, the out-of-the-body projection, even *rolang*, the corpse who dances—is in Madame David-Neel's books.

Madame David-Neel, unlike Norbu Chen, remained very skeptical of most of the stories she was told. In speaking of *rolang*, she says (*Magic and Mysteries in Tibet*, p. 135):

Had that fantastic struggle [with the dancing corpse] not been purely subjective? Had it not taken place during one of those trances which are frequently experienced by Tibetan naljorpas [an ascetic possessing magical powers], which they also voluntarily cultivate. I doubted and asked to see "the tongue." The sorcerer showed me a desiccated blackish object which might have been "a tongue," but it was not sufficient to prove the origin of the hideous relic.

* * *

According to Colin Dangaard (writing in the Chicago *Daily News* of August 27, 1973, p. 15), "Norbu Chen sees about 20 patients a week." If he does in fact average twenty patients a week, then his income—at $500 a patient, which is, he told me (and patients have confirmed this), is minimum fee—is $10,000 a week, or $520,000 a year.

Charles Alexander, Norbu Chen, is doing very nicely for himself.

I haven't written about Norbu Chen, his background and his credentials to discredit him; his record speaks for itself. I've written this chapter about him because he affords an excellent example of the fact that intelligent people, well-meaning people, can easily be persuaded by "healers," particularly when those intelligent people want to believe.

Dr. Edgar Mitchell told me, "Norbu Chen is one of the greatest of the healers." Mitchell is quoted by the *National Enquirer* as saying, "Mr. Chen has developed a truly phenomenal ability to heal. He is performing some cures that will astound the medical world." If any of the many intelligent people who have gone as patients to Norbu Chen had made any real effort to investigate the man, they could have learned, as I did, that his "powers" are far from extraordinary. But they didn't investigate him; they wanted to believe.

Now, assuming they read what I have written, are they going to be angry with Norbu? Of course not. Norbu will probably tell them some amazing story about how it was really his astral body that went to Sikkim, and they'll believe him. Instead, they'll be angry with me because, in effect, I've said "the emperor has no clothes." They may hate me for it. I hope that won't be the case, but I'm afraid it may be.

12

I had been assured, by John White of the Institute of Noetic Sciences, that Norbu would let me watch him treat patients, but apparently this was not to be.

"I'm not treating anyone this week," Norbu said. "Besides, I don't like anyone watching when I treat my patients. Do your patients want people watching when you operate on them?"

Since I had seen Norbu treat the mice, and since Randy Lewis had assured me that, technically, the treatment of patients followed the same routine, it wasn't critical that I watch Norbu work on patients. But it was essential, if I was going to evaluate Norbu's healing powers, that I get from him the names and addresses of some of the patients he had cured. I pestered him about this frequently during my four-day visit, and finally, just before I was to leave, he jotted down the names of some of his patients and had his secretary go through his files—such as they were—and get me others.

"I'm going to give you some of my failures, too," he said. "I'm not perfect."

"No." I told him, "that won't be necessary. I'll assume there have been some patients you couldn't help. Just give me names of patients you've cured, preferably patients who had diseases that would otherwise have been fatal."

When I left Houston I had the names, addresses and/or phone numbers of eight of Norbu's patients. Next to each patient's name Norbu had written his "diagnosis."

133

It had been apparent from our early conversations that Norbu knew almost nothing about medicine. He threw medical terms around—cirrhosis, dialysis, even "vaghys," an abbreviation surgeons occasionally use when speaking of vaginal hysterectomies—but on those occasions when I dared to press him to elaborate on a disease he immediately shut me up. "I don't care about all that bullshit," he said. "Vibrations lead me to the patient's trouble and my power flows into him and heals. It's perfectly natural."

The list of cures which he gave me confirmed my impression that he knew little about medicine. There was only one cancer, a skin cancer, on the list. The others included migraine headaches, whiplash pain and a variety of kidney and liver diseases—none of which were malignant. There was even one patient who was listed as "hysterectomy." Nevertheless, I wrote or called them all, and six of the eight gave me their stories. I missed only one migraine headache and one whiplash but both these problems are represented by the cures I did get. Here are the results—I've changed only names and identifying characteristics.

1. Louise Rawlins, a fifty-nine-year-old woman with cirrhosis of the liver.

Mrs. Rawlins had been a heavy drinker for thirty-five years. She admitted to "about a pint a day," and as is true of most alcoholics, she underestimated her intake by a wide margin. "She drinks at least a quart of bourbon a day," her son told me, "or at least she did, till Norbu started treating her."

Her alcoholic consumption hadn't been this high for all of the thirty-five years. She had drunk regularly and heavily from the age of twenty-four, but her "pint a day" estimate had probably been reasonably accurate until 1969, when her husband died. It was then that she'd moved up to a quart a day, and simultaneously, had stopped eating well.

The liver can take a lot of punishment. Some people who

are blessed with naturally strong bodies can drink a pint, even a quart, of liquor every day for years and never show any evidence of liver disease, as long as they eat a sound, well-balanced diet. But once the heavy drinker stops eating—watch out. Even the hardiest liver will degenerate on an "alcohol only" diet.

The liver has superb recuperative powers. In the early stage of cirrhosis, the liver cells become loaded with fat. If, at this time, a patient will stop drinking and start eating, the liver cells will lose their fat and become healthy again. And even if 50 percent of the liver cells are so far gone that they can't recover, the patient can still get along nicely. Patients who have had half of their liver removed because of tumors or injuries live perfectly normal lives.

When Mrs. Rawlins went to Norbu Chen she had the signs and symptoms of liver disease. She was jaundiced, her bilirubin (bile pigment) was 4.0 mgms per 100cc of blood (a normal level is about 0.5 mgms per 100 cc), and she had a swollen abdomen and swollen ankles. Jaundice and fluid retention are both associated with liver disease.

In September 1972, Norbu treated Mrs. Rawlins. She went through the usual routine—bed rest and grapefruit juice—and then Norbu "hit" her with his power. After he treated her, Norbu told Mrs. Rawlins to go home, stay in bed for four days, and of course, abstain from alcohol. She followed Norbu's directions, she lost a lot of fluid and her bilirubin dropped to 1.4 mgms—still elevated, but much better than it had been. "Norbu cured me," she said.

Unfortunately, three weeks later Mrs. Rawlins fell off the wagon. When she did, her jaundice and swelling returned. Her son insisted that she go back to Norbu Chen.

Norbu treated Mrs. Rawlins again. This time he demanded that she remain in bed for ten days after her treatment. Again, Mrs. Rawlins improved.

Over the last year Mrs. Rawlins has been treated by Norbu five times. After one treatment Norbu insisted that she stay in bed for six weeks. After each of Norbu's "hits,"

Mrs. Rawlins improved. The improvement lasted just as long as she followed Norbu's instructions. Unfortunately, as soon as Mrs. Rawlins started drinking again, all of Norbu's good work came undone. But, as Mrs. Rawlins said, "That certainly isn't Norbu's fault—it's mine."

Any doctor who treats alcoholics with liver disease has dozens of patients like Mrs. Rawlins. He has heard her story and watched her course many times. He has even prescribed the same treatment Norbu uses: all that is lacking is the "hit"; most doctors don't go through the Tibetan rituals that Norbu uses (although, and we'll get to this later, M.D.s often use rituals of their own). But rest and diet are not just ideal treatment—they are virtually the only treatment for a sick liver. Doctors don't cure alcoholic liver disease; the liver cures itself, if we can persuade the patient to stop poisoning himself.

Norbu's "hits" certainly didn't harm Mrs. Rawlins. In fact, since Mrs. Rawlins' belief in Norbu's mysterious powers may have persuaded her to follow his instructions, Norbu's rituals probably helped. But certainly there is no evidence in this case to show that Norbu has any miraculous unexplained healing power.

Sadly, as this book goes to press, I've learned that Mrs. Rawlins is back on the bottle and her liver has begun, once again, to fail. This may well be the final time; she can't have many healthy liver cells left.

2. Sarah Riley, a thirty-seven-year-old woman with a "whiplash" injury.

One evening in February 1970, Sarah Riley and her husband, Jim, were driving along a street in Miami during a rainstorm. When they stopped at a traffic light, the car behind them skidded and struck theirs in the rear. Sarah's head snapped back and she immediately noted pain in her neck and shoulders.

Sarah had had trouble with both her neck and her back for many years. "I'm loose-jointed," she told me. "It doesn't take much of an injury to hurt my spine. Once, when I threw my back out bowling, I was in traction for ten days. Another time I just bent over to pick up one of the kids' toys and I was laid up for almost two months. I've had lots of back trouble.''

Following her whiplash injury, Sarah spent eleven weeks in the hospital, not all at once, but over the next two years. Even though the X-rays didn't show any evidence of a fracture or a dislocation, Sarah had a great deal of pain. First she had traction, which helped for a while, but after she went home and tried to do her housework, the pain recurred. She went back into the hospital for three weeks of traction and physiotherapy, but two weeks after her discharge, her pain recurred. Finally she had to resort to a neck brace.

Then, a year and a half after the accident, Sarah began to have severe headaches and she had them almost every day. All her doctor would prescribe was aspirin, and this wasn't enough to relieve her pain. Sarah felt the headaches were due to the whiplash but her doctor didn't think so. He called them "tension" headaches.

In September of 1972 Sarah, desperate for relief from her headaches, flew out to Houston to see Norbu Chen. Norbu treated her and the next day her headaches were gone. She was even able to get along nicely without her brace. She flew home, and as Norbu had suggested, went to bed and rested for thirteen days. She had no more headaches.

Until a month later, when she slipped on a freshly waxed floor. She landed on her backside, jolting her spine, and her headaches returned. She flew back to Houston, Norbu treated her again and this time prescribed five days of bed rest. Again, Sarah was cured.

Unfortunately, five months later, Sarah backed into a parked car. This required another treatment by Norbu. Again, success.

After listening to Sarah's story, I said, "I hope you won't think me too nosy, Mrs. Riley—if you do, just tell me it's none of my business—but would you mind telling me if you have been able to collect medical expenses from these people who caused your whiplash?"

"I don't mind answering you. No, we haven't. The suit still hasn't been settled. Their insurance company is fighting us every inch of the way. But eventually I think we'll win."

Did Norbu Chen cure Sarah? There's certainly no evidence to show that he did. Her headaches, whether due to the whiplash, as Sarah insists, or to tension, as her doctor suggests, still come and go. There are few complaints as susceptible to suggestion as "headache."

And there are few patients more difficult to cure than the patient with a whiplash injury who is trying to collect from an individual or an insurance company. Doctors dread these cases. The patient is reluctant to get well until the settlement is made, for fear the medical expenses—and compensation for suffering—will be cut down drastically or even denied entirely. A friend of mine, a specialist in orthopedics, says, "The only satisfactory treatment for a whiplash injury is a greenback poultice." Cynical, perhaps, but only too accurate.

I'd be happy to send my whiplash injuries to Norbu Chen—if only he didn't charge so darn much.

3. Dr. John Smith, a fifty-two-year-old M.D. with severe kidney disease.

Dr. John Smith lives in New York, where he works as a medical examiner for an insurance company. "Until five years ago," he told me, "I practiced pediatrics. But then my kidneys really went to hell and I had to give it up. I didn't think I was as alert and as mentally sharp as I should have been, and I felt it wasn't fair to my patients for me to stay in practice. The strain of working as an insurance examiner is minimal and I can handle it, but I do miss my patients.

"My trouble began ten years ago—in 1963. I developed several stones in my left kidney, and by the time the

138

diagnosis was made, I'd lost a good part of the function in the kidney. Even with the stones out, the kidney function didn't come back much.

"Then stones formed in my right kidney. I had all the usual work-ups—parathyroid tests [malfunctioning parathyroid glands can cause kidney stones], X-rays of all sorts, everything they could think of at the university hospital—and no one could figure out why I was such a stone-former. We still don't know.

"Things went downhill fast over the next five years. I had three operations on my left kidney and two on my right. All the time, my kidney kept getting worse. Finally my B.U.N. [blood urea nitrogen, a waste product that the kidneys should excrete] went up to 240 [normal ranges between 10 and 20] and I was hardly putting out any urine at all. No one wanted to operate on me. I insisted they take one more crack at the stones, in my right kidney but it didn't work. I was damn near dead.

"So, much as I disliked the idea, I went on dialysis [the artificial kidney]. I've been on it three times a week every week for five years. I don't like it, as you'd suspect, but I get by."

"Why don't you have a kidney transplant?" I asked him.

"I've thought about it," Dr. Smith said, "but I'm not impressed with the results. I'd have to get a cadaver kidney, since I don't have a close relative with my tissue type, and the chances of a successful take are only about fifty percent. The chief of the kidney service at the university hospital is a good friend of mine—we graduated from medical school together—and I talk about the transplant idea with him occasionally. At the moment, he doesn't think it's proper treatment for me."

"What about Norbu Chen—is he helping you?"

"Sorry," Dr. Smith answered. "I should have gotten to him sooner. I suppose you think it's kooky—an M.D. going to a healer—and I guess it is;. but I'll tell you how it happened.

"A friend of mine, a surgeon, is sort of a promoter of Norbu's. He has always been interested in things like E.S.P. and the occult. Anyway, about two years after I started on dialysis, I began to develop a skin disease. It was a scaly, warty eruption and it broke out on my forearms, my face and my neck. I went to dermatologist after dermatologist and none of them could do a damn thing for me. I looked like Frankenstein.

"This went on for two years. The rash kept getting worse and I was getting desperate. Then, a couple of months ago, my friend stopped by and told me about Norbu Chen. He suggested I might try him. I figured, 'What the hell—no one else has helped me, so why not.' I flew out to Houston.

"And, damn it, he has helped me. My dermatitis has improved a lot. My face is almost completely clear and my arms are definitely better. I've flown out to see him five times and I'm a little better after every visit. It's cost me a bundle, but it's worth it."

"How about your kidneys? Has he helped them?"

"No sign of it yet. I'm still not putting out more than a trickle of urine. But Norbu keeps treating my kidneys and he says he'll cure them yet. I'll call you and let you know if he does."

Dr. Smith never called back. Six months later I called him. "My rash is still improving," he said, "but my kidneys aren't any better. I guess I'll be on dialysis as long as I live."

We've already talked about skin diseases and how susceptible they are to suggestion, so I won't dwell on that subject. The point to be learned from this case is that medical knowledge certainly doesn't protect anyone from succumbing to the lure of a miracle worker: Dr. John Smith, despondent because he sees in the future only years of treatment on a kidney machine, is willing and able to ignore his scientific training and medical education and grasp at the straw that Norbu seems to offer.

Most doctors might try to dissuade Dr. Smith from

seeking irrational help, but no doctor, with any compassion, would criticize him. I extend to Dr. Smith only my sympathy, I'm sorry that the straw Norbu offers him has not been more helpful.

4. Willard Hopkins, a sixty-eight-year-old man with skin cancer.

In the fall of 1971 Mr. Hopkins developed a rough spot on the skin of his neck, just below his left ear. He ignored it, thinking he might have nicked himself while shaving, but when it hadn't healed after three months he went to see his family doctor. By this time the rough area had become an ugly sore with rolled edges and a punched-out center. It measured about one by one and a half inches.

Mr. Hopkins' doctor told him he thought this was a skin cancer, and under local anesthesia, removed a small piece of the growth. A week later the doctor called his patient, told him that the pathologist had confirmed the diagnosis of cancer and referred him to a surgeon, who subsequently removed the skin tumor. However, when Mr. Hopkins came back to the surgeon's office ten days after his operation to have his stitches removed, the surgeon said, "The pathologist reports that all the tumor is out. Unfortunately, the tumor had grown in quite a distance, so at the bottom we haven't got much of a margin. I think, just to be safe, you should have some X-ray treatment."

Mr. Hopkins agreed, and over the next two weeks he had a series of ten X-ray treatments to his neck. "Two weeks after the treatments were finished," Mr. Hopkins told me, "my neck looked terrible. The skin was red and sore and I even had some trouble swallowing. I was a hell of a lot worse off then I had been before I ever went to a damn doctor."

At that point Mr. Hopkins went to Norbu, who treated him four times over a two-week period. "By the time Norbu had finished treating me, my neck looked normal and I felt fine," Mr. Hopkins said. "I'd take him over an M.D. any day."

Mr. Hopkins' case history, with the exception of his visits to Norbu Chen, is much like the case history of anyone with skin cancer.

The cure rate for skin cancer should be almost 100 percent. The only patients likely to die of the disease are those who ignore it for years. (I am speaking now of the routine forms of skin cancer: basal and squamous cell cancers, which comprise about 95 percent of all skin cancers. Malignant melanoma is another matter. I learned, from his doctor, that Mr. Hopkins had a basal cell cancer.)

Skin cancer can be treated successfully with either surgery or X-rays. Usually the decision depends on the extent of the lesion, its location, and the preference of the doctor and/or patient. Sometimes, as in Mr. Hopkins' case, after surgical treatment, the surgeon may decide that X-rays should also be used. This is done when the pathologist who examines the tumor under the microscope says that the surgeon has not removed a "safe" margin or normal tissue with the specimen. The X-ray treatment is given "prophylactically," to kill any cancer cells that my inadvertently have been left behind in the wound.

X-ray treatment of the skin invariably causes redness and swelling of the tissues. Sometimes the reaction is severe, sometimes not. The severity of the radiation burn depends largely on the X-ray dosage, but it also varies between individuals; just as some people are more likely to suffer from severe sunburn than are others, so some people are more sensitive to X-rays than others.

Usually, as in Mr. Hopkins' case, the full skin reaction doesn't develop until a week or two after the X-ray treatment has been completed. Then, unless the radiation burn is so severe that the tissue actually dies, the reaction will gradually subside.

Mr. Hopkins went to Norbu just as his radiation burn reached its peak. As Norbu treated the skin, the burning and

142

swelling—naturally—subsided. Nature "cured" Mr. Hopkins' radiation burn: Norbu got the credit.

The M.D.s who treated Mr. Hopkins are, fundamentally, responsible for the fact that Mr. Hopkins spent some $2,000 in Norbu's care. Somewhere the course of his treatment one, or all, of Mr. Hopkins' doctors should have sat down and explained to him what was being done, why it was being done, and what he was to expect. The swollen red skin, developing two weeks after the X-ray treatment was completed, came as a complete surprise to Mr. Hopkins. It's easy to understand why he'd interpret this reaction as a return of his cancer.

One of the major reasons why patient go to "healers" is the M.D.'s failure to communicate.

5. Janet Thorsen, a twenty-eight-year-old woman with "irregular menstrual periods."

For three years Janet suffered from irregular periods. "Sometimes I'd have periods three weeks apart, sometimes I'd go five weeks. I might even skip a month. But when they came they were always heavy and usually I'd have bad cramps. I'd actually have to go to bed with a heating pad on my stomach. And I needed codeine to get through them.

"For three years I went to doctors. I had a D&C that made me regular for five months, but then my periods started going all haywire again. One doctor put me on birth-control pills but the pills made me sick. One week every month I was practically an invalid.

"Finally, four months ago, I went to Norbu. One treatment was all it took. I haven't had any trouble since. He's a miracle worker."

What can I say? How can I argue? Norbu "cured" Janet Thorsen. She's happy and I'm happy for her. I only hope she stays cured.

Every doctor—and every woman—knows dozens of women who have had problems like Janet's. Menstrual periods do get "mixed up." Emotional people—and Janet is

143

a very tense person—are particularly prone to menstrual irregularities. But even normally placid women, at times of stress, will develop menstrual problems. If I had a dollar for every woman whose period arrived days or weeks late because that woman was terrified that she might be pregnant, I could retire.

The stress of an operation frequently precipitates an early menstrual period. I often find that women who have had their gall bladder or appendix removed will begin a menstrual period a day or two after the operation, even though they aren't "due" for another two weeks.

And just as almost anything can produce menstrual irregularities, almost anything can cure them. Tell a woman who is two weeks overdue that her pregnancy test is negative, and her menstrual period will most likely begin that afternoon. Tell her that a pill or an injection will make her regular, and tell her in a voice and in a manner that exudes confidence, and she'll often become regular.

Of course Norbu Chen cured Janet. Norbu is as reassuring and as confident a man as I've ever met.

6. Steve Black, a thirty-eight-year-old man with "kidney problems."

"I developed kidney problems twelve years ago, when I was twenty-six," he said. "I had a lot of burning when I passed urine and had backache as well. I'd get treatment, improve, and then get worse again. Over a ten-year period I was in the hospital seven times, without any relief. In fact, I developed prostatitis [infection in the prostate gland] and seminal vesiculitis [inflammation of the seminal vesicles, two small sacs in which sperm is stored; they lie adjacent to the prostate].

"Finally I read about Norbu in the paper and decided I had nothing to lose by going to him. One treatment and I was better. In the last twelve months I haven't taken any antibiotics and haven't been back to the hospital. And my wife is pregnant."

"Just one treatment from Norbu cured you?" I asked.

"No. It cured me for a while, but my symptoms returned. Now he treats me about twice a month, whenever I notice any burning."

"Have you been back to your doctor for any X-rays or urine examinations to document your cure?" I asked.

"No," Steve Black replied. "I don't need to; I can recognize the symptoms when they arise. I go to Norbu and he treats me; I'm tired of doctors and hospitals."

I have one patient who has a history much like Black's. He developed prostatitis in the Army and every now and then it flares up. He gets back pain and notices burning when he passes his urine. Sometimes when he's having trouble, he comes in to see me and I massage his prostate. This, supposedly, squeezes any accumulated wastes out of the gland and usually relieves the patient. It often helps my patient.

Some men will develop sore prostate glands if they refrain from intercourse for several weeks. Usually nocturnal emissions, or masturbation, will relieve them. Most of the seminal fluid which is ejaculated at intercourse is produced by the prostate gland. When the prostate doesn't get a workout once in a while, it may become swollen and sore.

I don't know what is going on with Steve Black. Since he has never had a medical follow-up, it's impossible to pin anything down; it might be difficult even with a medical follow-up because prostatitis, as I've mentioned, comes and goes frequently. But I can venture an opinion: I think Norbu Chen reassured Steve Black and gave him confidence. This, in turn, made Black more sexually active—he positively beamed when he called my attention to his wife's obvious pregnancy—and his increased sexual activity relieved his prostatitis. This is all conjecture, I admit, but I've seen this sort of case often enough to make what I think could be called an "informed guess." At any rate, Steve Black is happy and Norbu Chen is pleased.

Norbu Chen, like all other "healers," does not claim to know about Western medicine and makes every effort to treat only those patients who consider themselves doctor failures. By so doing, the healers can assure themselves that the patient will have no cause to blame them if something goes wrong. If any patient feels he has been helped at all, such as Dr. John Smith or Steve Black, he is eternally grateful to the healer.

IV

FILIPINO PSYCHIC SURGEONS

13

In June 1973, I left for the Philippines, where I was to meet Manny Hofman. I went at that time—even though in "reading up" on the Philippines, I had learned that the rainy season usually begins about the middle of June—because that month worked out best for Manny. He had to go to Greece on business on May 26, and instead of returning to Detroit he'd simply continue on around the world to Manila.

I hated the idea of going to the Philippines. Just before I was to leave, I called Joan from the Minneapolis airport and said, "Do you really think I ought to go? Don't you think I can learn enough about the psychic surgeons by talking to people who have been there and watching their movies?"

"Come on, now," she said. "You know that won't work. You've already seen a lot of films and you still can't make up your mind. You've got to see them in person."

"I guess you're right," I said, "but it's so damn far away!"

I hadn't realized the vast distance before I started planning the trip: about 7,500 miles from Minneapolis to the Philippines. You can get there via Hawaii, but out of Minneapolis the most direct flight is by way of Seattle. From Seattle you fly to Tokyo in one of the jumbo jets. Then, after a three-hour layover in the Tokyo airport, you board a conventional plane, a 727 or something like that (I'm no good at telling one plane from another), and fly first to Okinawa, then to Manila. Altogether the flight from

Minneapolis to Manila takes about twenty hours, but since you're flying west you pick up a day. I left at noon, Minneapolis time, on June 6 and got into Manila at nine o'clock the night of June 6—Philippine time.

At the Manila airport I got the first of many jolts the Philippines had in store for me: as we approached customs I saw a big sign which said: HAVE YOU HAD YOUR CHOLERA SHOTS?

I hadn't. Cholera shots weren't required, according to the brochure I'd read, so naturally, I hadn't had any. Shots hurt, and cholera shots often cause a fever. "Are cholera shots necessary?" I asked the customs inspector.

"They're not required," he said, "but we advise strongly that you have them. You can get them here at the airport if you want."

I thought it over for a minute and then decided to take my chances. I didn't want to run the risk of three of four days in the Philippines with a sore arm and a fever. But for the two weeks I was over there I never drank a glass of water without wondering if it might not be my last.

Manny and I had planned to meet at the International Hotel, which Manny assured me was the best in Manila. I expected to take a cab, but was delighted as I came through customs to find Manny waiting for me. "I rented a car," he said. "I thought it would be more convenient and less expensive than hiring a chauffeur."

"Sounds fine to me," I said, "as long as you know where we're going. I'd certainly hate to find my way around a strange country."

"Nothing to it," Manny said. "I've been here before, remember? And besides," he added, "I'm one of those people with a built-in sense of direction. I never get lost."

With that we piled into the Volkswagen and spent the next forty-five minutes driving to the hotel, which is about three miles from the airport. The delay wasn't caused by traffic—there wasn't any—it was caused by Manny's getting lost. Three times, aftr negotiating a series of turns, I had to say to him, "Manny, isn't that the airport we're coming to again?" And Manny would mutter something about "Confusing signals" or "Why can't they give their streets decent names? In Detroit you'd never find a crazy name like 'Santo Domingo Drive.'" For some reason—I suppose it was because we were on the other side of the world, sort of standing on our heads in comparison to people in Detroit and Minneapolis—Manny's built-in direction finder never did work during the time we were in the Philippines.

The Intercontinental Hotel is a very cosmopolitan hotel—businessmen from coutries all around the world stay there—and it's air-conditioned, so you don't notice the Philippine heat. We had one drink in the cocktail lounge at the top of the hotel, and then we went to our room and I collapsed into bed. It wasn't until the next morning, when we were on the road to the lowlands, that I began to learn what the Philippines are really like.

First, it is a very hot country. Not just in June, but all year round. And if you think that because they are a bunch of islands (this is not going to be a formal lecture on geography, so I feel free to use words like "bunch") there will be breezes most ot the time, forget it. I don't, as I think back on my visit, remember even one little zephyr. The Philippines are hot and still. Except, they tell me, when there's a hurricane.

They are also humid. Very humid. In fact, I'd suggest that if you're thinking of visiting the Philippines—that is, if after you've had your head examined you still want to go—you lock yourself in a sauna for two weeks instead; weatherwise, you'll know exactly what it's like to visit the Philippines (one exception is Baguio City) and you'll have saved yourself about $2,000.

But I wasn't in the Philippines on a vacation; I was there to study the psychic surgeons. Hence, as we drove along the narrow roads I tried not to mind the fact that every time we had to wait while a water buffalo crossed in front of us, I became soaked with perspiration. In choosing the car,

Manny had had to decide between an automatic shift and air conditioning and he had chosen—wisely, as you'll see later—the automatic shift. But only as long as we kept moving with all the windows open could I stay dry.

Pangasinan province, about a hundred miles north of Manila, is the region in which most of the psychic surgeons are concentrated. A hundred miles should be about a three-hour drive, but with Manny at the wheel we managed to make it in five hours. We were able to see several small towns twice, and one three times, as we doubled and tripled back after the homing pigeon had made a wrong turn. All this weaving in and out gave me a chance to look over the countryside.

The housing on the outskirts of Manila is, to an American, unbelievable. When I was doing my residency at Bellevue Hospital in the fifties, I got a close look at the worst housing in New York City; in comparison to the shacks outside Manila the New York slums are a collection of luxury hotels.

The homes—and I use the word loosely—on the outskirts of Manila were made of junk: doors from automobiles, old wooden crates, strips of discarded linoleum, everything you might find in a dump was tied or nailed together to form semi-enclosures. All of these shacks had dirt floors. Most had roofs of thatched grass. Small children, most of them naked, ran in and out and around these clusters of homes while the women cooked, usually in pots over open fires, outside the shacks. I suppose the men had jobs of one sort or another in Manila, because I rarely saw in these slums any men who looked healthy or young enough to work.

The average pay for a day's work in the Philippines is 25 pesos (about $1.50 in American money) but a lot of Filipinos work for less. Average per capita income is $215 a year. A laborer can't afford the luxury of passing up a job even when it barely allows him to subsist, not with unemployment in the Philippines running at about 15 percent. Most of the available jobs involve manual labor, since mechanical and electrical equipment is in very short supply. In the Philippines, roads and buildings are constructed with picks, shovels, wheelbarrows and perspiration—the way roads and buildings were built in the United States a hundred years ago.

The poverty can be attributed to a large extent to the tremendous population growth—3.3 percent annually. In case that doesn't sound like much to you, I'll put it in another way. In 1945, at the end of World War II, there were 8 million Filipinos; in 1973 there were 40 million. And since birth control, for cultural and religious reasons, is not popular in the Philippines, it's expected that in another ten or twelve years the population will reach 65 million. Things are bad in the Philippines now, and as the population continues to increase, they are almost certainly going to get worse.

At noon Manny and I stopped at a gas station for a Coke and Manny took his Bible and went off by himself to pray for about ten minutes. Manny has been praying for his daughter, Charlotte, three times a day ever since he first visited the Philippines. No matter where he is or what he is doing, he never misses. Manny has become a deeply religious man. I admire and envy him.

At half past two we drove through Asignan, a city of about 200,000 which looked to me like one massive slum. About five miles outside the city we turned off on the dirt road which led to Toboya, the barrio where David Oligani lives. David Oligani is the healer in whose home Manny and his daughter lived for eight weeks in the summer of 1972.

A barrio is a rural village. There are thousands of them scattered about the Philippines. They are clusters of homes built of bamboo with thatched-grass roofs. Those near rivers are built on poles, off the ground—otherwise the heavy rains of the wet season would wash them away. Each cluster of huts is separated from the next by paddies where the villagers grow rice. For each group of huts, scattered over an area of a couple of miles, there is one marketplace with, perhaps, a gas station, a garage, a store and a village school. In the marketplace there may even be a village hall in which there is a telephone, though this was not true of Toboya. The nearest phone was in Asignan, five miles away.

Almost no one who lives in a barrio has electricity or running water. Usually there is one well for several huts, and the women carry water to their homes in buckets. Kerosene lamps are used for light. Since there is no refrigeration and no ice, when the villagers want fresh vegetables or meat they have to go to the market and buy it on the day they expect to eat it. Usually their diet consists of smoked fish, bread and rice, and the fresh fruit—papayas, mangoes, pineapples and bananas—which grows in the villages.

In the barrios there were always lots of chickens running around, scratching out a living as best they could. The chickens in the Philippines, and the occasional dogs, are the skinniest examples of those species that I've ever seen. I suppose that's because no one in the Philippines has any food to waste on an animal, with one exception—the water buffaloes, which they need to cultivate and harvest the rice. Every villager like to have at least one water buffalo, and these animals are well cared for. Only when the buffalo is too old to work is he slaughtered; then everyone has a feast.

David, as the healer and local head of the Espiritista Chruch, is wealthier than most of the other residents. He has a compound—about an acre of land—on which there are three buildings. One is his church, about twenty-five feet by fifty feet; the other two are homes. In one home live David and his wife and his children; in the other live David's three sisters, Clorita, Juanita and Margarita. David is forty; his sisters look ten to twenty years older. There were also a sprinkling of cousins, brothers and grandparents around David's compound. David never made any formal introductions, so I never found out who each was or where everyone slept. Manny couldn't identify them either, although he had lived in the compound for two months.

David's homes were, by local standards, very nice. They were built of wood and had wooden floors. In his home there was a pump in the kitchen, and there was even a toilet. To flush it, one had to first ladle water from a bucket into the toilet bowl and then pull the chain. Where everything flushed to I never learned, nor did I have any burning desire to know. Sometimes a lack of information may be a blessing.

When we arrived at David's compound Manny was greeted, warmly but shyly, by all the residents. Clorita assumed the role of spokesman (spokesperson) for the group. (I learned during the days I spent with David Oligani that Clorita was the organizer, David's assistant and generally the strong one in the family.) She asked after Charlotte and expressed delight when Manny said she was doing well. Then she told us that David had gone to Baguio for the day and asked if we could stay and have supper with them. Since it was now about four o'clock and we had an hour-and-a-half drive to Baguio left, we declined with thanks. We promised to return by nine the next morning and have breakfast with the family. Then with everyone standing in the yard smiling and waving at us, we got into the Volkswagen and left.

We had decided to stop over in Baguio, at least for the first night, because it is high on the mountains and reliably cool. Manny's wife, Helen, had stayed there at the Pines Hotel during the time Manny and Charlotte spent in David's compound, and she had told me, "It's the only place in the Philippines where you can breathe."

She hadn't told me about the road to Baguio, which is probably just as well, because if she had, I'd probably never have seen Baguio. The road is two lanes—two narrow lanes—cut out of the side of a cliff. It goes up for about thirty miles at what must be a sixty-degree angle. Every now and then you encounter a pile of boulders lying on the road, the result of one of the rock slides which occur by the dozen every day during the rainy season. The road is a series of curves, and most of the way you can't see more than thirty feet ahead. Trucks and buses come hurtling down the mountain but they have to crawl up it, since most of them are at least twenty years old. Many have been kept going, with string and glue, it often appeared, since the 1940s when they were left behind by American troops. Every now and then, after crawling along at ten miles an hour behind one of these ancient vehicles, Manny would gamble on passing, even though he couldn't see far enough ahead to do so safely. (Incidentally, it was because he knew about this road to Baguio that Manny had forgone air conditioning for an automatic shift.) When Manny would take these wild gambles at passing, with a drop of several thousand feet just off the road, I'd grab onto my seat, hold my breath, and occasionally, shut my eyes. I don't know what new levels my blood pressure may have reached on the drive to Baguio and it's probably just as well that I don't.

Baguio, a city of 85,000, is comfortable—it's at least thirty degrees cooler there than it is in the lowlands. The Pines Hotel, where we stayed, doesn't have air conditioning and none is ever necessary. The temperature ranges between sixty and seventy degrees.

The hotel is, reportedly, owned by President Ferdinand Marcos, who also maintains a luxurious home in Baguio. Any conventions of government workers are held at the Pines, naturally, and this keeps the hotel busy all year round.

Since Helen had stayed at the Pines for two months, Manny knew Mrs. Laros, the manager of the hotel, and we were given a beautiful room with a magnificent view. While Manny took his shower I turned to the television set, and after watching the last few minutes of an old movie starring Bruce Cabot as a Mountie, I listened to the news.

I use the word "news" loosely because the Philippines have, since early 1972, been under martial law. President

Marcos rules with an iron hand. As Manny said, "About the only way you might criticize Marcos and get away with it would be to criticize him for not appointing more of his family to high-paying positions." As a result of Marcos' complete control of the country, including the news media, the nightly "news" is nothing but a hymn of praise for everything the government is doing.

To be fair, I'll have to say that in the two weeks I spent in the Philippines I never met anyone who was against the Marcos government (even though there is always the possibility they would be afraid to voice criticism to a stranger). Apparently, before he took over as dictator, the country was coming apart at the seams. For example, most of the people in Manila carried pistols, and gunfights on the main street were commonplace. Marcos stopped that by confiscating all weapons and imposing an eleven o'clock curfew, rigidly supervised by the army. The people lost some freedom, but everyone breathed more easily.

Before Marcos became dictator, inflation had been out of control The wealthy, who owned most of the land, controlled the price of rice and regulated it so that the poor people, who worked the rice paddies as tenant farmers, could earn just enough to subsist. Marcos was working hard to get ownership of the land back to the poor.

Education, before Marcos, was not for the masses: children of the poor went to work in the fields as soon as they were strong enough to do so. And there were always plenty of children because birth control was all but unknown. Under Marcos, more schools were being built and birth-control information was becoming much more readily available, not only through television, on which programs devoted to birth control are frequent, but through health clinics which Marcos was building in most of the provinces.

Everything considered, conceding that martial law and dictators are not the ideal, it seemed to me that everyone in the Philippines (admittedly, I met mostly the poor and the

157

apolitical) was delighted with Marcos' regime. They knew he was probably putting aside a nice little fortune for himself and his family, but the people were so much better off themselves that they didn't begrudge him his graft.

Our plan was to talk with the observe as many psychic surgeons as possible. Manny knew David Oligani and Joe Mercado best, since they had treated Charlotte, but he also knew of several others. Most worked in the lowlands but there was one, Placido Palitayan, in Baguio. That first evening at the Pines, tired as we both were, we decided to talk to Placido, if we could find him. Manny didn't know how to reach him directly but he did have the phone number of Donald Winslow, who works with Placido. Manny called Donald, and he agreed to meet us at the Pines. We had dinner, and at eight o'clock Donald arrived. We talked with him in the lounge.

Donald Winslow is thirty years old. He is, as far as he or anyone else knows, the only American with the gift of "material healing," i.e., the ability to perform psychic surgery. That evening, he told us about his powers, how he had acquired them, about the Espiritista Church and psychic surgery. Later, visiting with other psychic surgeons, I found that their stories—their explanations—of the phenomenon of psychic surgery were essentially in agreement with Donald's. His story can stand for theirs.

Here is what Donald told us.

14

"I first heard of psychic surgery in 1971," Donald began. "At that time I was a member of the fire department in Eugene, Oregon. One night a friend of mine invited me to go with him to Portland to see some films that had been taken in the Philippines; he knew I had always been interested in the occult. I went, saw some amazing movies of Tony Agpaoa performing psychic surgery, and then and there I decided I had to go to the Philippines. Those films were a message to me from God.

"Until that night I'd lived a completely routine, dull, boring life. I grew up in Oregon, went to San Diego State for two years, California State for one year, and had finally graduated, in 1967, from the University of Alaska in Fairbanks. My degree was in psychology and sociology. I worked six months for the Office of Economic Opportunity, but the job bored me to death and it didn't pay very well. I was married then and we had a little boy, so I took a job with the Eugene fire department. That job turned out to be boring too, but at least it paid reasonably well.

"The morning after I'd seen the films I wrote to Tony and asked if I could come and study under him. He said yes, so I quit my job and went to the Philippines. I got there in November of 1971.

"At that time Tony was working in Manila and I spent six weeks observing and sometimes assisting him. He has a very busy practice. He treats about two hundred patients a month.

"After six weeks with Tony I felt I had learned all I was going to learn from him, so I decided to move on and study with another healer. A Swiss woman whom Tony had treated was driving down to the lowlands and she invited me to come along. I went with her to Asignan, where Joe Mercado practices. Joe agreed to let me study under him and I spent two months there. Joe is a fantastic surgeon—probably the best in the Philippines. You'll have to see him while you're here.

"By now, after four months in the Philippines, I'd learned quite a lot about the Espiritista Church—the church to which most of the healers belong—and one thing I had learned was that if I wanted to be a healer, all I had to do was believe hard enough and God would direct me along the proper path. That is exactly what happened. After I had been with Mercado for two months, a voice inside me directed me to go to David Oligani. On March seventh, 1972, I said good-bye to Joe, went directly to David's compound, and he accepted me. Though I had never seen him before, he had known I was coming. The voice of a spirit had told him to expect me.

"I stayed with David for six months. David worked in the rice paddies in the morning, as Brother Manny has probably told you [all the healers call each other and their friends "Brother." In the two weeks I spent there, I just couldn't bring myself to call any of them "Brother." It just didn't seem natural to me.] In the afternoons and evenings he'd heal. Sometimes patients would come to him, at other times he'd go to their homes. One week out of every month, we'd go out into the mountains. David has a jeep now—thanks to Brother Manny—and all five of us, David and I and all his sisters, would go on these trips together. While Brother Manny and Charlotte were staying with us, though, we didn't make any trips. David's 'protector' told him to stay at the compound and heal Charlotte.

"In December of 1972, after Brother Manny had left, David and I went on a mission to Isabella, an isolated place far off in the wilds. While I was there, on December twenty-second, I went to pray in a place known to the natives as the Holy Cave. While I was meditating, I heard a voice say, 'Now you will go to Baguio City and study with a healer whose initials are P.P.' I've only heard voices a few times and usually they seem to be within me, but this voice was outside. I was alone but anyone who had been with me could have heard it. It rang out clearly and distinctly. I knew it was the voice of God.

"When we were back at the compound I told David what I had heard and he, of course, told me I must follow this order, so I packed up what little I owned and went to Baguio City.

"There I almost lost my faith. I spent two weeks wandering around Baguio, and never heard of or met anyone, much less a healer, with the initials P.P. I finally got discouraged and went back to Manila. I thought the Lord had deserted me—that I had gone as far on my pilgrimage as I was to do. I was very depressed.

"I should have known better. While I was in Manila I met a man from Oregon, Dick Wright, who was trying to arrange a group of sick people to come over from the United States to visit the healers. I worked with him for a few days and then I met a man named Romos who knew most of the healers. Without me ever mentioning my orders he said when he saw me, 'You ought to meet a healer in Baguio City—a man called Placido Palitayan.' He had barely uttered the name when I realized I had at last found the man I had been seeking. The next day I left for Baguio. When I went to Placido's home he said immediately, 'You are to work with me. You're late.' He had known all along that I was being sent to him.

"That was January 1973—just six months ago. Since then I've worked with Placido constantly. He is very poor. He's one of the few healers who doesn't have a church, so while he's in Baguio he has to heal in his home. But most of the time we are out on missions, out in the mountains, so it doesn't matter so much.

"In fact, for me, I guess it's probably just as well that I

have had to go out on missions; it was on a mission, in March, just three months ago, that I was granted the gift of material healing. Shall I tell you about it?"

"Please do," I said. "Your story is fascinating."

"Well," Donald continued, "on our missions Placido first conducts a service where he preaches and everyone prays. This lasts three or four hours. Then, when he feels he has the power, he begins to heal.

"By March I had progressed with my understanding of the Bible to the point where Placido would often let me do some of the preaching. I had even, at times, been able to heal magnetically—that is, I could draw illness out of a person simply by passing my hands over them. It's an odd sensation, almost as if your hands are no longer part of you.

"On this particular mission, near the end of March, I had a strange feeling that my powers had increased. As I was healing magnetically I was almost in a trance. Then, suddenly, I looked down at the patient lying on the table and I saw that my hands had actually gone through the flesh and were inside her abdomen. The blood was running out around my fingers but the patient felt absolutely no pain. I, Donald Winslow, was actually performing psychic surgery.

"As soon as I became completely aware of what I was doing, my power disappeared. For a few second I panicked—I couldn't get the hole in the abdomen to close. I looked over to Placido, pleading with my eyes for help, but he just smiled. 'Make your mind a blank, Brother Donald,' he said, 'think of nothing. Let God do your work.' I did as he said—I thought only of God—and in seconds the wound had closed and my patient was cured.

"Since March I have operated many, many times and I have gotten much better. Now I know that I must keep my ego out of it, simply let my 'protector' take over and everything will be all right. Last week I took a growth out of the neck of the wife of a doctor from Germany and I've removed many tumors from the stomach. I am very grateful to God for the wonderful gift He has given me."

"I can certainly understand your gratitude, Don," I said.

"I'm a surgeon, as you know, but I have to use a scalpel and clamps and sutures and a lot of other things. I'd love to be able to operate without gloves or anesthesia, and have the incisions I make heal immediately and without infection. But I'm afraid it's a gift I'll never acquire—I'm too steeped in our Western medical tradition. But even if I can never acquire the gift of material healing, I'd like to learn as much as I can about it. Would you be willing to tell me more— how it all started, how it's related to the Espiritista Church, what it all means? I'd like to know because if it is as wonderful as it sounds, we M.D.'s should either try to acquire the gift or send the patients we can't help to you people who can."

"I'll be glad to tell you more," Donald said, "but I won't be able to explain everything. I don't understand it all—no one does. How could we? We'd have to know as much as God."

Donald ordered another cup of coffee, Manny ordered milk, and I ordered a pot of Sanka. Then Donald continued his story.

"The ability to heal is, as you probably know, one of the gifts the Lord promises us in the Bible; read the first book of Corinthians, chapter twelve, verses one to twelve.*

"The ability to heal had always been a part of the Christian tradition, but for several centuries it was present only sporadically. A resurgence of healing powers is a sign that we are nearing the Second Coming of Christ.

"The Espiritista Church was founded in 1850 in France. It's a fundamentalist church—we accept the Bible literally,

*I Corinthians 12:1–12

Now concerning spiritual gifts, brethren, I would not have you ignorant.

Ye know that ye were Gentiles, carried away unto these dumb idols, even as ye were led.

Wherefore I give you to understand, that no man speaking by the Spirit of God calleth Jesus accursed: and that no man can say that Jesus is the Lord, but by the Holy Ghost.

Now there are diversities of gifts, but the same Spirit.

Now there are differences of administrations, but the same Lord.

And there are diversities of operations, but it is the same God which worketh all in all.

163

as it is meant to be accepted—and we know from our readings that the Second Coming is not far off. However, the sign of His coming—the gift of material healing—has appeared in only two places: Brazil and the Philippines. God has chosen these two small, out-of-the-way places, populated mostly by poor people, to show the sort of life He expects us to live if we are going to be saved.

"The Espiritista Church is not very strong any more, except in Brazil and the Philippines, probably because these are the only two places where the gift of material healing has been manifested. I only know at first hand about the healing here, but I've talked to members of our faith who have lived in Brazil, and apparently the healing is the same in both places.

"A man named Terte was the first of the material healers. He received the gift in 1943 and for many years he was the only one who had it. He's still alive but he doesn't heal much any more. His powers seem to be weakening, which is one of the problems with which all we healers must contend; at times we have great powers, at other times they aren't as strong.

"The second healer to appear in the Philippines was Tony Agpaoa, the healer whose films drew me here in the first place. Tony's about thirty-seven now, and he has been healing for twenty years. Some say he began to heal when he was only eight, but most believe he first acquired the gift at the age of fifteen.

"Tony is still the busiest healer on the island. As I told

But the manifestation of the Spirit is given to every man to profit withal.

For to one is given by the Spirit the word of wisdom; to another the word of knowledge by the same Spirit;

To another faith by the same Spirit; to another the gifts of healing by the same Spirit;

To another the working of miracles; to another prophecy; to another discerning of spirits; to another divers kinds of tongues; to another the interpretation of tongues:

But all these worketh that one and the selfsame Spirit, dividing to every man severally as he will.

For as the body is one, and hath many members, and all the members of that one body, being many, are one body: so also is Christ.

you, he treats about two hundred patients a month. Most of his patients are foreigners—from Germany, Switzerland, and in the last few years, from the United States and Canada. He is easily the most famous of the healers.

"In the last two years, however, Tony has gotten farther and farther away from our religion. He has dropped out of the Espiritista Church and founded his own church—the Church of Science and Revelation. There are rumors that he is beginning to lose his powers—that God is punishing him for becoming too commercial—and that sometimes, when his powers are weak, he resorts to trickery; though I have to admit that when I was with him I saw no trickery. There were times, however, when he refused to let me watch him work, and I can't say that he didn't use trickery on these occasions.

"In the last ten years, about a dozen new healers have appeared; Joe Mercado, Juan Flores, David Oligani, a woman named Josephine, and Placido are among the best. I've seen or studied with them all. Placido and David Oligani, I think, are the most religious of the healers. Placido has even started his own branch of the Espiritista religion which we call the Progressive Spiritualist Church. We're recognized by the government.

"Altogether, I'd guess that only about two percent of the people in the Philippines belong to the Espiritista Church: most of the population is Catholic. But far more than two percent go to the healers for help when they're ill. We have Catholics coming to us all the time. The healers provide all the medical care for a large part of the population, particularly down here in the lowlands, where so many have received the gift of material healing."

It was after eleven o'clock now and Manny and I were both worn out, but I hated to let Donald go as long as he was willing to talk to us. So when he paused to drink his coffee, I asked, "Can you tell me more about what it's like to heal—how you tell what to take out and what to leave behind . . . that sort of thing."

"It's difficult to explain," Donald said. "You see, when I

165

work I'm always partly in a trance. Each healer has a 'protector,' usually a saint, and the protector takes possession of the healer's arms and mind when he's working. Some healers are completely unconscious when they're operating, some only partly so. As I improve I find I'm more and more conscious of what I'm doing.

"Our protectors guide us all the time, not just when we're working. It was my protector who brought me to Placido, remember? And he tells me things from time to time; for example, he has told me not to do any material healing in the United States, that I will lose my powers if I try to heal there. At least for now, anyone who wants me to heal them will have to come to the Philippines."

"Who is your protector?" I asked.

"I'm different than the other healers," Donald answered. "I don't have a particular saint to guide me. My protector is God Himself."

Finally I asked, "What about your family, Don? Doesn't your wife want you to come home?"

"No, not any more. She understands me. She and my mother have both been over here to visit. In fact, I took out my wife's appendix and I removed a growth from my mother. My mother is going to come back and study here, but my wife wants to stay in the United States. I really shouldn't call her my wife any more, because we've recently been divorced. We just didn't seem to have the same interests. But we're still friends, and when I go back to the United States I'll certainly go and see her and my son."

In the hours it took Donald to tell us all these things he appeared very calm and matter-of-fact. He had apparently accepted his fantastic powers as something he had earned, something God wished him to have. And if it meant leaving home and family, so be it. He promised to meet us again in a few days and, hopefully, arrange for us to visit with Placido and watch him work.

It was midnight before Manny and I got to bed.

15

The next morning we got up early, had a quick cup of coffee and left Baguio at seven-thirty. We checked out of the Pines, planning to spend the next few days in the lowlands. Neither of us looked forward to another drive up the mountain to Baguio.

Going down the mountain was almost as exciting as coming up had been. There were fresh rock slides, the result of a heavy shower during the night, and on several occasions we had to stop and wait for an oncoming car to get by before we could move down. Since there were always trucks or buses of ancient vintage behind us, driven by wild Filipinos who took the mountain for granted and passed us in spots where we couldn't see more than ten feet ahead, we were doubly glad we had had the good sense to check out of the Pines. We got to David's at eight-thirty, by which time the temperature was already well into the nineties.

Brother David greeted Manny with a warm embrace and then, after I had been introduced, we all went in to breakfast. David, Manny and I sat down and the women served us rice, fruit and smoked fish. The rice came in several forms, among which were sweet glazed cakes, loose boiled rice, and rice mixed with bits of vegetables.

The flies buzzed around constantly as we ate, even though the women stood behind us waving fans. At first the sight of the flies sitting on the fruit and rice disturbed me, but then I thought—what the hell, it's eat or starve—and I ate. Everything tasted very good. (In all the time I was in the Philippines, drinking water from questionable sources and eating food which flies had just left, I never had any digestive troubles. Neither did Manny. Just lucky, I guess.)

After breakfast David, Manny and I went out on the porch while the women ate and cleaned up; women's liberation hasn't made much headway in the barrios of the Philippines. While the women worked, David brought Manny up to date on what had happened in the year he had been gone. With money that Manny had given him, David had installed the toilet I've already described, had done some repairs on the church and had purchased the beautiful jeep which he now showed us. Like all the other jeeps I'd seen in the Philippines, David's was brightly painted—red and yellow primarily—and the vehicle had a variety of doodads, the sort of things given as prizes at carnivals, attached at every available point. The jeep was obviously the apple of David's eye.

David is a very pleasant, soft-spoken man. He has the typical dark complexion and black hair of the Filipinos. I'd guess that the average height of the Filipino man must be about five six, but David is shorter than average, about five two. David was very polite and treated Manny and me with deference.

After the women had finished cleaning the kitchen, David told us that he had to make a house call and invited us to go along. We, of course, accepted and David, Clorita, Juanita, two other unidentified relatives, Manny and I all piled into the jeep and set off for another barrio, which proved to be about twenty miles from David's house. As David had no phone, I asked him how he had learned that the patient was sick; he told me that the sick man's wife had come to his home the previous evening. Since David had promised to make the trip, she would invite whoever else was ill in her barrio to come to her home for treatment.

The roads were unpaved and the jeep bounded around a

lot. It was dry and dusty, but this didn't seem to bother anyone but me.

When we arrived at the barrio I found that it looked just like the others I'd seen—lots of scrawny chickens and smiling children around—and the house in which his patient lived was simple but adequate. Off the living room to one side were two small bedrooms, and beyond the living room was a kitchen. There was a small yard with a bamboo fence around it and a couple of fruit trees—mangoes, I think. It was hot in the house. (This is the last time I am going to comment on the weather, I think. If I don't tell you what it was like, assume it was hotter than hell.)

We all sat around the living room while our hostess, a woman in her late fifties, scurried around, smiling, bringing us rice cookies and glasses of orange pop. David and the man who was ill talked together in Tagalog, the principal Indonesian language in the Philippines. David and his sister Clorita both spoke English reasonably well, and after he had talked to the man for a while, David sent him into one of the bedrooms and then beckoned to me. "This man, Mr. Bandio, has trouble with his legs." David said. (I shall not attempt to write in broken English.) "They are swollen and painful. This is caused by blood clots and I am going to operate on him."

"May I watch?" I asked.

"Certainly," he said. "In fact, I would like you to examine the patient."

I did. Mr. Bandio, a moderately obese man whom I judged to be in his mid-sixties, had swelling of his legs from just below the knees down and into his feet. The skin on both legs was superficially eroded. I felt the man's abdomen, looking for signs of liver enlargement, listened to his heart and lungs and checked his pulse to see if he might have heart failure. There was no evidence of either liver or heart disease. I concluded that David might well be correct in his diagnosis—Mr. Bandio probably did have clots in some leg veins. He apparently had what we M.D.'s call a postphlebitic syndrome, a condition in which the valves in the veins of the legs become incompetent as a result of inflammation. Then closts may develop, and since blood and fluid can't get out of the lower extremities, the legs and ankles swell. The swelling causes the skin of the legs and feet to break down, forming ulcerations. There are many operations which have been developed to treat this condition, none of which are routinely successful. I was anxious to see what operation David would perform.

Much to my surprise, David had the patient turn over and lie face down as he prepared to operate on him. I was surprised because the major veins that drain the legs run on the front of the thigh. Behind the knee there is a vein (the popliteal vein) which some surgeons used to tie off hoping to alleviate the postphlebitic syndrome, but David was preparing to operate on the back of the thigh, just below the buttock. The only blood vessels in that area are tiny superficial veins, of no importance as far as the postphlebitic syndrome is concerned.

Manny, who was standing in the bedroom doorway with me, had become very excited. "Watch closely now, Bill," he whispered, "and you'll see how David works. I've seen him remove blood clots before."

While the patient stripped to his shorts in preparation for the operation, Clorita, who always acted as David's assistant, set out several rolls of cotton on a small table at the bedside, and a bottle which apparently contained rubbing alcohol. When everything was in readiness, David sat on the bed beside the patient and went to work.

First Clorita and he bent their heads in silent prayer. This took only a few seconds. Then David swabbed the back of the thigh with alcohol, using his left hand, passing it over the spot where he intended to work. Next he pointed the index finger of his right hand at the patient's thigh and made a quick slashing movement about six inches above the skin. I had my camera with me, and having received David's permission, filmed all this.

170

At this point I stopped filming—I had been about eight feet from the patient—and went up to look more closely at the thigh. With his fingers on either side of the thigh, David was pulling the skin against itself, and between his fingers I could see a fine red line about three inches long. It looked like the sort of scratch one would make with a pin, but David had evidently made it appear without ever touching the patient.

After he had stretched the skin as far as he could, Clorita handed David a water tumbler and some cotton. He stuffed the cotton into the bottom of the glass, set fire to it, and then inverted the tumbler over the scratch in the thigh, pressing it down hard. Immediately the skin and underlying tissue popped up about a half inch into the tumbler so that inside the tumbler the flesh took the shape of an igloo. A few seconds later dark blood began to ooze from the scratch, which was located at the top of the puckered tissue. David looked up at me, quite somberly, and said, "That is one of the clots that is causing trouble." I said, "I see."

What David had done, I explained to Manny later, was to treat his patient with a technique called cupping which is hundreds of years old: the fire in the glass causes a vacuum, the skin puckers, the scratch stretches, and blood is drawn out by the negative pressure in the glass. When I was a surgical resident at Bellevue I had occasionally seen patients who came to the hospital with the telltale round circles still imprinted in their skin from a recent cupping. If I looked carefully at the skin of these patients, I could often find the scratch on the flesh near the middle of the circle. Usually they were young people, Europeans generally, who were new to the United States, and before their mothers or grandmothers would send them to Bellevue for treatment they'd try the "old country" remedies—like cupping—first. Only when cupping, or sometimes leeches, didn't effect a cure would these people turn to physicians and hospitals.

David apparently wasn't satisfied with the amount of blood he had drawn on his first cupping because he was now

171

preparing to cut the patient again, this time higher up on the buttock. The buttock, like the back of the thigh, is an area where there are no superficial blood vessels of any significant size.

So far the only thing David had done which seemed mysterious to me was the scratch. How had he made it without touching the patient?

Perhaps this is the time to interject a pertinent note. I am easily deceived by magicians. I say this with some pride because it has been demonstrated that the more intelligent you are, the more likely you are to be blind to sleight of hand. I don't know why this is so, but perhaps it has something to do with the ability to suspend one's critical faculties at will, a characteristic also found with greatest frequency among the more intelligent people. (This is the reason why intelligent people are more easily hypnotized than dull people; more about this later.)

To repeat, I am usually deceived by magicians. Not just the professionals, who, as far as I can tell, can actually pull rabbits from empty hats, but even the amateurs who make coins disappear and can pick a card I've selected out of a deck. My fourteen-year-old son Julius can execute card tricks that baffle me.

Once, when I was about six, my gullibility got me into trouble. A fifteen-year-old boy who lived next door took a cinder in his right hand, apparently stuffed it into his right ear, and then pulled it out of his left ear. I didn't know much about anatomy at the time and it seemed reasonable to me that the head might be hollow (there are occasions when I still wonder if this might not be the case) and that one might be able to shove a cinder in one ear, pass it through the head and pull it out of the other ear.

So I tried it. I took a cinder and shoved it into my right ear. I still remember the sensation; it hurt like hell. When I found I couldn't reach in and pull it out of my left ear, I tried to pull it back out of the right. Unfortunately, it was stuck. I told my mother, who called my uncle Bill—my father was in court at the time—and my uncle came up from the law office he shared with my father and drove me to the doctor. Just before he took me into the doctor's office he decided to try getting it out himself, using a matchstick, and much to my relief, he did. As you can probably understand, I remember that episode as vividly as if it had happened yesterday.

Now, however, watching the psychic surgeons in the Philippines, I had one big advantage over all the others who were watching: I was a surgeon. I've done about six thousand operations. I've taken out lungs, gall bladders, appendices, uteruses and various other organs. I've operated on the head, the neck, the chest, the abdomen and the extremities. I've had my hand inside all the cavities of the body. I know quite a lot about surgery, and when I watch someone operate I'm able to evaluate what he is doing. This is the background that most others lack who have observed and been treated by psychic surgeons. And as I learned over and over again during my two weeks in the Philippines, it's almost essential to have experience as a surgeon to appraise the psychic surgeons with accuracy. If you haven't done or watched many operations—if you haven't seen a lot of blood—you can easily be fooled.

As David and Clorita again went through their preliminary prayer I handed Manny the camera and moved up so I could look over David's shoulder. While he swabbed the patient's buttock with alcohol I looked carefully at his left hand; it seemed to be empty. But as he withdrew his left hand from the patient I peered intently at the buttock and I could see a barely perceptible scratch. I looked back at David's left hand as he dropped it onto the patient's bed and I could see, almost hidden between two of his fingers, a tiny but sharp piece of mica.

Then David lifted his right hand and again made the slashing gesture in the air, about six inches above the buttock. He left the mica on the bed sheets as he replaced his left hand on the buttock and began stretching the skin

173

between his hands. After about twenty seconds of stretching, the scratch, which had been almost imperceptible, became obvious. It was also obvious—to me, but not to the others who were watching—that David had made this scratch during his preliminary preparations and not with the showy, slashing gesture six inches above the buttock. (Later, when I explained to Manny what David was doing, he watched more carefully, and in the course of several other of David's operations, he was able to confirm my observations.)

After David had finished treating Mr. Bandio, his patient dressed, shook hands with David and joined the others in the living room. Mrs. Bandio then came into the bedroom and started talking to David in Tagalog and pointing to her upper abdomen.

When she had finished talking, David directed her to lie down on the bed. She removed her sandals, and Clorita helped her pull her skirt down and her blouse up a few inches, exposing the upper abdomen. Brother David pushed and probed with his hand for about a minute, Mrs. Bandio occasionally wincing with pain.

When he had finished examining the abdomen David went to the end of the bed and picked up Mrs. Bandio's right foot. Holding the foot steady with his left hand, he squeezed the great toe in his right, watching the woman as he did so. The pressure on her toe didn't seem to bother her. David lowered her foot back to the bed and came over and spoke to me.

"Stomach trouble, Doctor," he said. "I will operate."

"What sort of trouble?" I asked.

"Pain," David said. "Pain in the stomach. She has had it a long time."

"Why did you squeeze her toe?" I asked.

David smiled. "To see if the trouble is natural or unnatural," he answered. "Sometimes the trouble comes from evil spirits; this is difficult to cure. Natural trouble much easier."

"Oh," I said.

While we talked, Clorita had been laying out wads of cotton, about the size of a hen's egg. She also placed the bottle of clear liquid, presumably alcohol, on the bedside table. As soon as David was ready he first bowed his head in prayer, then washed the abdomen with the liquid. Clorita put three of the pieces of cotton on the patient's abdomen, and David, with bare, wet hands, began kneading the abdomen, just as one might knead dough. A few seconds later the cotton, which he had also kneaded, was no longer visible; and a few seconds after that, dark-red liquid started to ooze from between his fingers.

By this time the only part of David's fingers that were visible were the first phalanges, from the knuckles up to the first joint; the last two phalanges were doubled up almost into a fist. Then the first phalanges were shoved into the fleshly folds of the abdomen. Someone who had never seen an operation and who was eager to believe that something mysterious was happening might be persuaded that the ends of the fingers were actually in the abdomen and that the red liquid which we could see was blood. No one who had ever seen an operation would be misled for a moment.

After a minute or so David pulled something up from the abdomen with his left hand, keeping his right hand shoved into the abdomen. He held it up so we could all see it, a dark-red sloppy piece of material about two inches long. "Blood clot," he announced and we all nodded our heads. He returned his hand to the abdomen and began kneading again; Clorita placed more cotton on the abdomen and this quickly disappeared into Brother David's "operating" hands. Soon he pulled out another, longer mass of material, dark-red, wet and sloppy. "Bad tissue," he said, and again we all nodded.

Finally, perhaps three minutes after it had begun, the "operation" ended. David withdrew his hands and the abdominal wall resumed its usual shape—no cut, no scar, no blemish of any sort. One more piece of cotton—dry

175

cotton—was used to mop up the residual red liquid on the abdominal wall. The cotton used in the operation had apparently disappeared, but no one seemed to worry about it.

Two or three minutes later Mrs. Bandio joined us in the living room, to which we had retreated when the operation ended. She was all smiles as she went over and spoke to David. When Mrs. Bandio left David and went to the kitchen, David said to me, "She tells me she is very happy now. All her pain is gone. She only wishes she had called me two years ago." That's a line I've heard—every doctor has heard—many times from grateful patients who want you to know you're much better than any other doctor they've ever been to. It's a line I always like to hear.

While Mr. and Mrs. Bandio, completely recovered from their operations, worked happily out in the kitchen preparing a meal for all of us, another patient entered the house. This man, Mr. Conatos, looked about sixty years old. He had a big belly but the skin of his face sagged, as if he had lost a lot of weight. His eyes were dull and he walked slowly, as if every step were a burden. David listened to him for about five minutes, asking an occasional question, and then sent Mr. Conatos into the bedroom.

"I saw this man three weeks ago," David told me. "He was having trouble passing his water and I treated him. He was supposed to come back a week later for another treatment, but he didn't. He is poor and he didn't want to bother me. Now he is sicker and I will treat him again."

I followed David into the bedroom where Mr. Conatos, stripped to his undershorts, was lying on the bed. David walked around to the left side of Mr. Conatos and started pushing on his abdomen. After about a minute he said, "Doctor, would you examine this man?"

I sat on the edge of the bed and looked at the abdomen. There were streaks around the navel that looked like the blue lines on a road map: distended veins, the sort of thing we sometimes see in patients who have an obstruction in the large veins that flow into the liver.

I pressed gently on the abdomen, trying to feel any enlarged organ or tumor mass that might account for the swelling of the abdomen and/or the distended veins. It didn't take me long to find one. On the left side of the abdomen was a stony hard mass that began at the rib margin and extended down below the level of the navel. It felt to me to be about the size of a football. I tried to move it, but couldn't: it was fixed to the back wall of the abdomen.

"What do you think, Doctor?" David asked me.

Since I knew Mr. Conatos couldn't speak English, I was able to speak frankly. "This man has a very hard, large tumor in his abdomen," I said. "I'm not sure what it is, but it's probably a tumor of the kidney. I suspect it's malignant, though I suppose it might possibly be a gigantic infected kidney."

"What would you do with him?" David asked.

"If he were my patient," I replied, "I'd send him to the hospital right away. I'd have some tests done which I think would tell me what organ this growth is in. Then, after I prepared the patient—I suspect he's anemic and needs a transfusion—I'd probably operate and try to get the tumor out.

"I realize, however," I added, "that you probably don't need to do all this. I suspect you can operate and remove this right away." Actually, I suspected nothing of the sort; after the two operations I had witnessed I didn't believe David had any magical or miraculous operative skills. But I wanted, as gently as possible, to put him on the spot.

"No," David said. "I shall not operate right now. This man has two problems, one unnatural, one natural. First, I shall treat the unnatural. I shall prescribe some herbs. Then, next week, I will treat his natural problem—the tumor you describe."

I said, "I see." What else was there to say?

Mr. Conatos got dressed and departed, taking with him a

piece of paper on which David had written instructions as to which herbs to take and when. Then we all went into the kitchen, where a long wooden table had been set. We were served rice, fruit, smoked fish, scrawny chicken and black, inky squid. I didn't eat the squid.

After lunch I went out on the street for a few minutes just to look around. While I was there I noticed David, out in the yard, talking with a young boy. David gave him some money and the boy went out into a shed and came back a few minutes later with a bucket of reddish green fruit, each about the size of a plum; I learned later that these were betel nuts. David tucked them under the seat of his jeep and went back into the house through a rear door. He hadn't seen me.

It was about five o'clock when we got back to David's. Everyone went into the chapel to pray; Clorita and David took turns in leading the prayer and reading from the Bible. We gave thanks for our blessings and prayed particularly for Manny's daughter, Charlotte. We also said a prayer for President Marcos.

While the women prepared supper Manny, David and I sat on the porch talked and smoked. David smokes a lot of cigarettes—a couple of packs a day, I'd guess—and Manny and I smoked cigars. David asked me about my practice, I told him, and then he told me about his.

"I have been a healer for seventeen years," he said, "since I was twenty-four years old. My father was a healer before me.

"My powers come from God, but I have a protector too—a saint who guides my hands. Usually I know what I am doing, but sometimes I operate in a trance."

"If you are in a trance at times, how can you recognize diseased organs?"

"I tell by the temperature," he said. "When my hand is in the body a diseased organ feels hot. Then I take it out."

"How many patients do you treat in an average day?"

"Seventeen or eighteen, usually. But on Sundays I treat

fifty or a hundred. Today was a slow day because we had to travel so far. But you will see on Sunday."

Manny had told me that all healers acted as dentists as well as physicians. I asked David about this.

"Yes," he said, "there is no dentist in the barrio, so I pull teeth when it is necessary."

"Do you ever fill them?"

"No," he answered, "just pull. I have a special chair in the church where the patient sits."

"It must be wonderful," I said, "to have all this power from God, not to have to read and study and worry about complications all the time."

"It is wonderful," David said, "but there is one problem: sometimes my powers are great, sometimes not so great. I always worry that my power will be weak."

"Well, today you seemed fine," I said.

"Yes," David answered. "Today was a good day."

16

After supper Manny and I left for the Hotel Lis in Asignan. Since Manny is a knowledgeable hotel man, I had left the hotel selection up to him. However, I must say I was disappointed. I can hardly blame Manny because after we later looked at the other hotels in Asignan, I had to agree the Lis was apparently the best of the lot. But the best was certainly none too good.

There were, for example, lizards all over the place. On the floor, on the ceiling, on the toilet, in the drinking glasses. Frankly, I'm not fond of lizards. Manny assured me these weren't poisonous, but that didn't help me enjoy their company.

The bathroom, too, left a lot to be desired. For one thing, there was no hot water, and for another, there was no seat on the toilet. Manny explained to me that toilet seats are a luxury in the Philippines, found only in the plush hotels or the homes of the wealthy. Later experiences proved to me that once again, Manny was correct.

The hotel dining room was called. "The Hut," and one could hardly think of a more appropriate name, since it was, indeed, a straw hut set beneath some trees about fifty yards from the hotel proper. We discovered this when I, naïvely, suggested a night cap before retiring and went to look for the bar.

Another thing we discovered, when we went looking for a bar, was that there was no key to the door of our hotel room. "We lock hotel at eleven," the man who served as bellhop, desk clerk and general manager told us. "No need to lock room." Perhaps he was right, but being from the United States, we weren't sure. We decided not to go out at all, since, we learned there was no bar in The Hut, there was no reason to go out.

The manager did manage to get us some ice cubes. I had a bottle of Scotch in my bag and we each had a drink. Manny insisted on rinsing his glass out once with the Scotch before he refilled it ("as a precaution against cholera") but I just went ahead and drank. I figured if I could live with lizards, I could live with cholera germs.

Once during the night, about two o'clock, I woke and decided to get a drink of water and, incidentally, empty my bladder. Much to my dismay I discovered that now not only was there no hot water there was no water at all. Nothing to drink, no way to flush the toilet. At the Hotel Lis they expect the patrons to sleep through the night, so the water is turned off between 11 P.M. and 6 A.M.

In the morning Manny and I tried to decide whether to spend the next week at the Hotel Lis or risk the drive up to and back from Baguio every day. Our deliberations lasted about three seconds; we packed up and said goodbye forever to the Hotel Lis. Let me make one positive statement about the hotel; it is inexpensive. Our double room cost us $1.50 for the night.

That morning at breakfast with David and his family Clorita asked us if we would like to go and see Josephine operate. "Tomorrow [Saturday] Joe Mercado and Juan Flores heal in their churches, but Josephine heals in her home every day." Since we wanted to observe as many healers as possible we accepted Clorita's offer.

On the way to Josephine's home, as we drove through downtown Asignan, Clorita pointed out the churches of Flores and Mercado. Both were on the outskirts of town, plain frame houses with chickens and dogs wandering around on the ground outside and occasionally venturing into the buildings. "Mercado begins his service at ten,"

Clorita said, "and Flores starts at noon. As you see, they are close enough together so you can easily visit both. Mercado doesn't mind if you take movies, but Flores has forbidden any film making. However, they will both be happy to let you observe."

On the edge of Asignan there is a river which, like all the rivers I saw in the Philippines, is muddy, with water buffaloes stomping around the shallow areas and occasionally some Filipinos bathing in it, and along the edge of the river there is a dike-like elevation with a narrow road on top. We turned off the highway onto this road and drove about five miles off into a barrio much like the other I have described. Across the street from Josephine's home was a school, and while we waited for Josephine to return—she had gone to market—we watched the children playing in the schoolyard. I took films of them, and like kids everywhere, they were delighted and made faces and giggled at the camera.

Josephine is twenty-four years old, pretty and obviously light-hearted; she laughs a lot and when she isn't laughing she smiles. She has a cute little girl, about three years old, and a husband whom I didn't meet. Josephine doesn't speak much English, but after Clorita had introduced us, she said "Welcome" and waved us on in.

Josephine works in a room on the ground floor of her home. The room is dark, the only light coming from the door, which is left open, and a window up front, where Josephine stands. There is a table in front of her and a bucket in the corner behind her. Visitors and patients sit on chairs or benches, facing Josephine. I stood near the head of the table. There was a cubicle—it looked like a laundry room of some sort—just off the room where Josephine worked. I could see a bucket of betel nuts on the floor.

Josephine kept a pad and pencil on the table. As each patient approached and told Josephine about his or her ailment, Josephine wrote on her pad. This writing looked simply like a lot of doodles. "It is 'spirit writing.'" Clorita told me later.

The first patient was a fat man, about fifty, who pointed to his stomach as he told his story in Tagalog. Josephine wrote constantly while he talked. Then the man climbed up on the table and Josephine pulled his shirt up and his pants down. She swabbed his abdomen, placed some cotton on it and went to work.

I watched very closely and saw about what I had seen as David worked, except that Josephine apparently pulled some straw out of the abdomen (or out from under the patient's shirt, if you were standing and watching from my location) along with the "clots" of cotton. "Witches did this," Josephine said as she stopped for a moment and held the straw up for me to see, before tossing it into the bucket. In about two minutes Josephine finished her operation and wiped the abdomen clean, and the fat man—all smiles—tucked in his shirt and got off the table.

The next patient was a thin woman who pointed to her lower abdomen as Josephine listened and wrote. Then Josephine operated on this woman, in the usual fashion. About half a minute after she had started to operate, Josephine held up a blood-soaked specimen for me to see, saying with a smile, "Appendix." I've removed several hundred appendices in my surgical career. What Josephine was holding was a wad of cotton, not an appendix. Josephine threw it in the bucket and a few seconds later she completed the operation. Her patient—no scar, no pain, all smiles—stepped down off the table.

The third patient was a woman about fifty. She complained of a pain in her left cheek, and for this problem Josephine performed what I later learned is her specialty: she took a wad of cotton, shoved it into the left cheek and pulled it out of the patient's left nostril. "Sometimes," Clorita whispered to me, "Josephine will push the cotton into one ear and pull it out of the opposite ear. The cotton takes the poison with it." All I could think of was my own experience with the cinder.

This was Josephine's last patient of the day. Now all the patients and their families left, smiling and waving at Josephine. As each patient departed, he or she placed an envelope containing a donation on the table. Josephine spoke a few words to Clorita and then smiled at us. Clorita translated. "Josephine says she is sorry she had to rush through the operation so fast, but her little girl is fussy. She says you can come back any time and she will go slower so you can see better." Manny and I thanked Josephine and we each put a dollar's worth of pesos on the table. This amount, Clorita had assured us, would be ample payment for the hospitality Josephine had shown us.

We left Josephine's, drove back to David's, and then, even though it was only two in the afternoon, decided to go back to Baguio. "I'm exhausted," Manny said. "I only got two hours' sleep last night. I kept worrying about those lizards."

"I thought you told me they weren't poisonous," I said.

"I meant to say I didn't think they were poisonous," Manny replied. "About three in the morning I began to wonder about them."

"I'm certainly glad I misunderstood you," I said. "If I'd thought they were poisonous, I wouldn't have slept at all."

By now I was doing all the driving to and from Baguio. I hate to drive, but if there's one thing I hate worse than driving, it's riding with someone whose driving I don't trust—and I didn't trust Manny's. He looked at the view too often to suit me. When I'm riding on a narrow mountain road subject to rock slides, with nothing but a skinny little fence between me and a drop of several thousand feet, I like a driver who keeps his eyes glued to the road. And I certainly don't want a driver who has had two hours' sleep the night before. Manny didn't seem to worry much about my driving, so this arrangement worked out nicely.

Back at the Pines I showered, watched an old cowboy

movie on television for an hour and then slept until seven. Manny was still asleep when I went down to dinner.

After dinner I called the hotel manager, Miss Taros, a very pleasant woman to whom Manny had introduced me, and asked her if she knew of a doctor in Baguio who could speak English and who might be willing to talk to me about the psychic surgeons.

"Certainly, Dr. Nolen," she said, "I know just the man—Dr. Raul Otillo. He is my family doctor and he speaks English very well. He took some of his training in the United States. I will call him for you." She did, and Dr. Otillo agreed to meet me at the Pines Hotel after he had finished dinner.

When Dr. Otillo arrived we ordered drinks and then sat in the lobby on a couch in front of the fire. Dr. Otillo is about thirty-eight years old, thin, intense, personable and intelligent. He had two years of surgical training at a hospital in Detroit, Michigan, and he spoke English fluently.

"So you're interested in the psychic surgeons, too," he said with a smile. "We're used to lay people coming here to see them, but rarely doctors. I hope you're not here for treatment?"

"No, not that," I said. "Actually, I'm a writer as well as a surgeon. I'm hoping to write a book about the psychic surgeons. I'm over here to observe them and to try to decide exactly what is going on."

"Good luck," Dr. Otillo said. "We tried to investigate them off and on for years, but couldn't get anywhere. Lately we've just given up. Thousands of patients come to the Philippines for treatment from these 'surgeons.' Chartered flights come in from Germany, Canada, Japan and, lately, the United States. We tried to warn people that these surgeons were fakes but no one would listen. So now, generally, we just ignore them. It's a shame to see people wasting so much money on nothing. If you can do anything to warn patients off, I'll be delighted."

"If you tell me exactly what you know about them," I said, "it may help me understand them."

"Sure," Dr. Otillo said. "First, you should know I've been practicing here for ten years. I do some general practice, but mostly surgery. There are four private hospitals and one county hospital in Baguio and there are five surgeons practicing here. The population is eighty-five thousand—bigger during holidays seasons—so we all keep very busy.

"In 1967, when I was the president of the local medical society, Tony Agpaoa was the big name among the psychic surgeons. He worked out of his home here, and as I said, hundreds of patients came here every month for treatment. They came from all over the world. His wife, as you may know, owns a travel agency, and it was through her organization that most of the visits were arranged. Between them they must have been raking in fantastic sums of money. He always claimed he didn't charge anyone—but he'd accept donation. I talked to a few of the people that came to see him; none had given less than a hundred dollars and many gave a thousand. Even if you figure he averaged only two hundred dollars a patient—and I'm sure he does better than that—he was taking in forty thousand dollars a month. Add to that the money his wife earned with her travel bureau, and you can see why those who know him think he's probably one of the wealthiest men in the Philippines.

"When I took over as president of the medical society I knew all this, but I also knew it wouldn't do any good to condemn him—people would say doctors were jealous—so I went to Tony and told him we'd appreciate it is he would demonstrate his healing abilities for us. If he could show us that he was honestly capable of performing bloodless surgery, without instruments or anesthesia, we'd be glad to let him practice in Baguio. We'd even send patients to him. Tony agreed and I lined up a fine pathologist to watch with me as Tony operated.

"The first time we came to watch, Tony didn't show up.

He claimed later that he had confused the date. So we rescheduled his appearance.

"The second time we went to his church, Tony claimed to be ill; he had temporarily lost his 'powers' and couldn't operate. We made another appointment.

"The third time Tony just didn't show up—no excuse, no explanation. He had left town for a while. We never could get him to show us his skills. There was nothing we could do except kick him out of Baguio. It didn't bother him, of course. He owned a beautiful beach resort, Cresta Ola, not far from here, and moved his church up there."

"What about his patients?" I asked. "Surely some of them must have been dissatisfied with the treatment. Couldn't you get them to sue?"

"You'd think so, wouldn't you," Dr. Otillo said, "but it doesn't work that way. I've been called here to the Pines Hotel dozens of times to treat sick patients that have flown in for Agpaoa's help and have then gotten into desperate straits; not one of them was willing to testify. They're all embarrassed because they've been taken. No one wants to go to court and say they've acted like an idiot. They're all foreigners and they just want to get home.

"The saddest are those who die here, and there have been several. It's not very pleasant talking to a parent who has brought a little girl with leukemia all the way from the United States only to have her die in the Philippines. When that happens I'd like to wring Agpaoa's neck; but until someone will take him to court there's nothing we can do."

"The guy must be clever," I said.

"He's clever, all right," Dr. Otillo answered. "Hell, he's been practicing this crazy surgery for twenty years, and do you know how often one of the 'specimens' he had removed has reached a pathologist? Just once. Every other time he either managed to lose the specimen or he burns it up immediately; he tells the patient 'the tissue is evil.'"

"What happened with the one specimen that got to the pathologist?"

187

"That was interesting," Dr. Otillo said. "A man who had come here from Canada for treatment of a kidney stone became a bit skeptical after watching Tony operate on other patients. When Tony removed his 'stone' the patient managed to grab it before Tony could throw it away. He brought it to me and I had our pathologist examine it; it was a piece of sugar."

"And the Canadian wouldn't protest?"

"He would not. He refused to pay Tony, but that's all he'd do. He was a prominent businessman and he was afraid his reputation would suffer if his friends and associates knew he'd been taken in by a charlatan. He'd learned his lesson, but he refused to help us warn off others."

"What's Tony up to now?"

"He's still around," Dr. Otillo said. "He has a home here and he's back often. But he keeps his practice out of Baguio; he knows we'd be on his neck in a minute if he tried working here. He practices mostly in Manila.

"In fact, it's kind of funny—do you know one of the reasons Tony often comes back here?"

"No," I said, "why?"

"For medical care. He has some problems with his health and one of the doctors here in Baguio is his family physician. I'm not at liberty to tell you which doctor, but he takes care of Tony, his wife and his children. We laugh about it often: it's either that or cry. People are so gullible. I wish you luck in trying to remedy the situation, but I don't have much hope for your success."

"I don't either," I said, "but I'm going to give it a try."

We shook hands, Dr. Otillo left, and I went up to bed.

17

On Saturday morning, as we hurtled down the mountain, I related Dr. Otillo's story to Manny.

"Sounds awfully suspicious, doesn't it, Bill?" Manny said. "It begins to look as if I've been a fool."

"Let's try to keep our minds open for a while," I said, "though I admit it doesn't look promising. So far all I've seen is a lot of sleight of hand, and not very clever sleight of hand at that. The only actual blood I've seen came from those cuppings David did. All the blood clots and appendices and tumors he and Josephine waved at me were nothing but lumps of cotton soaked in a red dye of some sort and twisted into different shapes. I've seen too many appendices, too much real blood and too many blood-soaked surgical sponges and wads of cotton to be taken in by fake operations. So far it looks like one big hoax to me, but I'm still willing, even eager, to be shown differently. Maybe Joe Mercado will be the man who convinces me. Didn't you say he was supposed to be the best operator of all the psychic surgeons?"

"That's right," Manny said. "And if you remember, even Donald Winslow, who works with Placido, thinks Mercado is the best. If he doesn't convince you it's real, then I doubt if anyone else will."

"And didn't Donald also say that Joe Mercado is one psychic surgeon who never fakes anything?"

"Right," Manny said. "Agpaoa has been caught faking it several times, when his powers were weak. Mercado has

189

never been know to lose his power. He must do at least a thousand operations a year and no one has ever accused him of cheating."

"Manny," I said, "I've got an idea—a way to settle once and for all, at least as far as I'm concerned, whether these psychic surgeons are for real. I'm going to let Joe Mercado operate on me."

Manny turned to look at me. "You're kidding," he said.

"No, I'm not. Frankly, Manny, I haven't seen anything yet to convince me that these psychic surgeons are actually putting their hands in the body. I'm certain that both David and Josephine were faking it. I just can't believe Mercado will do anything different."

"It's your life," Manny said, "but I'm glad you're running the risk and not me."

"So now I need some advice," I said. "How do I get Mercado to operate on me?"

"That shouldn't be too difficult," Manny said. "After the service, which is usually very brief, everyone who needs help gets in a line. First, Joe gives them spiritual injections—you'll see what they're like—and then his assistant, a woman who speaks English, asks each person what is wrong with them. If it's something that needs an operation, she writes the name down. After the injections are over, she calls people up one by one for their operations.

"Joe operates on kidney stones a lot. Maybe if you tell him you have a kidney stone, he'll decide you need an operation."

"I haven't got a kidney stone," I said, "but I do have high blood pressure and often that's caused by kidney disease. I'll tell him about that problem and see what he decides."

We arrived at Mercado's church at nine-thirty. Services wouldn't start until ten, but already the room, which held about two hundred people, was half full. We wandered around the compound and Manny pointed Mercado out to me—a husky, dark-haired, cheerful-looking man who appeared to be in his early forties. He was chatting with visitors and his family. His assistant, Maria, a woman in her early thirties, spotted Manny and came over to us.

"Brother Manny," she said, "it is so nice to see you. How is Charlotte?"

"Just fine, thank the Lord," said Manny. "She's doing very well." He introduced me and then Maria brought us over to say hello to Joe. Joe speaks no English, but he grinned and patted Manny on the back—he obviously remembered Charlotte—and shook hands with me. We sat down and Joe resumed his conversation in Tagalog with a Filipino visitor. I struck up a conversation with a tall, thin white man who was sitting next to me.

"I've come from Brazil," he said. "I'm a member of the Espiritista Church. We used to have a fine healer in Brazil, a man named Arigo, but he died a few years ago. I'm here in the Philippines for two reasons: I'm on vacation, but I also wanted to see some of the healers. Really, I guess, there are three reason. I have a very bad tooth that needs extracting and I've asked Brother Mercado to pull it for me. I've watched him work before, and he's as good as Arigo was."

I hadn't seen a tooth extraction yet, so I looked forward to this one.

At ten the service started, and after prayers which only lasted about ten minutes, I learned who one of Mercado's visitors was: Joaquin Cunanan, the head of the Espiritista Church in the Philippines. He spoke for about ten minutes, giving thanks for the wonderful healing powers of the healers, Mercado's powers in particular. He held up articles from various magazines—among them *Time*—which purported to show evidence that the healers did, indeed, have supernormal powers. The *Time* magazine article included photographs of Joe Mercado's fingers done by a special technique known as Kirlian photography. The pictures supposedly showed a field of power radiating from Joe's fingers before he operated, and a diminution of the radiation after he had healed someone. This was interpreted to mean that Joe's powers left his body through his fingers and flowed into the body of his patient, healing the ailment, whatever it might be.

Mr. Cunanan then read excerpts from an article by former astronaut Edgar Mitchell praising miracle healers. Finally he read a report signed by several men who had observed the healers in action. It was sort of "white paper" proclaiming the fact that psychic surgery involved no fakery.

After the prayers and the "sermon" by Mr. Cunanan, Joe and his assitants went up front. Maria said, "All who want spiritual injections may come forward." About sixty people got in line in the aisle. As each one stepped forward Mercado, pointing his left index finger as if it were a needle, pushed at various points of the body, wherever anyone had a ache or pain. He laughed and chatted in Tagalog as he did this. His patients smiled and laughed too. It was certainly a much happier collection of patients than those to whom I gave injections in my office.

After I had photographed the procession for a few minutes I joined the line. When I reached Joe I pointed to my arm and my buttock and he gave me two quick "injections."

When Joe finished with me I went over to Maria. "What problems can we help you with?" she asked, using the very phrase that most of the nurses in our clinic use when they show a patient into an examining room.

"I don't know if you can help me," I said. "I hope so. I have high blood pressure." Then I pointed to my left lower abdomen. "Kidney trouble, possibly."

"The blood pressure is no problem," Maria said. "The other, we shall have to see. Please be seated. I will call you." I went back to Manny and said, "I think I'm going to have an operation."

"Great," Manny said. "I'll have to remember to send you flowers."

I wasn't number one on the list of surgical candidates, so I had a chance to watch Mercado in action.

In a corner, next to the kitchen table which served first to hold the Bible used in the religious service and later as an operating table, one edge of a white bed sheet had been nailed to the wall. As a patient's name was called he stepped up and Maria held out the opposite edge of the sheet so that the patient could stand in front of it. Then Joe would bounce around the patient, with a bath towel stretched out between his hands, peering at it as though he were looking through it and into the patient. This, Manny explained to me, was the healer's equivalent of our X-ray procedure. Supposedly Joe could see through the towel into the patient's body and spot any abnormality or diseased organ.

After "X-raying" then, he operated first on a man with stomach pain and then on a woman with pelvic cramps. The alcohol, the cotton, the red liquid were the same as in the other operations I've described, but Joe added an extra touch; he sometimes produced masses of tissue, mostly yellowish blobs but sometimes stringy and reddish yellow. Once he held up a specimen and Maria said, "Hysterectomy." This was like no uterus I'd ever seen; it, and all the other specimens Joe produced, looked like viscera of small animals—probably, I thought, of chickens.

When my name was called I stepped forward. I stood in front of the sheet and Joe jumped around me with his towel. When he had finished Maria said, "You need operation."

"All right," I said, "go ahead."

Joe decided, however, that I was too long for the operating table and elected to operate on me while I stood. He pulled up my shirt and lowered my pants, exposing my abdomen, and went to work. I was able to look down on his hands as he pulled and tugged. From my vantage point I could see, as he began, that he had some reddish yellow object palmed in his right hand.

After a few seconds of pushing on my abdomen, the skin was covered with "blood"; supposedly he was in my

193

abdomen. He pulled out several wads of dark red cotton and held them up for me to see. Maria said, "Clots." Then he busied himself with some serious poking and tugging, and finally, after a few seconds, smiled and held up a blob of reddish yellow tissue for me to see. At this close range—it wasn't more than six inches from my nose—I recognized it definitely as clumps of fat, soaked in whatever this reddish liquid that passed as blood was. Maria looked at me, proudly, and said, "Tumor. Very serious. You are very lucky man." I'd have loved to grab that specimen, but Joe immediately threw it into the bucket behind him, where another assistant doused it with alcohol and set it on fire. This was the treatment given to all the specimens Joe removed.

Seconds after Joe had produced the "tumor," he wiped the "blood" off my abdomen with fresh cotton and pointed to my abdomen. No scar, no nothing. He beamed with pride and I smiled and thanked him. "Will that cure my blood pressure?" I asked Maria.

"That was much worse than blood pressure," she said. "That was bad tumor. You are lucky. But we cure you blood pressure too. Just sit down and we will give you massage to cure your blood pressure."

I sat in a chair and first one of Joe's assistants, an elderly man, and then Joe himself tugged on my neck and shoulders. Apparently it was a funny sight because all the parishioners giggled or laughed, as did Joe, Maria, the assistant, Manny and—once I got into the spirit of the thing—I. It was all a lot of fun. When Joe finished, Maria said, "Now sit down and rest for a few minutes. Then we'll give you some oil you can rub on later." I rejoined Manny in our second-row pew.

I knew with certainty that Joe's hands hadn't been in my abdomen. The rectus abdominus muscles run from the rib cage to the pelvis; they are two bands of muscle about a half inch thick and four inches wide on either side of the midline of the abdomen. I've cut through or across these muscles hundreds of times. When Joe "operated" on me I tightened these muscles, and even at moments when I couldn't see his fingers because of the way he kept his hands turned, I could feel the pressure on my skin, outside the rectus muscles. Joe Mercado, "one of the best of the psychic surgeons" and "one operator who never has to fake it," had just performed a sham operation on me.

After one more "appendectomy," the Espiritista believer from Brazil sat in a chair and Joe proceeded with the tooth extraction. The man opened his mouth and Joe reached back; we couldn't see exactly what he was doing. After a few seconds of tugging he pulled out a piece of white material. It was about twice the size of an ordinary human tooth and it was flabby, obviously not a tooth at all. The Brazilian tried to take the "tooth" from Mercado, but he quickly tossed it to an assistant who immediately threw it in the bucket and set fire to it. The patient stood up, stuck a finger into his mouth and said with dismay, "But my tooth is still there!"

Mercado just shrugged and walked over to some friends who were standing near the table. Maria said to the man, "The roots—those are what Joe removed. Tooth is okay—only roots were bad. You will be fine now." The Brazilian tried to prolong the discussion but Maria left him. He stood there, poking in his mouth, shaking his head in dismay, obviously shaken. "Poor guy," I thought, "he's going to find it difficult to remain a believer. Particularly when that tooth starts aching again."

Now the healing was over, and Mercado left the chapel and strolled outside, smiling and talking with Joaquin Cunanan and his associates. One of Joe's helpers piled a stack of bottles on the operating table and said, "Those who wish to purchase holy oils may do so now." A dozen or so people came forward to buy the oils.

"How much are they?" I asked.

"No special price. Whatever offering you want to make we shall be happy to have. It all goes to support our chapel." The chapel looked like nothing more than a slightly oversized garage. It couldn't have cost more than $500. If all the money Joe collects goes into the chapel, then its foundation must be made of solid gold.

Manny and I each made a $20 donation to the chapel, which seemed to please Joe's assistant. I caught Mr. Cunanan as he was leaving, asking him for a reference to the *Time* article. "Here," he said, "take this." And he gave me an envelope containing reprints of all the articles from which he had quoted in his sermon. I thanked him, shook hands with smiling Joe Mercado, and Manny and I piled into the Volkswagen and drove the few blocks to Juan Flores' church.

Since it was only eleven-thirty and Flores' service didn't begin until noon, Manny and I stopped at a small neighborhood store and had a Coke. "What did you think?" Manny asked me.

"I'm sorry, Manny," I said, "but the more I see, the less I see. So far, it's all a fake."

"I'm sorry too," Manny said. "I have to admit, though, that I'm inclined to agree. Last year I was all shaken up, emotionally. Learning that Charlotte had a brain tumor simply floored me. I was ready to grasp at anything. Now that I'm able to be more objective, it all looks different. I'm afraid I don't believe any more either."

"I hate telling yo this, Manny," I said.

"It's not your fault, Bill. I wanted to come back and I wanted to know the truth. That's why I asked you to come with me. I've got to be a realist. It it's fake, it's fake. There's not sense in kidding myself."

"Come on," I said, "let's go see Flores."

The church was packed. All the windows and doors were open but it was still very hot in the building. The temperature hovered around a hundred degrees and there was no breeze at all. Yet every pew was filled.

Manny and I stood in the back so that we could step out for air when we felt like it. To our surprse, Joaquin Cunanan had come to Flores' church too and opened the service by giving the same speech, praising the Espiritista surgeons, that he had given at Mercado's. He even waved the same articles at the audience. He spoke twice—first in English, then in Tagalog.

Manny and I stood outside during Cunanan's talk. We met a British journalist from Hong Kong and his wife (I'll call them Roger and Sarah) who had stopped by on their way back to Manila from Baguio. "I'm doing an article on Baguio for my magazine," Roger said. "The government is very anxious to attract more tourist to the Philippines. I spent some time in Manila with President Marcos and I also met a newspaper reporter who suggested that I stop by and watch Flores work. He thought I might get an interesting article out of it."

"I'm sure you can," I said. "This psychic surgery is, if nothing else, fascinating."

After Cunanan's speech, and after a brief reading from the Bible, patients lined up for diagnoses, spiritual injections, and if necessary, operations. Flores worked about as Mercado had worked, except that Flores, instead of nailing one edge of a sheet to the wall, wrapped the sheet around each patient. Then he jumped around him, rather like a bullfighter, peering at the patient at various angles. After he had made his "X-ray" diagnosis, Flores would administer a series of "spiritual injections." The patient would then leave a donation on the table and return to the pew.

Flores, unlike Mercado, was a very serious, intense man. He was tall by Filipino standards, about five feet nine, and thin. He never smiled. It was well known that he did not like foreign observers—though foreign patients were welcome—and he would allow no one to bring a camera into his church. I watched the spiritual injections from the back of the hall, but when he started to operate, as he did after about an hour of injecting, I slowly worked my way toward the front of the church. Roger, the journalist from Hong Kong, came with me. Flores performed two abdominal operations in what I now recognized as the usual fashion, and then Mr. Cunanan sat down in a chair. Flores was to perform an eye operation on him.

Roger and I wanted to get a really good look, so we tried to get close to the altar. "No," a little old woman said, "you cannot come up here. You may interfere with the powers. I think you are not believers."

"We have come to learn," I said. "We won't interfere."

"No," she said, scowling, "stay down." We had to retreat.

As he began the operation Flores interposed his body between us and the patient. When he stepped aside he had his closed left fist over Cunanan's eye. Then, as he spread his fingers of the hand we could see the eye in his fingers.

Everyone gasped. Roger and I noticed that the little old lady had left the church, so with everyone's attention riveted on Flores, we were able to get to the alter. Finally, we weren't more than five feet from Cunanan, who had his left eye closed. His right eye had apparently been pulled three or four inches out of its socket. It was open and staring between Flores' fingers. It was, to say the least, a weird sight. Cunanan was obviously not the least bit uncomfortable. While Flores worked, Cunanan occasionally made a brief comment in Tagalog. Sometimes he chuckled. He seemed to find the operation on his eye a pleasant experience.

Flores took a handkerchief from his pocket and began to wipe the eyeball, about the way you might wipe off a windshield.

"Amazing," Roger whispered to me, "how can he possibly pull the eye out that far?"

"He hasn't," I whispered. "Watch what happens when he finishes the operation and goes to put the eye back. Watch how he does it."

After three or four minutes of polishing, Flores had apparently accomplished to his satisfaction whatever it was he was trying to accomplish. Now he put down the handkerchief, and bringing his right hand up to the nasal side of the eye, he closed his fist around the eye and then pushed down, as though shoving the eye back into the socket.

"Watch his left hand," I whispered to Roger. As Flores took his hands away, and Cunanan opened both his perfectly normal-appearing eyes, Flores kept his left hand closed. "He has the eye in that hand," I whispered.

Flores walked around his operating table and swung his left hand nonchalantly onto a shelf behind it which no one in the church could see. A second later the left hand appeared, open and empty. I retreated even farther, so that I was completely behind the altar, and managed a glimpse of the shelf: the eye was lying on it.

Flores, his big operation finished, went outside for a cigarette. Mr. Cunanan spotted me and came over. "Did you see an eye operation or did you see an eye operation?" he asked with a smile.

"Amazing," I said, avoiding an outright lie.

"Not to us Espiritistas, it isn't," he said. "Our psychic surgeons have fantastic powers."

Roger and I went out and joined Manny and Roger's wife, Sarah.

"Bill," Roger said, "I have to admit—till you told me to watch his left hand—he had me fooled. I was almost ill watching him work on that eye."

"That's why that operation—in fact all the operations, work so well," I said. "You are, I'm sure, a critical, skeptical man; a journalist has to be skeptical. And Manny's a critical, skeptical person too; he has to be in order to remain successful in business. But when you see an operation—all that blood and gore—you suspend your critical faculties. You become believers.

"Surgery is my profession. I can watch operations with an objective, critical eye. I'm able to look dispassionately at what these psychic surgeons are doing. I knew damn well that wasn't Cunanan's eye. There's no way the optic nerve could stretch to allow the eye to come out that far. And what the hell kind of an operation was it, anyway? You don't polish up an eye as you might a mirror. I spoke to Cunanan at Mercado's and had a good look at his face. His eyes are perfectly normal—no cataracts, no nothing. Flores had simply palmed an animal eye, probably one he'd removed from a dead dog. He kept it in his fist and he kept his fist over Cunanan's eye. You'll notice that never, absolutely never, do any of these psychic surgeons take both hands off the body. If they did, it would be immediately apparent that there was no cut, no incision, no nothing. They have to keep their hands on the body to sustain the illusion. Everything I've seen is pure illusion. I'll bet if Mercado or Flores knew I was a surgeon, they'd have figured some way to keep me out of their churches."

"Having it an illusion sure as hell kills a good story," Roger said.

"Don't I know it?" I said. "I've flown almost eight thousand miles trying to find something miraculous to write a book about, and all I've found so far are a lot of sleight-of-hand artists. And not very good ones at that. They wouldn't last a week on television. But as long as I'm here, I'm going to keep looking, and I'm going to get at the bottom of all this if I can. I'd like to know what makes all these people tick."

"Good luck," Roger said. "And if you get to Hong Kong, look us up."

"Thanks," I said, "I will."

We shook hands and Roger and Sarah left. A few minutes later we learned that Flores had decided to quit work for the day, so Manny and I left, too. At five o'clock we were back in Baguio and I checked my blood pressure to see how effective Mercado's massage had been. It was up five points, from 160 over 90 to 165 over 90. I wondered how many more "cures" I could stand.

18

On Sunday morning we arrived at David Oligani's at nine-thirty. By ten the church was filled and the service began.

First, Clorita went into a trance. She was to act as the medium, receiving messages from heaven during the service. Sitting near the altar, with her eyes shut, Clorita opened a Bible on the table in front of her, supposedly at the direction of her spirit guide. Then, eyes still shut, she passed the Bible to Juanita, standing beside her. Juanita read the selected passage to the congregation. She then closed the Bible and handed it back to Clorita. She reopened it and returned it to Juanita, who read from it again. This sequence was repeated a third and final time. There was no obvious interrelationship between the three readings. They were purely random selections.

Next, David spoke to his parishioners. Out of deference to Manny and me he spoke in English. The gist of his sermon was that although it was important to heal the body, it was even more important to heal the spirit. David spoke for about ten minutes; then, to my surprise, he asked me to say a few words. I thanked David, his family and the Filipino people in general for the courtesy they had extended to me during my visit to their country. I don't suppose many members of the congregation understood English, but they all smiled and nodded anyway.

Manny gave a brief talk along the same lines I'd chosen, and then Clorita stood up, eyes shut, still in a trance, and walked over to a pennant labeled ESPIRITISTA CHURCH which stood in a corner of the room, near the altar. She took the pennant in her hands and twisted it as if she were wringing out a wet towel. Juanita held a bucket beneath the pennant to catch what Clorita was supposedly wringing out. Whatever it was, was invisible.

After she had wrung out the pennant, Juanita waved excitely to Manny, beckoning him to come to the front of the church. "Instructions for Charlotte are coming through," Juanita said. Then Clorita began to speak, but what she said sounded like gibberish to me; she was allegedly speaking in tongues. After the service, when Clorita was out of her trance, Manny asked her to write out the message. Fortunately, she was able to remember it all. This was the message:

June 10, 1973

DIRECTIONS:

FOR CHARLOT

For her sickness had warm on her eyes and her body, full of warmest of all parts of her body She need a *shot 3 time a week 3 times for flouido. Monday Wednesday Friday*

She don't need to go out every early in the morning cause its too cold. Cause she need to be protected the kind of sickness *pholnoria.* She don't need to take a bath with cool water. She need warm water to take a bath. And then she is not required to be expose outside after her bath.

DIRECTIONS: FOR INJECTIONS:*

1st INJECTIONS—Viens

2nd INJECTIONS—heart

3rd INJECTIONS—BRAIN

(BIYENTE) Proof

1st injections —the color is violet

---

*These are spiritual injections, which Manny gave by pushing his finger against the designated area and praying.

2nd   "   —pink
3rd   "   —yellow
One big needle given for shots 3 inches long fluido
given on his hands.

After Manny had received this message from the other
world, Clorita came out of her trance. It was healing time
now and she had to take up her duties as David's assistant.

David performed three or four of the usual abdominal
"operations" on patients with stomach pains and pelvic
cramps, but he also treated a number of patients with
diseases of unnatural cause. "Unnatural cause" meant that
the disease or pain had been caused by a devil who had
gotten inside the patient's body. In effect, he was performing an exorcism.

One such patient was an elderly woman with huge floppy
breasts. She stripped to the waist in a corner of the church
and lifted her breasts up so that David and I could look
beneath them: the skin under the folds of the breasts was
cracked and there were superficial weeping sores over a
large area. While we examined her the woman told her story
to David in Tagalog. David then sent the woman over to
Clorita, who helped her onto the operating table.

"For six months this patient has been treated by regular
M.D.s," David said, "but she is no better—do you know
why?"

"I can't be certain," I answered. "The woman appears to
have what we call intertrigo, a skin infection which occurs
in areas that are continually moist. Usually, medicated
powders that dry the skin and stop infection will cure the
ailment, but it can take a long time. Either the doctor hasn't
given her the proper medicine or the patient hasn't followed
instructions; I can't tell which."

"Neither," said David, looking very serious. "This
woman is not better because she has an unnatural disease.
She needs a different treatment. Watch."

David walked over to the table where the woman lay. He

lifted her left foot and began squeezing and bending her great toe. As he did, the woman let out a blood-curdling scream and began to writhe around on the table. The more she screamed and twisted, the tighter David held her toe. "Ha, you devil," he shouted, apparently at whatever spirit was emanating from the woman, "scream away. Begone from this woman!" After two or three minutes, when the woman's screams subsided, David put the foot down and walked over to me.

"She won't remember any of this," David said, "but her devil has left her and soon she will be better."

Another of David's patients was a Japanese man, about fifty, who told David in English that he had stomach ulcers. They had been treated by M.D.s in the usual fashion without any relief of pain. David asked him to lie on the table and pull his pants down and shirt up. Then David put his hand on the abdomen as if preparing to do one of his usual "operations."

Suddenly he stopped and waved to me to join him. "Doctor," he said, "feel here; this man has an abnormal pulse. This stomach trouble is not natural—it is unnatural."

I put my hand on the center of the patient's abdomen and pressed down. "You feel it?" David asked.

"Yes, I do," I said. I was feeling the aorta, the big artery that runs from the heart down through the chest and abdomen. The aorta lies in front of the spine, and in thin people—and this Japanese man was very thin—it is often palpable. I checked the pulse in the man's wrist; the rate was, as it should be, the same as the aortic pulse.

"Come here, Doctor," David said, moving from the abdomen to the patient's feet. He grasped the toe and squeezed it; the Japanese said nothing. "This is a different sort of devil," David said. "This devil will not scream, but you will feel a wind rushing out from between the toes. That will be the devil leaving." After ten or fifteen seconds David said, "Now, put your hand next to mine." I did.

"Do you feel the wind? It is very cold."

204

Perhaps I should have said, "No, I feel nothing," which would have been the truth, but I didn't have the courage. Instead I said, "Yes, I feel the wind; it is very cold."

David smiled and turned to his patient. "How do you feel now, sir? Is your pain gone?" The Japanese man pushed on his stomach, gingerly at first and then with greater pressure. Finally he said, with a happy smile, "Yes. My pain is gone. I am much better."

David put the foot down. "Your devil has departed," he said. "You are cured of your ulcer."

The patient was, understandably, very pleased.

A little later David led me over to look at an elderly man whose fourth and fifth fingers were flexed into a semi-fist; he couldn't straighten either one. "This is unnatural arthritis," David said. "I am very successful with unnatural arthritis, but some cases take time. I have treated this patient for three months and he is much better. Watch what I do." He lifted the man's hands and bent his fingers as far as he could. The man winced.

Since the joints of the man's fingers weren't swollen, I thought this was indeed a rather unnatural case of arthritis. I asked the man to turn his hand over and I examined it as David watched. Beneath the skin of the palm I could easily feel thick bands of gristly tissue. These bands were what prevented the man from straightening his fingers.

"Do you not agree he has unnatural arthritis?" David asked me.

Since I knew I had discovered something he had missed, this was a tricky question to answer. "I would say he has a condition we call Dupuytren's contracture," I said. "There are thick bands beneath the palm which keep the fingers from straightening. In the United States I would operate on this patient, cut the bands, and he would be better. But we don't really know what causes the bands to develop; perhaps it has an unnatural cause and therefore your treatment works as well."

"Yes," said David, "probably so." But he seemed a bit depressed.

After an "appendectomy," which he performed with great aplomb, David's spirits seemed fully restored, and since he was near the end of this treatment session, I decided to risk one more bit of my anatomy.

"David," I said as he and Manny and I stood together in a corner, "I have a bad tooth. I planned to have it pulled when I went back to the United States but I dread the pain. Will you pull it for me now?" I asked the question quietly so that only David and Manny could hear me. I didn't want to embarrass David in front of any of his parishioners.

"I am sorry," David replied. "The healer that pulls the teeth is not here today."

David said this to Manny and me without any trace of embarrassment, even though two days earlier he had told us explicitly that he could pull teeth and even though, a year earlier, he knew that Manny had watched him, apparently, pull teeth. It did not seem to David that this apparent contradiction should disturb either of us. In fact, the contradiction didn't upset me at all and it bothered Manny now much less than it might have a week earlier. We were beginning to understand how these healers reasoned: believers believed and nonbelievers didn't believe, and in most cases there was nothing that would convert one to other.

The service ended about one o'clock. While we waited to have dinner I chatted with David, and Clorita spoke briefly with Manny. Later, as we drove back to Baguio, Manny told me what she had said. "Clorita was worried about you. She wanted to know what you thought about the operations. I told her you were still trying to evaluate things. After that she tried to hit me for some more money—they need new pews in the chapel, all that sort of stuff. I told her I'd think about it. I can tell she's afraid she may have lost a good source of revenue and she'd like to get one last payoff before we leave. She doesn't know it, but I'm not going back there at all."

"Wait till tomorrow before you make up your mind," I said. "We'll go and see Placido Palitayan and then head up to Manila. We've got to go by David's, anyway, and maybe you'll have a change of heart by then."

"Not a chance," Manny said, "not a chance."

I let it drop.

19

When we got back to Baguio, Manny called Donald Winslow and made an appointment for us to observe Placido at nine o'clock the next morning. "He has five patients coming in for operations," Donald said, "so you'll get to see some representative cases."

The next morning we checked out of the Pines Hotel and drove to Placido's home. We had difficulty finding it and arrived about ten minutes late. "I'm sorry," Placido said as he greeted us, "but since you were late, all my patients have been here and departed." From the appearance of Placido's home—in a slum area, curtains rather than doors between the very tiny rooms, furniture that would have been turned down by Goodwill Industries, a pump in the yard rather than running water—I guessed that in all probability there had been no patients that morning, nor could he have had many on other mornings. Placido, obviously, had a very limited practice.

"As long as you are here," he said, "I will give you each a complete physical examination if you like."

"Fine," Manny and I agreed.

Placido led us into a bedroom, and while I sat on a chair to watch, Manny stripped to the waist and stretched out on his back on the bed. Placido pushed on Manny's abdomen and chest for about a minute, then had him turn over while he pushed on his back Placido said, "You are in good health but slightly run down. I shall give a spiritual transfusion." With that he put his extended index finger on Manny's arm at the elbow crease and pushed silently, with his eyes closed, for about thirty seconds.

"There," he said, withdrawing his hand. "That will make you much better."

"Thank you," Manny said and got up.

Then Placido examined me, following the same routine and reaching the same diagnosis of "good health but slightly run down." I too received a spiritual transfusion. There was no sensation associated with the transfusion other than the feeling of pressure at the elbow where he was pushing on my arm. I thanked Placido, and as I dressed, said to him, "Placido, I noticed a picture of you in the other room—you seemed to be pulling a tooth—do you do that often?"

"Oh, yes," he said with a smile, "I pull many teeth for my patients."

"I'd like to ask you a favor for me then," I said. "I have a bad tooth. It gives me a great deal of trouble and I plan to have it extracted when I return to the United States. Would you please pull it for me now?"

Placido hesitated momentarily, then said, "Yes, I will pull the tooth for you. Sit here a moment, I will be right back," and with that he left the room.

When he was gone I said to Manny, "Maybe this is it. I don't really believe he can do it but it should be interesting. This tooth has been giving me hell off and on, but it's probably just a cavity and I expect it could be saved. However, if I'm going to lose it, I guess I may as well sacrifice it in the interest of research. I just hope that when Placido comes back he isn't carrying a hammer and chisel or a big pair of pliers. I like painless dentistry."

A minute later Placido returned. To my great relief, he was empty-handed.

"I'll show you the tooth," I said and pointed to the third tooth from the rear in my upper left jaw. I wasn't going to rely on Placido to diagnose the bad tooth; if he was going to yank one, I wanted to lose the right one.

"I see," he said. "Now sit on the edge of the bed."

I did and Placido, facing me, pushed against my cheek, over the tooth, with the index finger of his right hand. Then he put his left index finger into my mouth and pushed that against the tooth, so that he had the tooth squeezed between his index fingers. I could feel him pushing back and forth but the tooth remained solidly fixed in my mandible.

After pushing for about a minute Placido withdrew his hands.

"I am sorry," he said, "I used up too much of my strength giving you spiritual transfusions. I cannot remove your tooth."

"That's all right," I said. "I understand. Perhaps if I return another time you can help me."

"Certainly," Placido said, "some other time."

Manny and I thanked Placido, gave him a $40 donation for the chapel he was planning, and departed.

I'd guess that Placido and his family ate better that day than was their usual custom.

As, for the last time, I drove down the mountain from Baguio I said to Manny. "I was sorry to put Placido on the spot like that. I didn't want to embarrass him. He's a nice little guy. [Placido is about five feet tall.] But I thought I ought to give him a chance to do his stuff if he could.

"To tell you the truth, Bill," Manny said, "I don't feel sorry for him at all. I don't feel sorry for any of them. They're not real healers and they're using a lot of innocent sick people. I have no sympathy for them."

"They're not really bad, Manny," I said. "They don't hurt people, except, in a sort of negative way—by not doing them any good. All this fooling around with cotton and chicken guts isn't going to kill anyone. And those tiny scratches they make and the cupping routines they go through won't bother anyone either. Physically, at least, they're harmless. Emotionally—well, that's something else again."

"Emotionally," Manny said. "Yeah, I guess that's the problem. That's where they hit me and that's why I'm so

210

bitter. I believed in them—bought the whole thing—and now I feel as if they were playing games with me. It hurts.

"You know," he continued, "when I was here with Charlotte last year, I was really strung out. I'm sure, having kids of your own, you can imagine how horrifying it is to have a doctor tell you that your four-year-old daughter has a malignant brain tumor and that it's incurable. My whole world collapsed.

"Then I came over here, and suddenly everything was going to be all right again. Brother David and Brother Joe Mercado were going to make Charlotte well. Originally, you know, Charlotte and I were to spend only two weeks in David's home—not that two weeks in that heat with all those flies didn't seem like a long time to me—but at the end of two weeks Clorita had a vision, she said, saying we would have to stay two more weeks. And when those two weeks were up she had another vision saying we'd have to stay three more weeks. Clorita kept having visions till she had kept us there for eight long weeks.

"They made those eight weeks hell for me. Sometimes, in the evening, Clorita would go into a trance. When she came out of it she'd say to me, 'Brother Manny, you don't yet have enough faith. If you don't get enough faith, your daughter will die.' I'd actually cry myself to sleep, I'd be in such despair. Then the next night Clorita would say, 'you have a little more faith now; maybe we can cure Charlotte,' and I'd be so elated I'd run off to the chapel and offer prayers of thanksgiving.

"It was tough on Charlotte. One or the other of them would wake her and me at midnight, and again at two and at five in the morning. 'Those are the best times to pray,' they'd say. Charlotte would cry because she was so sleepy and hated to get up, but I didn't dare let her stay in bed. I wanted her cured, damn it, and I had to see that she did what was best for her.

"You know what they made me do sometimes?—hold Charlotte while Clorita or Juanita or one of the others pulled out strands of her hair. 'To make charms with, to cure her,'

211

they said. The poor kid would kick and scream and I'd hold on, almost crying myself but afraid not to do everything they said. They'd made a believer of me, all right.

"And of course all the time I was there they bled me for everything they could get. 'Brother Manny,' Clorita would say, 'see how poor our school is. We wish we could get some swings for the playground'; 'Brother Manny, see how the chapel pews are rotting. Could you help us?'; 'Brother Manny, we wish we had water in our home. It would be so nice to have more comfort to offer our patients when Brother David is doing his spiritual work.' And every time she asked, I gave in. In that two months I gave David and his family over three thousand dollars in cash, plus that jeep, and I paid for the food we all ate as well.

"That bothers me nowhere near as much as the pain I caused Charlotte of course, but still, I hate to feel like a sucker. I'm supposed to be a sharp businessman, not a gullible idiot. I was really blind.

"And you know what else bothers me—really bothers me? All the talking I've been doing. At churches, at business meetings, to my friends. Telling them all about the wonders of the Philippines. I don't even want to know how many trips to the Philippines I've been responsible for. It's damage I can't undo."

"Listen, Manny," I said, "I know how you must feel, but for heaven's sake, don't blame yourself. You're not the first desperate person to go looking for a far-out cure when there wasn't anything else to try. You won't be the last either. In fact, you're one of the few people—the only one I know—who has dared to go back and take another look at the cure he grasped at. Most people won't do it because they're afraid they'll find they've been misled; they don't want that knowledge."

"Maybe so," Manny said, "but it will be a long time before I can forgive either myself or the 'healers' who misled me. I feel as if I've been betrayed."

As we approached Toboya, Manny didn't suggest stopping at David's and I decided to let it go; Manny had

212

obviously had about all he could take. We talked some more about Charlotte. I reassured Manny that even though the psychic surgeons weren't miracle workers, that didn't mean Charlotte wasn't going to be well. After all, Dr. Lawrence hadn't biopsied the tumor; he couldn't be absolutely certain it was the sort that would inevitably prove fatal. I also told him that the X-ray treatment might actually have cured Charlotte; sometimes that happens. And there was always the possiblity that the tumor might regress spontaneously. By the time we reached Manila, Manny's spirits were very much improved.*

I could hardly wait to get to the Intercontinental Hotel, but Manny wanted to buy some rattan furniture at a place our journalistic friend had mentioned, so we went first to the store. I hate to shop and had no idea what anything made in the Philippines would cost in the States, but as long as I had to wait for Manny, anyway, I bought some book ends, hand-carved out of monkey wood, and had them sent home. I like things made out of wood.

When we finished our shopping and got back to our car, it was almost five and traffic was heavy. It occurred to me that perhaps we ought to ask someone the most direct route to the hotel, but Manny demurred. "No need for that," he said. "You can almost see the Intercontinental from here. It's just down the boulevard about ten blocks."

Idiotically, I believed him, and of course we proceeded to get lost immediately. Half an hour later we found ourselves at the Manila airport; somehow that airport seemed to act like a magnet on Manny. An hour later we finally found our way to our nice air-conditioned hotel.

By now, after a week together, Manny and I were getting

*In May of 1974, two years after her brain tumor had been diagnosed and twenty-two months after radiation treatment had been completed, Charlotte Hofman developed symptoms that suggested the tumor had begun, once again, to grow. Diagnostic tests, including an X-ray examination of the blood vessels in her brain proved that this was, sadly, what had happened.

By August, Charlotte was unable to walk. Both of her legs were paralyzed—as a result of increased brain pressure. She received treatment with two new, experimental anti-cancer drugs, but in September 1974, Charlotte died of her brain tumor.

213

to be a bit like "The Odd Couple." "I've never seen anyone who can leave a bathroom as steamed up as you do," he said to me after I showered the night before. "And I've never seen anyone who ties up a bathroom as long as you do every morning," I snapped back. Hardly a vicious exchange, but symptomatic of what might be coming if we stayed together too much longer. We were both damn sick of the Philippines, and Manny in particular was very unhappy with what we had learned. We were still good friends but we were both anxious to get home.

As soon as we'd cleaned up, Manny called the airport. He couldn't get a flight back to the United States but he could get one to Hong Kong in the morning, with a connection out the following day. He rather wanted to visit Hong Kong, anyway, so he made the reservation. I would have liked to go along with him but I hadn't finished my research, so I resigned myself to another few days in the Philippines.

The next morning, after Manny had left, I returned our rented car and then took a cab to the Philippine General Hospital, the city hospital of Manila.

Philippine General is like most of the city hospitals in the United States, and it reminded me of Bellevue in New York. There were more patients than the buildings could comfortably accommodate—there were beds in all the corridors—and it was clear that funds for operating the hospital were inadequate; the whole place was very dirty and paint was flaking off the walls. Patients, in the striped bathrobes that all city hospitals seem to acquire, wandered along the corridors and out in the courtyards onto which many of the corridors opened. I presume the purpose of the open corridors is to allow more air to get into the hospital. It was very hot in the hospital, and without the open corridors the heat would have been unbearable.

Philippine General is a one-story hospital which stretches over two city blocks. I rambled around until I found the psychiatric ward, where I managed to find a resident

Filipino doctor who spoke English. I told him who I was and what I was doing in the Philippines and asked him what he knew of the psychic surgeons. "Nothing, really," he said. "I've heard of them but I've never met a patient who has gone to one. My understanding is that they work mostly on tourists, though I have to admit I'm not sure about the people who live in remote barrios. Maybe some of them go to faith healers."

"Do you know anyone here who does know something about them?" I asked.

"I'm afraid not," he answered, "but ask around—maybe you'll find someone with an interest in that sort of thing."

I asked around. Over the next three hours I talked to a dozen different doctors. Each was willing to talk to me but no one had any information; most of them had never even heard of the psychic surgeons. As far as they were concerned, such stuff belonged in the field of quackery or entertainment, not in the field of medicine. They reacted about the way I'd expect a professor of medicine at Cornell to act if I were to ask him to tell me about the witch doctors practicing in Manhattan; he wouldn't have any idea what they were doing. Finally a young obstetrician gave me a lead. "There's a psychologist named Louis Martinez here in Manila. I know he does some clinical hypnosis and it seems to me that he has had dealings of some sort with faith healers. You might try him."

He was able to get Martinez's number for me. I went back to the hotel, called Dr. Martinez, and to my great delight, he agreed to have dinner with me that evening. Since there wasn't much else I could do that afternoon, I took a swim, read for a while, then took a nap. The heat and humidity in the Philippines (I know I promised not to mention the heat again) kept me near exhaustion most of the time I was there. Even now, in the midst of a Minnesota winter, I can warm up just thinking how hot it must be in Manila.

20

At five o'clock Dr. Martinez phoned my room and I went down to the lobby to meet him. He is a stocky man in his mid-fifties, a practicing clinical psychologist. M.D.'s in Manila refer patients to him for psychoanalysis, and obstetricians often send him pregnant women who need training in preparation for natural childbirth. "I practice what I used to call hypnosis," he said, "but I don't call it that any more. I simply make a patient more sensitive to suggestion—that's really what hypnosis is. Have you read *The World of Kreskin?* He says the same thing." (At the time I hadn't read Kreskin's book, but subsequently I did. On the matter of hypnosis, Martinez and he are in agreement.)

We found a table in a quiet corner of the lobby, and after we had ordered drinks and I had explained my mission, Dr. Martinez told me what he knew about the psychic surgeons.

"I know most of them personally," he said. "There are only about twenty altogether; three or four here in Manila and another fifteen or so in Baguio and the lowlands. Some of them move around, so it's hard to be certain where they are at any one time. Agpaoa, for example, used to work mostly in Baguio, but now he operates out of a hotel here in Manila. He's afraid to go back to Baguio for fear they'll nail him for taxes."

"Do you have any idea how much he earns?" I asked.

"I sure do," Martinez said. "He sees at least three hundred patients a month, almost all foreigners, and he charges each one a minimum of two hundred dollars. That's at least sixty thousand dollars a month, and I'm being conservative. A lot of his grateful patients give him a thousand or more. Almost all of it is in cash. He's probably one of the wealthiest men in the Philippines.

"But that's beside the point for the moment. You want to know what the psychic surgeons are all about and I'll tell you as much as I can. I've been studing them off and on for twenty years.

"To understand what they are doing you have to realize that large segments of the Philippine population are still very primitive. We're not many generations removed from the jungle, and even those of us who live here in the city realize that practices such as headhunting and witchcraft are part of our heritage. I'm dressed like a civilized man, and I am civilized, but I still fell as if I could be happy out climbing trees. Our culture hasn't been civilized as long as yours. Which may be a blessing." I agreed.

"The psychic surgeons claim they get their powers from Christ—that they're performing in His name—but that's just so much nonsense. We had miraculous healers and witch doctors in the Philippines long before anyone dreamt up the Espiritista Church. The church business adds a certain respectability to all that the healers do. They need that respectability when they're treating people from other countries. The poor people in the barrios, the primitive Filipinos, are willing to accept a healer on his own merit; they ask no questions. But 'civilized' people—people from France, England, Canada and the United States—require an explanation. They ask the healer where his extraordinary powers come from, and the healer has learned to answer, 'God'; he knows this will satisfy the foreigners.

"It all started with Terte, about thirty years ago. He was a healer just like many other healers out in the country. He said prayers, went through a lot of rituals, even used a little voodoo. He was, if you'll excuse the phrase, a witch doctor.

"Terte's patients did about as well as anyone else's. As

you know, about seventy-five percent of all ailments are, at least in part, mental, and many of the other twenty-five percent are self-limited [healed by the body itself]. With the neurotic disorders, if you can persuade the patient he's going to get better, he often will get better. With the other diseases, things like pneumonia or infected cuts, if you don't do any harm—and if you get the patient to eat and sleep sensibly—nature will cure him. I'm sure I'm not telling you anything you don't already know. Wasn't it Hippocrates who said, 'First, do no harm'? He was a wise man.

"When Terte's patients had something that wasn't mental or self-limited—cancer, for example—he used two dodges. Sometimes he'd spot these cases early and suggest that they go to a hospital, if there was one in the neighborhood. When the patient was too far gone for anything to help, Terte would tell the family, 'It's the will of God.' I bet you use that line a lot yourself?" I admitted that I do.

"That's nothing to be ashamed of," Martinez continued; "after all, we all die sometime. Apparently it is the will of God—if you believe in Him—that we humans remain mortal. Anyway, 'God's will' is an explanation almost anyone will accept. The healers use it whenever necessary.

"All the healers had their little gimmicks—exotic costumes, unusual rituals, sometimes little charms with special powers—and so did Terte. Thirty years ago, however, Terte came up with a new idea: the operation. He was and still is, though he has slowed down a lot now that he's older, clever with his hands—a pretty good magician. It occurred to him that he might increase his cure rate in those diseases that were mostly psychogenic by performing operations on his patients. Surgery—cutting into people and taking out diseased parts—has always impressed the layman. It still does. You're a surgeon, so I'm sure you know. I'll bet people often ask you, 'How can you bring yourself to cut into the human body?' Operating is your profession and you're used to it, but for the layman the blood and guts of

218

surgery is something he views with both apprehension and awe."

"It wasn't difficult for Terte to fake an operation. He started out using chicken guts and blood, and at times he still uses them. He always has an assistant and between them it isn't difficult to palm this stuff. Patients are shocked by the sight of blood and they don't look very closely at what an operator is doing.

"Later, because it was less messy, Terte started using cotton and a red dye that he made from betel nuts. Since you've seen a number of the healers now, you've probably noticed they always use wads of cotton, always keep the belly moist, and always have an assistant who can slip them things. If you looked, chances are you'd find betel nuts in their homes."

I told Martinez about David Oligani hiding betel nuts in his jeep, and about the betel nuts in Josephine's laundry room.

"Then you know what I'm talking about," he said. "Some of the healers use animal blood, some betel nuts, some a liquid that magicians use which, when mixed with bicarbonate of soda hidden in the cotton, turns red. You see, all of the healers go through much the same routines, though a few have specialities—like Josephine and the cotton she sticks in the cheek and pulls out of the nose or ear.

"Nothing much happened for a few years after Terte worked out his operative routines; other healers had their gimmicks and they left him his. He treated natives mostly, and though he made a decent living like the rest of the healers, he wasn't getting rich.

"Then, about twenty years ago, a couple of foreigners, vacationing Americans, saw him work. They were amazed by what he was doing—only rarely does anyone see through this sleight of hand—and since they had some minor complaints, they persuaded Terte to operate on them. As I've heard the story, one patient had a backache, the other had vague stomach pains, and Terte 'cured' them both. They told friends and soon there was a trickle of foreign patients coming to Terte; these foreigners paid him more money than he'd ever seen in his life.

"It was about this time that Tony Agpaoa was beginning his career as a healer. He watched Terte work—'studied' under him, so to speak—and being a clever young fellow, he caught on quickly to what Terte was doing. Soon he was even better at this operating business than Terte was and he went off on his own, setting up a practice in Baguio.

"But Tony was sharper than Terte in a lot of ways, not just as a magician. Tony had a nose for money. He could see that this routine had great potential if he could lure a stream of foreigners over here, and he went at it very smoothly. His wife set up a travel agency of her own and then worked out a deal with travel agencies in many cities, mostly on the West Coast of the United States. Someone—often it's a grateful patient, a true believer—rounds up fifteen or twenty people in the United States, people who are sick and who are dissatisfied with the treatment they're getting from their doctor—you know people of that sort aren't hard to find— and they fly them over here so that Tony can work on them. I don't know how her agency and the others split the commissions, but I'm sure there's plenty of money for all. And Tony, of course, gets at least a two-hundred-dollar donation for his chapel from every patient he treats. If Tony put one hundredth of his take into that chapel, it would look like the Taj Mahal by now. He doesn't, of course—his chapel isn't worth more than ten thousand. But you should see his home—it's supposed to be worth half a million dollars and I believe it. And the talk around Manila is that he just bought a mountain near Baguio where he's going to build a 'healing' resort; he paid seven million dollars just for the land. Tony, as I said before, is a very wealthy man.

"You've probably heard that the reason there are so many psychic surgeons in the Philippines, and so few anywhere else in the world, is because Christ wanted a sign of the

Second Coming to appear among the poor—and the people in the Philippine lowlands are certainly poor. That's more nonsense, of course. The reason we've got twenty healers in a concentrated area is because the healers aren't dopes. A few years ago, when they saw how well Tony was doing, other healers got into the psychic surgery act. Some of them are very clever—for example, Mercado and Flores in Asignan, and Juan Blanche here in Manila—but until recently they hadn't made much money. They didn't have the business savvy that Tony has. By the way, while I'm thinking of it—have you seen Flores do his eye operation?

"Yes," I said.

"Clever, isn't he? He worked out that routine himself and for some time he was the only one using it. Now Tony does it once in a while. He won't let anyone get ahead of him."

I mentioned that I had never seen Juan Blanche.

"That's too bad," Dr. Martinez said. "But since you've seen David Oligani, you don't really need to see Blanche. Blanche and Oligani both feature that 'incision at a distance' bit; I've seen Blanche use it often. A couple of times he has really botched it—the incision appears before he makes that cutting gesture. The trick is to make that scratch very lightly so that it won't become obvious till you start kneading the skin. But what were we talking about before I interrupted myself?"

"You were telling me about the other healers and money."

"Oh, yes, now I remember. Well, as I was saying, all these healers have gotten pretty clever, and they're all anxious to start making some real money. So, recently they've gotten a sharp man, Joaquin Cunanan, to take over as head of the Espiritista Church. Oh, so you've met him? Well, he's getting the healers organized, he's getting them publicity—he just had a television crew over from France, shooting a special on Flores—and he has gotten into the tour business himself. The travel bureau which he operates out of Portland, Oregon. They set up a package deal that

221

includes four days in Manila, eight days in Baguio, and treatment from ten different healers. The package, last I heard, cost one thousand and ten dollars. Tony's package is nine hundred and fifty dollars, but that's without his fee, so the Cunanan trip is a bargain. In fact, I know Cunanan pretty well—I'd be happy to recommend you to him. If you want to round up fifteen patients when you get back to the States, you can get a free trip back here out of it. That's the bonus you get for being a tour director."

"Thanks," I laughed, "but at the moment I'm interested only in getting out of the Philippines, not in coming back. No offense meant, but I just can't get used to the heat."

"I understand perfectly," Dr. Martinez said. "I'm sure I'd be miserable in Minnesota."

"How does the Philippine Medical Association and your government react to all this? I'd think these shenanigans might upset them."

"You've talked to the doctors, so you know how they react—they don't. If they know anything about the psychic surgeons, they certainly won't admit to it. In all probability they're telling the truth; legitimate M.D.s just don't pay any attention to psychic surgeons. How much time do you M.D.s devote to the doings of 'witch doctors' in the States? Not much, I'll bet. You're too busy practicing medicine to concern yourself with the quack down the street.

"As to the government, their policy so far has been strickly hands off. And unless someone really squawks, they'll stick to that policy. These psychic surgeons are one of the biggest—possibly the biggest—tourist attraction in the country. An executive at Philippines Air Lines told me recently that patients coming to visit the psychic surgeons account for a lot of their passenger loads. If anyone clamped down on the psychic suregons, Philippine Air Lines would be in serious trouble."

"I have another question," I said, "one that really puzzles me. Some of these psychic surgeons—I'm thinking particularly of David Oligani—seem like sincere, dedicated, religious people. How can they rationalize their behavior? Don't they feel guilty, duping all these sick people?"

"Not ordinarily," Dr. Martinez said. "First, they know they aren't doing anyone any physical harm. Since they aren't actually cutting into the body, no one is ever going to die of infection or complications after one of their operations.

"Second, they think they are curing some patients, and actually, they are. People with neurotic ailments are going to get better when they're convinced they've been operated on by a man who is in direct communication with God. Their symptoms will disappear.

"Finally the ones that come here are often patients who have been rejected by practitioners of orthodox medicine. Sometimes these are patients with terminal cancer, for which medical science has nothing more to offer; sometimes they're patients who have been labeled 'crocks' by doctors—the chronic complainers, the hypochondriacs. The psychic surgeons operate on these people, give them attention, and they feel better. No, I don't think many of the psychic surgeons feel guilty, and sometimes I wonder if they should.

"There are exceptions. Agpaoa, for example. I believe that man exploits some of his patients. But that's just my opinion; most of his patients love him. In fact, the only advertising any of these psychic surgeons need is word-of-mouth advertising. Patients who leave here thinking they are cured run right home and tell all their friends about the marvelous experience they've had. They speak at Kiwanis and church meetings and they show films of their operations; I'd bet that there are in this world a hundred times as many films of Tony Agpaoa's 'operations' as there are of any other surgeon's. The whole thing quickly snowballs. That's why Tony alone can attract three hundred patients every month from Germany, Switzerland, Canada, the

223

United States—damn near everywhere. If he wanted, he could probably have more.

"David Oligani is an exception in the opposite direction. David, I think, would like to get away from psychic surgery. He's a truly religious man and he'd like to heal people by helping them to have faith in the Lord, without all this cotton and blood and stuff. So far he hasn't been able to make the break, but eventually I think he will. His conscience won't let him fake operations much longer."

"How about Donald Winslow," I asked, "the American who is working with Placido? I can understand how a Filipino, brought up in a country where healers are part of the tradition, might be able to rationalize what he's doing, but Donald is an American—this is foreign to him."

"Donald is a master not only of deception but of self-deception. I suppose he has told you that he goes into a trance when he operates, that it is not really him but a sacred guide who is doing the work? Many of the psychic surgeons—most, in fact—say this.

"In part, it's true. They convince themselves—call it self-hypnosis if you want, though I don't like the term—that a spirit is guiding their hands as they go through the routines. Then they can feel completely guilt-free when they resort to sleight of hand. When Donald tells you that a spirit guide has worked through him to perform an operation, Donald, at least at times, really believes it. You've heard of proven killers who protest their innocence so long and so vehemently that eventually they convince themselves that they really are innocent? Well, that's the way Donald is. He's a deceiver, but he'd neither admit nor believe it."

I wanted to find out if he knew more about tissues than I had learned from Dr. Otillo, so I asked, "What about tissue? It would seem to me that sometime, over the years, patients would have brought the tissue removed from them to a pathologist for examination?"

"That's been done many times. Not as many as you might think, considering the volume of 'surgery' done here.

224

For example, in twenty years of operating, as far as I know no one has ever managed to get any of the tissue 'removed' by Agpaoa to a lab; he manages to lose it all. But once in a while, with the other healers, it happens.

"It's not human tissue, of course. Sometimes it's recognized as animal tissue, sometimes just as some sort of foreign material—cotton, frequently."

"Doesn't that destroy the faith of the patient?" I asked.

"Momentarily, perhaps, but not for long. When he gets caught, the healer explains to the patient that the tissue came from the 'astral body,' a sort of double that hovers around the real patient's body and that only psychics can see. That gets them off the hook."

I'd heard that explanation before, from Dr. Edgar Mitchell when we had talked, briefly, of the psychic surgeons. It's a perfect cop-out, of course; how can anyone argue with a tissue report on an organ taken from the astral body? No one in this world, certainly, has ever examined such tissue under the microscope. I can recognize an appendix from a human body, but I have no idea what the appendix from an astral body would look like.

"Don't the psychic surgeons ever claim to have taken out real, human organs?"

"Certainly," Martinez said, "almost all the time. It's only when they're caught that they have to resort to the astral-body explanation. They make a point of not being caught very often; that's why they keep a bucket near them in which to throw the organs and they burn them as quickly as possible. When the patient asks for the specimen, the standard answer is, 'It's evil tissue. It must be destroyed.' It's hard to argue with that."

"It sounds as if they have answers for everything."

"They do," said Dr. Martinez, "they do. Over the last thirty years they've learned to explain away every objection anyone might raise. I don't envy you the job of trying to pin them down."

"I'm not really trying to pin them down," I said. "I just

want to find out what they're doing and how it's affecting patients. I haven't yet seen a psychic operation that appeared to do a patient any good. But neither have I had a chance to follow up any of the patients."

"I can help you with that," Martinez said. "I have the names and addresses of many patients from the United States who have been treated here. If you like, I'll make you up a list."

"I'd be delighted to have it," I said. "I can't tell you what a great help you've been, Dr. Martinez, I'm very grateful."

"Glad I can help," he said. "I'm a Filipino and proud of it. This psychic surgery business is getting out of hand; it may be bringing money to our country, but it is also giving us a bad reputation with respectable people from abroad. Something needs to be done. I hope you can do it."

"I'm certainly going to try," I said.

On that note, we went in to dinner.

Over the next few days I called fifteen M.D.s in Manila. Of the fifteen, only three admitted they had even heard of the psychic surgeons, and only one—a psychiatrist I'll call Dr. Xavier—knew much about them. I spent a couple of hours visiting with him, and in all essentials he confirmed what Dr. Martinez had told me.

Dr. Xavier also offered me another insight into the government's attitude toward the psychic surgeons. "The government's tolerance doesn't stem solely from the fact that the psychic surgeons attract tourists—though, admittedly, that's a factor. The chief reason, as I see it, is the poverty of our country. We have seven medical schools and we graduate a thousand doctors every year. Even though it's compulsory for every doctor to serve the government for two years, after that a lot of them leave. They can earn more money in other countries. You certainly know that many go to the United States. The net result is that we have only thirteen thousand doctors to care for forty million people—nowhere near enough.

"We have a socialized-medicine program, which is growing steadily, but at the present time if every eligible Filipino tried to utilize the system, we'd go bankrupt in a few months. Actually, at this stage in our development, the healers out of the barrios serve a very useful purpose; every patient that goes to them for help is one less our government has to worry about. If a patient complains to the Philippine Medical Association about a particular psychic surgeon—and believe me this doesn't happen very often—then the association might clamp down on that healer for a while. But eventually, and usually very fast, he'll be quietly allowed to go back to his practice. Perhaps someday we'll be wealthy enough to at least try and educate all our people so that they choose orthodox medical care; we haven't yet reached that point."

Dr. Xavier was a friend of Dr. Wilfred Marcos, the brother of President Marcos. Dr. Marcos is an obstetrician, a former president of the Philippine Medical Association, and currently heads the Philippine medical program. Dr. Xavier made arrangements for me to attend a meeting of the Medicare Committee and, afterward, to interview Dr. Marcos.

The committee meeting was interesting in that it so closely resembled meetings I had been to in the United States. There were ten committee members, all practicing specialists of various kinds: a surgeon, two internists, a pediatrician, etc. They listened to complaints raised both by the government and by patients and tried to resolve them.

One problem, for exmaple, was that under the Medicare program the government allowed a surgeon 150 pesos ($9) for performing an appendectomy. If, however the appendix was found to be ruptured at the time of surgery, the surgeon was allowed to charge 350 pesos ($21). Since the rule was established the incidence of ruptured appendices, as reported by surgeons, had increased from 15 percent to almost 50

227

percent. "Mr. Chairman," the reporting doctor said, "I hate to say it but I think some doctors are lying about these appendices just to get more money." The committee sadly agreed and decided to change the remuneration for appendices: in the future all appendictomies would be worth 250 pesos ($15) with no bonus for removing a ruptured appendix.

An internist on the committe complained about the fee allowed for treating a toxic thyroid gland. "Mr. Chairman," he said, "we allow two hundred pesos for the surgeon who removes a thyroid gland. Yet the internist who treats the toxic gland with medicines gets only a hundred pesos. I don't think that's fair. Actually, it's much more difficult to treat a thyroid medically than to operate on it." The committe chewed that one over for a while, the medical people lining up on one side against the surgeon representing all those doctors who earned their living with their knives. When the discussion began to get heated, Dr. Marcos intervened and appointed a subcommittee to discuss the problem over the next month and make a recommendation at the next meeting.

A third complaint was raised by a radiologist. "Mr. Chairman," he said, "since we've eliminated coverage for hospitalization for diagnostic studies only, we find many patients admitted with diagnoses of acute disease who then proceed to have diagnostic work-ups. For example, here's the chart of a patient admitted with a diagnosis of possible perforated duodenal ulcer and the next day the doctor orders X-rays of the stomach, the gall bladder and the colon. Here's another with an admission diagnosis of acute gastritis [inflammation of the stomach] and the next day the same batch of X-rays. No doctor would order these X-rays immediately if he really believed the patient had the disease on the admission card." For the next ten minutes the committee tried, without success, to devise a way of preventing doctors from faking admission diagnoses so that the patient wouldn't have to pay hospital costs out of his own pocket.

On the basis of this one meeting I'd have to conclude that government administrators in the Philippines run into the same problems with Philippine doctors as administrators do with a few of the doctors in the United States.

After the meeting, about five o'clock, Dr. Marcos invited me to join him and the radiologist on the committe for a drink. Dr. Marcos' chauffeur drove us a few blocks to the Armed Forces Officers Club, which has a rather bleak restaurant and bar.

Dr. Marco is fifty years old, about five feet five, stocky and very pleasant. He asked me what I thought of the meeting. "About like one of ours," I said.

"Yes," he laughed, "human nature doesn't vary much, does it?"

Dr. Marcos had visited the United States, had taken some obstetrical training here, and was interested in knowing more about coronary-artery surgery. "I had some angina about a year and a half ago," he said. "If I don't push too hard, I have no trouble. For example, I don't play doubles in tennis any more; I play triples instead. One man stays in the back court, two at the net. Not so much running involved."

"Sounds like fun," I said.

"It is," Dr. Marcos agreed, "but I don't want to slow down too much; so maybe someday I'll need a by-pass operation."

I told him what I knew about the by-pass procedure and we talked for another half-hour about medical matters. When I brought up the matter of the psychic surgeons, Dr. Marcos gave me the brush-off. "They're of no consequence," he said. "Simply a holdover from years ago. No intelligent Filipinos go to them." Then he changed the subject. Later in our conversation I mentioned the psychic surgeons again, and this time Dr. Marcos pretended he didn't hear me. I didn't want to aggravate him—his brother is, after all, "The Boss"—so I dropped it. I certainly didn't want to offend anyone who had the power to keep me in the Philippines even one extra day, let alone throw me in jail, and Marcos certainly has that power. The Philippine newspapers, for example, are nothing but pro-Marcos propaganda sheets. All antigovernment journalists are either in jail or in exile. I had no desire to join them.

We finished our drinks and Dr. Marcos was kind enough to drive me to my hotel. I'd never driven in a car with a dictator's brother before and I don't mind admitting I was a bit nervous; I kept a close watch out for snipers all the way back to the Intercontinental. It was with no little relief that I shook hands with and said good-bye to Dr. Marcos.

He's a nice man, but I'd be afraid to pal around with him.

21

The day after my visit with Dr. Marcos, I left the Philipines. The trip home, via Okinawa, Tokyo, Anchorage, Alaska and Chicago was—and I could hardly believe this was possible—more exhausting than the trip to the Philippines had been. As a sort of icing on the cake, our plane was late getting into Chicago, I missed my connecting flight to Minneapolis, and though I got on a plane an hour later, my luggage didn't. Standing in the Minneapolis airport after a twenty-six-hour trip, dirty, unshaven and exhausted, I almost cried; if I hadn't been so happy to be back in the United States, I might have. Joan, who had met me at the airport, drove us to a nearby motel where, after brushing my teeth with her toothbrush, I took a shower and collapsed into bed. My luggage arrived the next morning.

I spent the following month in Litchfield getting my surgical practice in order, and then I began tracking down patients who had gone to the Philippines for treatment by the psychic surgeons. It wan't difficult to find them. The list Dr. Martinez had given me contained twenty names, with phone numbers and addresses. I wrote to those patients who sounded as if they might give me solid information, avoiding only the ones who had been treated for such ill-defined ailments as bursitis and backache. Most of these patients responded and I interviewed them either by phone or personally. Since a number of them lived in and around San Francisco, I flew to California in September of 1973 and spent a week driving around the Bay Area, interviewing patients and looking into other matters related to healers. (California is a hotbed of healing activity. It is difficult to find anyone in California who does not know, or know of, a healer.)

I quickly learned that if I wanted or needed to do so, I could track down hundreds, possibly thousands of patients who had been to the Philippines; most of the patients on Dr. Martinez's list had gone there in groups, with a minimum of fifteen patients in each group. Most of the patients to whom I spoke were willing, even eager, to refer me to others who had been with them. It was as if they wanted to prove to me that spending $2,000 to travel to the Philippines for an operation by a psychic surgeon was a perfectly reasonable thing to do—that lots of people did it and that they, certainly, weren't unique.

In following up some of these leads I began to realize that the list Dr. Martinez had given me was a very selective one; it contained only the names of those patients who had come back from the Philippies happy, or at least satisfied, with the results of their treatment. Patients not on the list were usually disgruntled, often bitter, always disappointed with the results of their pilgrimage. Some were reluctant to talk to me—"I just want to forget the whole thing" was a frequent response; others, the bitter ones, wanted me to "get those crooks. They all ought to be in jail." One man whose eight-year-old daughter had died of a malignant tumor ten days after a "successful" operation by Tony Agpaoa said to me, "If I could afford to go back to the Philippnes, I'd go tomorrow; and I'd kill Tony Agpaoa with my bare hands." This man spoke calmly. He meant what he said.

There isn't any point in dwelling on the patients with multiple sclerosis who were pleased with the results the psychic surgeons achieved; I'll only mention here that as they do to Kathryn Kuhlman and Norbu Chen, multiple-sclerosis patients flock to the psychic surgeons. I checked on three of these patients, all of whom felt they were

232

"improved," and found that neither their doctors nor their friends had noticed any improvement at all. "But I haven't told her so," one doctor said to me, speaking of a twenty-three-year-old girl who had been "operated on" by three psychic surgeons. "She knows there's really very little I can do for her. If it makes her happy to think some nuts in the Philippines have helped her, that's fine with me."

From the fifty-three patients I tracked down, I've selected five to write about. I chose them not because they offer proof that the psychic surgeons actually do anything miraculous—there was no such evidence—but because these cases demonstrate other characteristics which I think are important in understanding why the psychic surgeons attract so many people, many of them very intelligent, to the Philippines. For the usual reasons—so I won't embarrass them and so they won't be bothered by crank mail—I've disguised the identity of these patients.

Case 1—Doris Landan, thirty-seven years old. She is a divorcee with one child, a fifteen-year-old girl. She is a college graduate with a degree in business administration, and she works as a buyer for a large department store.

"Three years ago," she told me, "in July of 1970, I went to my doctor for my annual checkup. My mother died of breast cancer when she was forty-two, so I've made a routine of annual checkups since I was thirty.

"Dr. Sullivan is my family doctor. As usual he did a Pap smear [scraped some cells from the cervix (the neck of the uterus); the Papanicolaou test for cancer] and a week later he called and told me that the test was highly suggestive of cancer. I had to go to the hospital for a conization. [This is a surgical procedure in which a cone-shaped piece of tissue is cut from the cervix of the uterus. The Pap smear is a screening test; with a conization the diagnosis of cancer can usually be established or ruled out, with certianty.] Three days after the conization he told me I had cancer—very early, but definite.

233

"Because it was in an early stage he told me I could be treated with radiation or an operation, that he thought the chances of a cure were excellent either way. I chose radiation and a few days later a radiologist inserted radium into my vagina next to the cancer. After forty-eight hours he took out the radium and over the next three weeks I had fifteen treatments with X-rays.

"For about three months everything was fine. Then I began to notice that I was going to the bathroom more frequently than I had before my treatment. I was getting up two or three times a night and had to go the ladies' room at least every two hours during the day. My urine burned a lot and I had difficulty passing it. I never passed much at any one time. I went back to my doctor and he catheterized me [passed a rubber tube into the bladder] and found out that my bladder was all shrunken down. He sent me back to the radiologist who had given me the radium and X-ray treatments and he said, 'Unfortunately, that's one of the rare side effects of X-ray treatment.' No one had ever warned me of this before.

"My life for the next year was a series of nightmares. I was referred to a urologist, who tried to make my bladder stretch but couldn't. Then for a while I had to wear a catheter all the time. That was really a mess. I hated it. Finally, and this was about a year after my treatment, my urine stopped flowing almost completely. The urologist got some special X-rays of my ureters [the tubes that carry urine from the kidneys to the bladder] and then told me that they were all caught up in scar tissue, another side effect of the radiation. He told me that I'd need an operation right away to relieve the obstruction. By this time I was sick—I couldn't even think straight—because all the poisons that my kidneys couldn't eliminate were piling up in my bloodstream.

"What could I do? I let them operate, but the scar tissue was too thick, so they couldn't remove it. When I woke up after the operation I had two tubes sticking out of my back, one in each kidney. I was in the hospital for a month recovering from the operation, getting rid of all the wastes that had accumulated in my blood, and learning how to manage these tubes. When I went home I felt terribly depressed.

"The doctors told me that I could never use my own bladder again. They suggested that as soon as I was strong enough I go back into the hospital and they'd make me an artificial bladder out of a piece of intestine. They'd run the unscarred pieces of ureter into this and I'd live the rest of my life with a bag stuck on my abdomen to collect my urine. Is it any wonder I was in a slump?

"About that time a girl friend told me about the psychic surgeons. A friend of hers, a man in his early forties, had been operated on by one of them for some sort of bowel disorder, and he was well. There was no scar, no pain and—after all I'd been through, this sounded wonderful to me—no complications of any sort. I didn't want to go with a group—I wanted personal care—so I got the name of the healer who had operated on this man, I borrowed two thousand dollars on an insurance policy, and I went to Baguio. I spent two weeks receiving treatment by Placido Palitayan and his assistant, an Oregonian named Donald Winslow. They operated on me six times, taking out scar tissue with each operation. Then they sent me to David Oligani, and I stayed with him for another week. He prayed for me a lot and he also operated twice. When I left for home they told me that in three months what was left of the scar tissue would be gone and I'd be able to pass urine from my bladder."

"What happened?" I asked.

"Nothing," she said. "Absolutely nothing. When the three months were up and no urine came through to my bladder I thought maybe it was just going to take a little longer. But when five months went by with no improvement, I lost hope. I went back to the urologist, he took more X-rays, and he tells me the scar tissue is as bad as it was a year ago. He also says that these tubes in my kidneys usually lead to trouble sooner or later and he wants me to come in for the artificial-bladder operation.''

"Are you going to do as he says?" I asked.

"I don't know," Mrs. Landan answered, with a sort of bitter half-smile. "I realize now that the psychic surgeons were fakes—that they really weren't doing anything for me—but I haven't got any faith in doctors, either. I did as I was told—got annual physicals so I wouldn't die of cancer—and then they discover an early cancer which they can treat 'easily.' What happens? I wind up deeply in debt, with a ruined bladder, doomed to live for the rest of my life with a bag full of urine pasted to my belly. Frankly, that kind of life doesn't appeal to me much. If it wasn't for my daughter I'd probably go out a window, but she needs me. I suppose I'll probably have the operation, though I haven't much faith any more that doctors will do me much good.''

I decided not to argue with her. I couldn't think of a decent argument, anyway. This was a case that M.D.s had fouled up. No one had explained the risks of radiation treatment to Mrs. Landan. Someone had miscalculated, or misdirected, the radium–X-ray treatment, and even though the cancer was apparently cured, the patient had been mutilated. When no rational hope of a normal life was offered her, Mrs. Landan had turned to what she would under ordinary circumstances have recognized as irrational help. Who could blame her? Not me.

Mrs. Landan is an example of the sort of medically mismanaged patient on which the vultures who offer quack cures feed.

Case II—Sam McCausland, a fifty-three-year-old man who had bowel trouble for ten years before going to the Philippines.

"Ten years ago," Mr. McCausland began, "I had my first attack of bowel trouble. Pain and cramps mostly, but it laid me up for almost a week. My doctor told me I probably

236

had diverticulitis and put me on a diet—no nuts, no corn—and gave me some medicine. I did okay for a while, but about six months later I had another attack and when that cleared up he ordered some X-rays. They showed, he told me, that his diagnosis of diverticulitis was correct. [Diverticuli, the small sacs on the large intestine, are present in about 15 percent of people over the age of forty-five. Usually they cause no trouble, but sometimes they become inflamed and the patient is said to have diverticulitis (-itis = inflammation). Once in a while these diverticuli bleed or perforate and surgery becomes necessary. Surgery is also often recommended if atacks of diverticulitis become frequent and severe.]

"Off and on over the next eight years I'd be bothered with belly pain, but if I watched my diet and took pills, it would clear up in a few days. Then, in the last two years, it seemed as if everything I ate gave me trouble, and the attacks lasted longer. We got some more X-rays and my doctor suggested an operation.

"Frankly, when it comes to operations, I'm a coward. My father died after an operation on his stomach, and my mother died after an operation for a broken hip. I didn't want an operation but my doctor said there wasn't anything else to do. He was afraid if I didn't have one soon, I'd get into serious trouble with my bowel. 'Not cancer,' he said, 'but a situation where you might need a colostomy for a while.' [A colostomy is a loop of large intestine which is pulled out into the abdominal wall and opened so that the patient evacuates stool through it. This defunctionalizes the bowel beyond the colostomy, and if the bowel is inflamed, allows it to heal.] He was afraid I'd develop a hole between my bowel and my bladder. [This condition, known as a fistula, is one of the complications that may develop as a result of repeated attacks of diverticulitis.]

"Even so, I didn't like the idea of an operation. I'd heard about the psychic surgeons through a friend who had a friend who had had a heart operation for angina in the

Philippines. This friend's heart pain had practically disappeared since the operation, so I decided to make the trip myself. I own my business and I've got enough money, so the two thousand wasn't going to hurt me. Even if they didn't cure me, I figured it would be an interesting trip.

"Six months ago I went over. Tony Agpaoa operated on me, and I haven't had an attack of bowel pain since. Oh, I have a little soreness now and then, but nothing serious; nothing at all like it was before Tony operated. I'm so damn grateful, I just sent him another five hundred dollars for his chapel."

"What does your family doctor think about all this?" I asked.

"He says I'm crazy," Mr. McCausland answered. "We're pretty good friends after all these years, so I don't mind what he says. You M.D.s are all alike, anyway," he added with a smile. "You don't think anyone but yourselves can cure anything."

"Maybe you're right," I answered. "We'll see."

Four months after this interview I called Mr. McCausland's doctor to find out how his patient was doing. "That damn fool," he said. "Three weeks ago he had a severe attack of diverticulitis. He perforated and we had to do an emergency colostomy on him. Fortunately, as you probably know if you met him, he's tougher than a boiled owl. He's doing fine now and we'll probably discharge him next week. But now he'll have to come back later to have that bowel removed and after that to have his colostomy closed. Because he went to those fakers in the Philippines he'll need three operations. If we'd operated earlier, we could have gotten away with one, but you know—people never learn."

Case III—Barbara Heinsohn, a forty-two-year-old housewife with three children, ages fourteen, seventeen and nineteen. Her husband, Harold, is an executive with a large manufacturing firm.

"When I went to the Philippines," Barbara said, "I had

no intention of being operated on. A friend of mine, Marjorie Simmons, has multiple sclerosis and she asked me to accompany her. We went down to Asignan and Joe Mercado operated on Marjorie three times. Each time I could see she had improved.

"On Saturday, during his religious service, when I saw people lining up for spiritual injections I thought 'Why not?' and I got in line. When Mercado's assistant asked me if there was anything special wrong with me I mentioned my gallstones; my family doctor has been after me for years to have them out. She told me that if I wished, Mercado would remove them. After watching him work on Marjorie I was a believer, so I said okay.

"He operated on me right there in the chapel. I could see the blood and watch his hands poking inside of me and finally he held up what I thought at the time were gallstones. I was so relieved to have that operation over, without any scar or any pain, that I gave him three hundred dollars for his chapel.

"When I got back here and told Harold what I'd done he said, 'You might just as well have thrown that money in the fire.' And to tell you the truth, now that I was away from the whole atmosphere of the Philippine healers, I had reservations myself. Ordinarily I'm a fairly level-headed woman, but just being around all those sick people, watching people going into trance and seeing dozens of bare-handed operations with blood and tissue all over, seeing what seemed to be miracles performed every day—all that had gotten to me. They'd made me a believer.

"I wasn't home two weeks when I had another gall-bladder attack. This one was so severe that I had to go to the hospital, and after it subsided I finally decided to let my doctor go ahead with the operation. My gallbladder was packed solid with stones—thirty of them. I've got one in a bottle in my closet if you'd like to see it. I use it to remind myself not to be gullible ever again."

"How is your friend Marjorie?" I asked.

"Sad to say, no better. For a while after she came home she seemed to walk more smoothly, but she's back to her usual gait now. I wish someone could do something for her."

"Maybe in the near future," I said. "A lot of people are working on the problem. Tell her not to give up hope."

"She won't," Mrs. Heinsohn said. "Marjorie is a tough girl."

Case IV—Neal Cook is forty-eight years old. He and his wife, Anne, have two children, both of whom are in college. Neal has a degree in both business administration and biology. He owns a very successful truck rental and leasing business. He earns $120,000 a year in salary and more in dividends.

Neal is a very influential man in the city in Texas in which he lives. He has served on the school board and has been very active in community affairs. He is, in brief, a successful, intelligent, pleasant person and, I gathered from his friends, a very sharp businessman. He founded and built his trucking firm from scratch.

"In August of 1972," Neal told me, "Anne and I went to Boston on a sort of combined business and vacation trip. The third day we were there I got up in the morning and started to shave when I noticed that things looked a bit blurred. I shut first one eye, and then the other, and decided it was my left eye that was at fault. I had Anne look at the eye and it seemed normal to her, but there was no question in my mind that something was wrong.

"I've never worn glasses—and I was forty-six at the time—so I thought perhaps it was just my age finally catching up with me. It didn't bother me much so I decided to live with it till we got back home before I went to a doctor. As you know, there are a lot of excellent doctors in my hometown and I know a lot of them personally.

"A week later I called an ophthalmologist friend, told him about my problem and made an appointment. He gave me a very careful examination—dilating my pupils and all that—and then told me he wasn't satisfied. He wanted me to see a neurologist. I asked him what he thought the matter was and he said, 'I'm not really sure. I'd rather wait till someone else checks you out before committing myself.' I didn't press him. I know my job and the doctors know theirs, I figured. The next day I went to the neurologist.

"It almost floored me when the neurologist, after examining me, said he wanted to admit me to the hospital. I couldn't believe I had anything that serious, since I didn't feel that sick. I needed a few days to get my business organized, and then went in. To make a long story short, after ten days of X-rays, blood tests and consultations, all these doctors decided I had a tumor in my pituitary gland. They weren't certain what kind it was, but they felt I should have it operated on.

"As you can imagine, this came as one hell of a shock. All I had for symptoms was a slight blurring in one eye—not too bad at that—and they wanted to open my skull. I decided, experts or not, I was going to have to think about that.

"I went home and while I was trying to decide what to do I remembered some films I'd once seen of Tony Agpaoa operating a patient; one of Anne's friends had brought them to a yoga meeting when Anne was interested in that sort of thing. We called Anne's friend and she made arrangements for us to see the film again. The operation certainly looked to me like the real thing, but it was an operation on the abdomen. It's funny how a mind works; I could accept the idea that this man could put his bare hands into the abdomen, but I had doubts that he could put them through the skull. I decided to call him and ask.

"I tried Baguio first, but Tony had gone to Manila. I tried the Manila number, and missed Tony again, but I talked to his wife and she assured me that Tony had often operated on the brain. She suggested that if I wanted to visit Tony, I call a Mr. Cortez at a certain travel agency in San Francisco. I called and the next evening we left on a Philippine Air Lines flight for Manila.

"I met Tony and liked him immediately—he's a very warm, personable guy. I told him that I was going to be honest with him—that I had reservations about his powers and that I wanted to watch him operate on others before I let him operate on me. This didn't bother him a bit. 'Certainly,' he said, 'perfectly understandable. You are from a different culture. Watch and take films if you like. I don't mind at all.'

"For the next three days I was his shadow. I saw dozens of operations and took thousands of feet of film. It was all so smooth, so painless, so marvelous that I could hardly believe my eyes. I know I wasn't in a trance—I talked to other patients and they saw the same things; it was all true. By the fourth day I was not only willing but eager to have the operation.

"I was staying at the Filipinas Hotel in Manila because that's where Tony stayed and worked. At ten o'clock in the morning I went up to his room. He was just finishing an operation on the back of a Mrs. Anderson whom I'd met a couple of days earlier. I asked her if she'd mind taking films of my operation and she agreed to do so. At ten-fifteen I lay down on the table and Tony went to work.

"As he began the operation he put cotton pads over my eyes, and from then on all I could feel was the power of his hands. He pushed and shoved and I could feel him, but it didn't really hurt at all. At this point Mrs. Anderson said, 'Oh my God! You should see what's coming out of your head!' Five minutes after he began, Tony completed the operation.

"I sat up, got off the table and looked in the mirror: there was no scar at all, no sign of an operation except a little blood on my hair. Imagine—it took Tony Agpaoa five minutes to perform what my surgeon friend in the States had told me would be a six-hour operation! And seconds after the operation I was up an around. My doctor had told me I'd have to spend at least three weeks recuperating if I were back here.

"Tony showed me the tissue he'd removed. It was grayish white, about two inches long and shaped like a worm. I told him I'd like to have it so I could get it examined back in the States and he said he'd have his assistant take care of it. Unfortunately, when the assistant was cleaning up for the next case, he threw the specimen out with some pieces of cotton. Tony and I spent half an hour looking through a bucket he thought it might be in, but we had no luck.

"I spent another three weeks in the Philippines watching Tony and getting to know him better. I also went down to the lowlands and observed Mercado and Flores. This entire business intrigues me, as you can imagine. I'm a level-headed businessman. I'm used to looking at situations from every angle before I commit myself. I've looked very carefully at Tony and the other healers. Let me tell you—this is real. I'm planning to go back again for three months next summer. I want to learn all I can about the psychic surgeons."

"How have you been since your operation?" I asked.

"Fine," Mr. Cook said. "Oh, once in a while, if I get tired, I still have a little fuzziness in my left eye, but it's much better than it was. Tony warned me that it might be some time before my vision clears up completely."

"What do your doctors have to say about all this?"

"You know doctors," Mr. Cook said with a laugh. "They're the most conservative, cautious, skeptical people on earth. With me they're noncommittal. They keep telling me not to be too optimistic; I tell them they ought to go to the Philippines and learn how to do real surgery. So far it's a stand-off."

"Would you mind if I talked to one of your doctors about your case?"

"Not a bit. I'd be happy if you would. Call Steve Fisher—he's the neurosurgeon who was going to operate on me and he's checked me over twice since I got back. He'll be glad to cooperate."

Mr. Cook signed a release form, giving Dr. Fisher permission to talk to me about his case, and I called Dr. Fisher. We met at his office the next afternoon.

"I'm glad someone's trying to do something about all this," Dr. Fisher said. "Neal Cook is a fine man, highly respected in this community, but he's becoming a sort of medical menace. He has all these films and he shows them at Kiwanis meetings, church meetings, meetings of all sorts all over the country. He's a very persuasive man and these films, to a person who has never been in an operating room, look like what they imagine an operation mush be. He doesn't tell people specifically to go to the Philippines for medical treatment; he just says, 'That's what I did and now I'm well,' and his audience gets the message."

"Is he cured?" I asked.

"In a word—no. His condition is exactly as it was before he went to the Philippines. He has a defect in the visual field of his left eye. X-rays show enlargement and erosion of the sella turcica [sella turcica = Turk's saddle; a hollowed-out area at the base of the skull in which the pituitary gland lies]. These pituitary tumors are usually very slow-growing. It may be several months before this tumor gets big enough to encroach on the optic nerve to such an extent that Neal's vision really gets bad. Then it's going to be a hell of a lot more difficult to get the thing out. But this screwball in the Philippines has got him so convinced he won't listen to me. All we can do is wait.

"Neal, as you probably realize, is a wealthy man. He gave this Agpaoa fellow fifteen hundred dollars as a donation to his chapel; he brags about it because he says it would have cost him more, when you figure in the hospital room, back here in the States. And he's probably right.

"But what he doesn't realize is that the fifteen hundred dollars, plus the three thousand or so he spent on transportation and hotels, have all been wasted. He doesn't realize that some of the people who have gone to the Philippines on Neal's say-so can't afford to blow three thousand dollars. I wish the hell someone could talk him into shutting up for a few more months. My guess is that by then he'll have changed his mind about Agpaoa."

"I'm afraid you're wrong," I said. "I asked Mr. Cook what he'd do if there were signs the tumor was returning. 'I'd go back to the Philippines,' he told me. 'Tony told me if I had any more trouble, to come back at once.' Mr. Cook, I'm afraid, is now a true believer."

"If that's the case, then our medical society will have to write to the A.M.A. Someone's got to put a stop to this nonsense."

"Good luck," I said as we shook hands.

"Thanks," Dr. Fisher said. "We'll need it. And so, I imagine," he added as an afterthought, "will Neal Cook."

Dr. Fisher, and dozens of other doctors, did write to the A.M.A. asking that action be taken to dissuade patients from visiting the Philippines. The A.M.A. did what it could, asking the Federal Trade Commission to intervene when travel agencies advertised the psychic surgeons as "healers," but, since the healers were citizens of the Philippines, the A.M.A. had no authority over them. Nor did the A.M.A. have any right to prevent a citizen of the United States from visiting the Philipppines for medical treament of any sort.

So Neal Cook continued to evangelize and send patients to the Philippines until, in December of 1973, his tumor became so large that he could no longer ignore his loss of vision. He returned to the Philippines and Tony reoperated and again, Neal gave Tony a $1,500 donation. This time, however, even Neal Cook had to admit there was no improvement. He returned to Texas, Dr. Fisher operated on him, removing a benign pituitary tumor. Neal Cook made a complete recovery.

He never speaks of his Philippine experience any more.

245

He has, in fact, become an active supporter of a charitable foundation devoted to funding research into the cause and treatment of tumors.

There are two aspects of Neal Cook's case that are worth emphasizing.

First, it demonstrates once again that intelligence and common sense don't necessarily protect one from charlatans. Although Neal is a successful businessman—some of his friends even described him as brilliant—once he was outside the field of his interest, in a foreign atmosphere that smacked of magic and the occult, he was easily deceived. He wanted to believe in the psychic surgeons, and in the interest of that belief, he had no difficulty suspending his critical faculties and swallowing whole all the nonsense he was fed. The same man who would go over every fine point of a business contract, ferreting out any possible snares, making certain that he was not being deceived in any way, was willing, after watching half a dozen phony operations, to lie down on a table and let Tony Agpaoa, whom he had met three days earlier, reach into his skull and pull out a piece of his brain—at least this is what Neal thought he was permitting Tony to do.

It would be difficult to believe that sophisticated, intelligent people would be capable of such irrational behavior in matters of life and death if cases like Neal's weren't so commonplace.

A second point that Neal's case demonstrates well is the fine job word-of-mouth advertising does for the psychic surgeon. When a man like Neal Cook, highly respected in his community, goes to Kiwanis meetings, church meetings and social gatherings, showing his films and preaching the merits of psychic surgery, it is inevitable that he will steer other victims to Tony and his friends. And they, in turn, will recruit others.

On occasion even internationally known personalities have promoted the psychic surgeons. For example, in *World*

Tennis (January 1974, p. 46) Richard Evans writes of visits that John Newcombe and Tony Roche, two world-famous tennis-players, made to the Philippines observing and / or seeking help from psychic surgeons, Placido Palitayan and Juan Blanche. The tone of the article is positive, leaving the reader with the distinct impression that these healers are, indeed, capable of performing miraculous, painless, curative, bare-handed operations. Several hundred thousand tennis buffs read *World Tennis*. Many of them have tendinitis of the elbow ("tennis elbow"), bursitis of the shoulder, bone spurs on their heels or other ailments to which tennis players are particularly prone. I wonder how many of these injured athletes, after reading Richard Evans' article, decided to follow in the footsteps of their idols Newcome and Roche. Only a few perhaps; but one would be too many.

Case V—Louise Andrews, fifty-one years old; before her death a schoolteacher with four grown children. Her husband, Roland, is a salesman for a kitchenware company.

"I was on the road most of the time for the twenty-five years Louise and I were married," Mr. Andrews told me when I interviewed him at his home in California. "In the evenings Louise was alone a lot, once the kids had left home, so I sort of blame myself for what happened. If I'd been around, we could have done things together—gone to the movies, taken up bowling or even skiing—but when you're fifty-five it's kind of difficult to change jobs and Louise was used to me being gone, so I never really gave it much thought.

"Louise was always very religious. We were Methodists at one time, but five years ago one of Louise's friends told her about a different church—a church where there were meetings three times a week with a lot of singing and incense, and people who even spoke in tongues. Louise went once, liked it and joined. She dragged me there one time but it didn't appeal to me, so I never went back, but I figured that if Louise enjoyed that sort of religion, and if it gave her something to do evenings, that was fine with me. I couldn't imagine it would do her any harm.

"Three years ago, when she was forty-eight, Louise developed a cough. She had smoked for years, almost two packs a day, and I kept trying to get her to cut down, but she never could. 'I'm too weak,' she'd say and laugh. But the cough bothered her a lot, so she really tried. She got down to a pack a day.

"After a month, when the cough didn't get any better, she finally agreed to go to a doctor. He took an X-ray and said she had a shadow in her left lung. He wasn't sure what it was but there was a possibility it was a tumor—a cancer. I told him I didn't think women ever got lung cancer, but he said, yes, they did. He wanted Louise to see a chest surgeon for some more tests and made her an appointment for a weeek later.

"That was on a Thursday afternoon. That night Louise went to her church and there was a young man there who had just come back from the Philippines. He gave a sermon on how Christ was coming again soon and as one of His signs He'd given the gift of 'material healing' to some poor people in the Philippines. Then he showed movies of them performing operations. After the service, while everyone was having coffee, Louise asked this man if the Philippine healers could cure cancer and he told her they certainly could.

"That was all Louise needed. I talked till I was blue in the face, trying to get her to go to the chest surgeon, but she wouldn't do it. 'Please, Roland,' she said, 'let me try the Philippine healers first. If they can't cure me, I promise I'll go to the chest surgeon.' I finally gave up and let her go.

"She came back all happy and cheerful. She told me all about the operation, how this psychic surgeon operated bare-handed and took out the tumor. She'd even seen the tumor; he showed it to her before he threw it in a fire. She was convinced she was cured. She wouldn't even go back to the doctor for an X-ray to make certain. "It isn't necessary,' she said. 'I've seen the cancer. Why waste money on an X-ray?'

"I had to admit she didn't cough much for about a month and began to wonder if she was right, if maybe she had been cured by this man in the Philippines. I was really getting hopeful when, on a Sunday night, the roof caved in. We were watching television, and suddenly Louise had a terrible coughing spell and coughed up what looked like a cup of blood. She looked at me and I looked at her and I think we both knew right away that she was in serious trouble.

"Louise went to the hospital that night. The next day they took more X-rays and found that the shadow was larger than it had been before. Worse, they found a lump just above her collar bone. The surgeon took that out under Novocaine anesthesia and the report came back 'cancer'; the tumor had spread from the lung to the glands, and there was no way to remove it.

"From then on it was six months of pure hell. They tried X-ray treatments but they made Louise so sick she could hardly stand it and they didn't do any good. She lost her voice—paralysis of a nerve to the vocal cord the doctor said—and she had trouble breathing. She was home for a while but her chest kept filling up with fluid and she'd have to go in and they'd stick a big needle into her back and draw out the fluid. God, how she dreaded those trips. Finally her chest was filling up about as fast as they could take the fluid away and she had to go back into the hospital so she could have oxygen all the time. I hate to admit it but when she died all I could think was—'Thank God.' She'd suffered enough. I think Louise felt that way, too.

"While Louise went through all this she never mentioned the Philippine surgeon and neither did I. We just didn't want to talk about it. But after she died I asked her doctor of the two-month delay in treatments had cost Louise her life. 'I can't say, Mr. Andrews,' he told me. 'Lung cancer is always a serious disease. There was no evidence that it had spread when I first saw Louise but maybe at an operation we'd have found it was already beyond cure. There's no sense in dwelling on what might have been.'

"I guess he's right, but I still have nightmares about what those two months cost us. If she hadn't gone to that healer in the Philippines, Louise might be sitting here today."

I could think of nothing consoling to say.

V

HEALING

22

During the year and a half I spent working on this book, whenever I was back in Litchfield practicing surgery (which was, of course, most of the time) I spent many of my spare hours reading books about "miraculous" healers. I looked through hundreds of volumes trying to find adequately documented examples of cures that could not reasonably be explained except in terms of miraculous powers. I couldn't find one such case.

Perhaps one example, a book published recently, may be helpful. It demonstrates the sort of thing I ran into constantly: cases that might—probably would—impress someone who hadn't had any medical training or experience, but which would not, even momentarily, suggest to an M.D. that something miraculous had occurred.

The book is *Born to Heal,* by Ruth Montgomery, a well-known writer with years of experience in investigating and writing about the paranormal. It might seem reasonable to expect that when she wrote a book about a man, Mister A, who she implies has miraculous healing powers, Ms. Montgomery would be able to provide some sort of weighty documentation—an impressive case or two, at the very least. She doesn't do it.

According to Ms. Montgomery, Mister A had for many years heard inner voices which directed his life. These voices explained, among other things, how diseases, including cancer, are caused. According to the voices, all problems are related to disturbances in one's personal magnetic field. By listening to a patient's chest, Mister A could tell what organ in the patient's body lacked the proper magnetic charge. Mister A would then recharge that portion of the patient's body by simply putting his hands on the patient's abdomen (the abdomen being the magnetic center of the body) and transmitting energy into him. Sometimes a series of treatments was necessary, but invariably the patient was improved and cured.

It wasn't even essential for Mister A to be in the same room as the patient. On several occasions Mister A saved the lives of patients by simply shooting evergy through telephone wires. Someone would call Mister A, explain the patient's problem and then point the telephone receiver in the patient's direction while Mister A shot his energy through the phone. In just a few seconds the patient would make a remarkable recovery.

Unforunately, in Ms. Montgomery's entire book there isn't one case with sufficient documentation to convince anyone, with even a moderate amount of medical sophistication, that Mister A had ever effected a cure.

For example, Ms. Montgomery's opening case—the case to which she devotes most space, evidently because she feels it is her most convincing example—is that of a young woman with a brain tumor. Mister A treated this patient and several years later she was still alive and well, apparently cured.

Regrettably for Ms. Montgomery's purposes, the patient had, prior to Mister A's treatment, been operated on by a neurosurgeon, an M.D., who had removed what in her book is described as an "encapsulated" malignant tumor. "Encapsulated" is a medical term applied to tumors which appear to be enclosed in a capsule—and this is, to any surgeon, a very hopeful sign. The chances of achieving a cure when you remove such a tumor is always much better than when the tumor is not encapsulated. Any doctor reading Ms. Montgomery's book would conclude that the patient she describes at such length was cured by the nerosurgeon and not by Mister A.

All the other patients Mister A cured, as reported in *Born to Heal*, fall into categories I've already described: desperate people yearning for good health, and highly suggestible. There is little doubt that Mister A is an impressive, eloquent man; there is also little doubt, as far as I could tell from reading Ms. Montgomery's book, that Mister A is a charlatan. Since, according to Ms. Montgomery, Mister A insisted on remaining anonymous, there was no way I could check him out further.

The rest of my research wasn't any more productive. I visited my friend Justin Oudal, who owns a secondhand bookstore specializing in the occult, and spent several afternoons looking through his collection trying to find some evidence that there are indeed healers around who can cure patients by using hidden powers. All the cases I found were like those in Ms. Montgomery's book—cases like those every doctor sees in his practice: self-limited diseases, cyclical diseases, diseases known to be psychosomatic or hysterical in origin. I could see how these flowery descriptions of "miraculous" cures might impress a layman, but there wasn't one case in any book where the author had proven to my professional satisfaction that forces other than natural forces had been brought into play.

Another thing I did, during the moments I could steal from my practice, was to follow up leads on other healers, healers not as well known nationally as Kathryn Kuhlman but with strong local reputations. These leads weren't hard to come by; in fact, I was deluged by them. It seems to me that about half the time I mentioned to anyone that I was doing research for a book about healers, that person would say something like "You ought to go and see Mrs. Jones over in Smithville. A lot of people around here go to her when the doctor hasn't been able to cure them, and I know for a fact that she helped old Mrs. Brown with her arthritis. Mrs. Jones has a healing touch." People who reputedly have a "healing touch" can be found in almost any city, town, or village in the United States.

I tracked down twenty-three of the most promising of these leads. I called or visited the healer and the patients he or she had supposedly cured, and talked or visited with both at some length. It was all to no avail. The cases I encountered resembled, except for minor, irrelevant details, cases I've already described. There were no miracles to be found.

And so, I finally gave up. After doing my very best for eighteen months to find some shred of evidence that somewhere there was someone who had miraculous healing powers, I concluded that no such person existed. I realize I could have pursued this will-o'-the-wisp forever, that I might have spent the rest of my life looking for a healing miracle,* but to do so seemed to be pointless. As some wise man once said, "It isn't necessary to eat the entire steer to tell if the steak is any good." I'd eaten all I could digest

---

*Harold Sherman, now seventy-five, is a man who has devoted his life to seeking out and writing about strange and occult powers and miraculous healing. Dozens of his books are still in print, many available in paperback. His 1942 book, *Thoughts Through Space*, has recently been reissued, with a laudatory foreword by Dr. Edgar Mitchell. In 1967 he wrote a book called *wonder Healers of the Philippines* praising the psychic surgeons.

Mr. Sherman claims that he has had extraordinary powers since the age of fourteen when he first sent a message to a school chum using mental telepathy. He also believes in precognition—the ability to predict what is going to happen in the future. In the February 1974 issue of *Psychic* magazine there is an interview with Mr. Sherman. Here are a couple of excerpts.

Psychic: Have you done any peeking into the future to find out what's in store for us?

Sherman: I wrote a book on this subject several years ago—*How to Foresee and Control Your Future*—and I think what was predicted in it is coming true, in large part today. . . .

Psychic: Do you see anything significant in its [the Comet Kohoutek's] appearance?

Sherman: Yes, I do. The spectacular advent of Comet Kohoutek is bound to have an immense effect upon man's mind. This issue of your publication is scheduled to be in the hands of your readers at the time that the comet is blazing in our skies.

I predict many will be struck with fear to the point of panic; others will regard this heavenly display as the most spiritual experience of a lifetime, and will look for new metaphysical and religious meanings. I also feel that the physical effects of the comet's passing may influence weather conditions on earth and lead to eventual meteoric showers and other astronomical happenings.

So much for Harold Sherman and sixty years of investigating, working with and writing about the paranormal.

of this particular animal; it was time for me to get on to other things.

But before I leave the subject of miraculous healing I think it may be helpful to write about some of the aspects of medicine and healing that lay people, generally, don't understand. I think it will be equally helpful to write about some of the things that doctors, though they don't always like to admit it, don't understand either. It seems to me that the more all of us know about the healing process the more likely we are to pursue life and health along channels that are apt to be productive. I spent the better part of two years looking for quick, magical, miraculous answers to problems of life and death, only to find that those answers do not exist. I'd like to spare others that pursuit.

Here are some aspects of the medical healing process about which some of us know nothing and none of us know enough. To start with the *body's ability to heal itself*: Kathryn Kuhlman often says, "I don't heal; the Holy Spirit heals through me." I suspect there are two reasons why Miss Kuhlman continually repeats this statement: first, if the patient doesn't improve, the Holy Spirit, not Kathryn Kuhlman, gets the blame; second, she hasn't the foggiest notion of what healing is all about and once she puts the responsibility on the shoulders of the Holy Spirit she can answer, if questioned about her healing powers, "I don't know. The Holy Spirit does it all."

Actually, we doctors could and should confess that in a certain sense we don't heal patients either. We may not give credit to the Holy Spirit (though that might be as good an explanation as any), but when pinned to the wall, we have to confess that all we do, in many instances, is help the body heal itself.

Broken bones afford an excellent example of what I mean. Let's assume a ten-year-old boy falls out of a tree and breaks his leg. I order an X-ray, to see where the break is located and in what directions the two ends are displaced, and then I reduce the fracture, i.e., manipulate the bones

257

until they are in proper alignment. Next I apply a plaster cast to hold the bones in this position. At this point, except to get follow-up X-rays to make certain the bones haven't slipped out of alignment, and to change the cast if it loosens, my job is done.

Have I healed the broken bone? Of course not. All I've done is align the bones so that healing may proceed. The body of this ten-year-old boy must heal the fracture for him.

Healing is a very complicated process. At the site of the fracture there is always some bleeding from the marrow cavity of the bone and from torn blood vessels in the fat and muscle that surround the bone. The blood clots and forms a hematoma (an organized collection of, among other things, blood cells and fibrin, a protein). Then specialized cells in the bloodstream (phagocytes; *phagos* = eat, *cyte* = cell) migrate to the fracture site and start cleaning up the debris, the tissue that has been crushed and destroyed by the injury which caused the fracture.

As the phagocytes clean up the fracture site other cells, osteoblasts (bone-building cells), begin to repair the bone. These cells, in some way we don't yet understand, pull calcium out of the bloodstream and place it in the hematoma at the fracture site. The mixture of hematoma and calcium is called callus; later, as healing progresses, the hematoma is absorbed and the callus gradually becomes bone. All this takes about six or eight weeks and at the end of that time, if things have gone well, the leg is solidly healed and the cast can be removed.

In children, bone healing is a particularly amazing phenomenon. Once in a while, because of the pull of the muscles, it's impossible to manipulate the bones into an end-to-end position. In those cases the doctor often leaves the bones in side-by-side position with the leg shortened by as much as one or two inches. No need to worry. As repair proceeds the body will mold those bones and lay down enough calcium so that when healing is complete, the broken leg will be the same length as the unbroken leg. And if, as sometimes happens, the doctor can't manipulate the two ends of the bones into a perfectly straight alignment, again the body will compensate for deficiency in his work. Many fractures that are immobilized at as much as a thirty-degree angle will, when healing is complete, be perfectly straight.

In all patients, bones heal in basically the same way, but as we get older our healing processes decrease in speed and efficiency. In the elderly it becomes much more important to restore proper alignment to bones, and it is usually necessary to keep casts on longer. A fracture of the tibia (the big bone in the leg) may heal solidly in six weeks in a child; it may take three to six months to heal a fracture, in a similar location, in a sixty-year-old woman.

The healing process in soft tissues is different but no less marvelous than it is in bones. Take, for example, an incision in the abdomen. When I cut into a patient, to remove a section of bowel with cancer in it or a gall bladder packed with stones, or an inflamed appendix, after I've finished the operation I close the abdomen in layers. First I sew together the edges of the peritoneum (the inner layer of the abdominal wall; thin, transparent, like cellophane), then the fascia (a tough, fibrous layer), then the subcutaneous tissue (fat), and finally the skin. Usually I don't sew the muscles, which lie between the peritoneum and fascia, because mucsle tissue is soft and doesn't hold sutures very well. Cut muscle edges will heal without stitches if they lie against each other.

For the first three weeks the incision is held together primarily by the stitches I've used. During that time—actually, beginning as soon as I've closed the incision—special tissue-building cells will have begun their work of laying down protein, removing debris and producing strong, sturdy scar tissue to solidly cement together the tissue edges which my sutures are temporaily holding together. If the sutures I've used are made of absorbable materials (catgut, for example), by the end of six weeks special cells, the phagocytes again, will have removed all of this suture material and healing will be complete.

My point in describing the healing process, accurately though admittedly in simple terms, is to make it clear that we doctors don't do the healing; the body does. And even though, by examining specimens of tissue in various stages of healing, we know something of how healing occurs, we don't as yet have any idea how to control it. We put things back together; the body—God, if you prefer—heals.

And excellent example of our lack of knowledge of the healing process is a complication of all surgeons dread: wound dehiscence (dehiscence = bursting).

About eight years ago I operated on a seventy-two-year-old man, Charlie Vargas, with cancer of the intestine. I removed the tumor-containing segment of bowel, sewed the two ends of the bowel back together, and closed the wound in layers, as I usually do.

Charlie tolerated the operation very nicely. He was out of bed on the first postoperative day and eating on the third day. His temperature remained normal and his wound looked fine. On the eighth day I took out his skin stitches, planning to let him go home the next day. When I removed the last stitch the upper part of his incision split open and about an ounce of bloody fluid gushed out.

This, as every surgeon knows, is a sign that a dehiscence may have occurred. I took a sterile clamp and gently inserted it into the opening at the top of Charlie's wound. Sure enough, I could move the clamp freely into the abdomen beneath the skin all along the incision. I strapped an abdominal binder on Charlie to make certain the whole wound wouldn't open up and allow his intestines to spill out, and half an hour later took him back to the operating room. This time I reclosed the wound—which hadn't healed at all except for the skin edges, which were lightly stuck together—with thick wire sutures that pulled all the layers together in one big bunch. Three weeks later Charlie's wound had healed solidly; I was able to remove the wire sutures and send him home.

Why hadn't Charlie's wound healed the first time? I haven't any idea. The surgical literature contains hundreds of articles on wound dehiscence and wound healing. We'd love to know why dehiscences occur and how to prevent them, but so far we don't have the answer. Healing remains a mystery.

So, in the sense that we don't heal bones or incisions, we doctors aren't healers; but in other ways, we are.

Take Charlie's bowel cancer. It's eight years since I removed that tumor and Charlie is still healthy, with no sign of a recurrence. Presumably, I've healed him of his disease—just as, by removing an inflamed appendix and gall bladders containing stones, I've healed hundreds of other patients. And my confreres who don't practice surgery heal pneumonia by giving the patients bacteria-killing antibiotics, cure anemias by prescribing appropriate blood-building ingredients, and cure (or at least control) duodenal ulcers, colitis and many other diseases by administering the proper advice and, when appropriate, medications. But in all these healing ventures we rely to a large extent on the healing mechanisms that reside in the body. Some patients could certainly die without our help, but we couldn't help them if they didn't first have the ability to help themselves.

Just as surgical incisions heal more quickly in some patients than in others, so some patients respond to infection and injury more vigorously. For example, sometimes I'll see a patient who has had the signs and symptoms of appendicitis for six hours, and already her white bloodcell count will have risen from the normal level of about 8,000 per cubic millimeter of blood to 18,000. In another patient, sick with appendicitis for twenty-four hours, the white blood count may be only 12,000. When I operate on the first patient I may find that the omentum (the fatty, apron-like membrane that hangs down from the stomach in the abdominal cavity) has, after only six hours, wrapped itself around the appendix, effectively sealing it off from the other organs in the abdomen. When I operate on the patient who has been sick for twenty-four hours, so such localizing movement of the omentum has occurred.

Why has one patient responded so vigorously to infection, the other so sluggishly? We know that a more vigorous response occurs in the young and the robust than in those who are elderly or run down, but among individuals in the same groups there are wide differences in response. Why the differences? We don't know. More research may give us the answers.

It is possible that "healers," by their machinations, their rituals, their sheer charisma, stimulate patients so that they heal more rapidly than they otherwise might; charismatic doctors do the same. In all probability, this is why doctors who have warm rapport with their patients seem to get better results than doctors who treat their patients briskly and impersonally.

Unfortunately all this is impossible to prove because responses to injury and infection vary so greatly, not only from patient to patient but even in the same patient at different times, depending on the nature of his disease and his general health when afflicted. But if we assume, as some researchers do, that charismatic stimulation of the healing process occurs, it seems probable that it would be mediated through the autonomic nervous system. We'll consider that system presently in some detail.

What it all amounts to is this. God—and I'm going to use that name freely; those who wish to substitute "nature," "first cause," "Jehovah," or anything else, may feel free to do so—gave us brains. Physicians spend many years using their brains, learning all they can about how the human body is constructed and how it works. We haven't begun to understand the body completely—perhaps we never will—but we have learned how to identify many diseases that afflict the body and have worked out methods that we can use successfully to help the body rid itself of these diseases.

God gave humans the faculties which, properly developed and employed, enable them to protect themselves from disease. These are the faculties physicians use when they heal.

Still, we have to admit that "healers"—and I use the term to refer to people outside the medical profession who profess to heal—do heal, in a certain sense. Kathryn Kuhlman "cures" the pain of a backache, Norbu Chen stops a migraine, David Oligani gets rid of a patient's stomach ache. How do these healers, without any medical training, manage to achieve these results? To understand the successes of healers we have to know something about the *autonomic nervous system* and *hypnosis,* or the power of suggestion.

23

Each of us has two nervous systems which, for purposes of this discussion, we can call the voluntary nervous system and the autonomic nervous system. The voluntary nervous system is, when we're healthy, under our control; the autonomic nervous system ordinarily is not.

Anatomically, the voluntary nervous system is composed of most of the brain, the spinal cord, and the nerves which run from the spinal cord to the muscles of our arms, legs, face, abdomen—all those areas where muscle movement is under our control. The nerves which are part of the voluntary nervous system vary considerably in size; close to the spinal cord they may be as thick as a pencil but as they continue to run farther and farther from the spinal cord they become thin as fine threads. These nerves, even as far out as in the fingers, can be seen by an operating surgeon and protect from damage or repaired if cut.

When you pick up a glass of water, it is your voluntary nervous system that you use. From the cerebral cortex of your brain, where the decision is made, a message passes down the spinal cord and through the appropriate nerves to the muscles of the arm and hand. These muscles contract and relax as necessary to permit you to reach out, pick up the glass and lift it to your lips. Simultaneously other messages, which enable you to tip your face properly and swallow, pass from the brain to your mouth, neck and throat.

Any voluntary act—walking, talking, writing—depends

on messages passing from the brain along the spinal cord and peripheral nerve pathway. Exactly how these messages originate and pass from one area to another, whether it is an electrical or chemical reaction, is still not resolved (research into the function of the nervous system has a long way to go), but at least we can see and understand the anatomy.

Anywhere along the line, the integrity of this pathway may be disrupted. Hemorrhage of the brain—a "stroke"—may prevent an individual from sending the message; a crushing injury to the spinal cord may interrupt the message at that level; a cut nerve in the wrist will not prevent the patient from lifting his arm, but because there is no path along which the orders may be delivered to the muscles of the hand, the patient will not be able to close his hand around the glass. Illness and injury may hamper the function of our voluntary nervous system; otherwise it's under our control.

The autonomic nervous system is another matter entirely. This system includes, besides some small parts of the brain, a network of nerves. These nerves, most of them fine as cobwebs and invisible to the naked eye, lie along the inner lining of the back wall of the chest and abdomen, and send branches out to the heart, lungs, eyes, blood vessels, intestines, bladder—all those many parts of our body which are not, normally, under voluntary control.

The autonomic nervous system can be subdivided into the sympathetic and parasympathetic systems, which sometimes oppose each other; e.g., the sympathetic system may cause a blood vessel to contract, the parasympathetic may cause that same blood vessel to relax. For our purposes we can consider them together as integral parts of the autonomic nervous system.

If you'd like to see the autonomic nervous system at work, step into a dark room with a friend and flash a light into his eye. You will see his pupil, which was dilated in the dark, contract when the light hits it. This is caused by a tightening of the iris, controlled by a muscle innervated by the autonomic nervous system. Your friend will not be aware of his pupil dilating and contracting any more than you are aware of this when it occurs, as it does hundreds of times a day in response to changes in the intensity of the light to which you are exposed. Nor can you order your pupil to dilate or contract; it is not under the control of the voluntary nervous system, but under the control of the autonomic, "self-governing" nervous system.

Another example. Check your heart rate as reflected in your pulse. If you're sitting and reading, as I assume you are, your pulse rate is probably running between sixty and ninety beats a minute. Stand and jump up and down as fast as you can for two minutes; now, if you count your pulse rate, you'll find it is ten, twenty or thirty beats a minute faster than it was when you were at rest. Your heart responded to exercise by increasing its rate. You didn't order your heart to do this. Unless you are a master of yoga, you can't order your heart to speed up or slow down. Your heart is under the control of the autonomic nervous system.

A third example. Go outside and run around a track or tennis court for half an hour on a hot day. You'll perspire. Your sweat glands will funtion in such a way as to help cool off your body and maintain your body temperature at 98.6 degrees. Can you order your sweat glands not to function? Can you remain perspiration-free despite the temperature? Can you order your body temperature to go up two or three degrees? No. Your sweat glands and the entire temperature control system of your body are not under your voluntary control.

Your intestine, when it contracts and dilates, churning and digesting your food; your skin, when it blushes in shame or blanches in terror; your penis, when it fills with blood and becomes rigid—you can neither will these things to happen nor prevent them from occurring. They are all under the control of your autonomic nervous system.

It is the faulty function of the autonomic nervous sytem that causes many symptoms and diseases. Asthma, duodenal ulcers, colitis, constipation, many menstrual disorders and skin rashes, impotency, high blood pressure, irregular heartbeats, diarrhea, headaches—all these things and many others may, and usually are, caused in whole or in part by a malfuntion of the autonomic nervous system. If we can correct malfuntion, we can (and do) cure the symptom or disease.

Let's consider the patient with an ulcer in the duodenum, the first part of the small intestine. This is the area where 90 percent of so-called stomach ulcers occur.

The cells of the stomach wall produce hydrochloric acid which helps digest food. When we eat, the vagus nerve (a part of the autonomic nervous system that innervates the stomach) stimulates these acid-producing cells. I don't order my stomach cells to produce acid; they do it because of stimulation from the vagus nerve, a nerve not under my voluntary control.

Now, suppose the vagus nerve begins to malfunction, i.e., to stimulate these acid-producing cells too often and for too long, so that the quantity of acid poured out by my stomach is far greater than is necessary to digest the food I eat. After a while that acid, as it flows from the stomach into the duodenum, will burn a hole in the lining of the duodenum. I will have an ulcer. If the acid continues to work on the duodenum, the ulcer may eventually go all the way through the duodenal wall and I'll have a perforated ulcer. Possibly the ulcer may erode a blood vessel in the wall of the duodenum and cause a hemorrhage. It's important to stop this excess acid production before I develop a severe, possibly fatal, ulcer problem.

How do I do this? Ideally, I'd order the vagus nerve to stop working so hard, but the vagus nerve is not under my voluntary control. As an alternative, I take antacids to neutralize the acid; take pills, which work on the stomach cells and reduce acid production; take sedatives, such as phenobarbital, which may make me less anxious and, indirectly, slow down the activity of the vagus nerve. If none of these things work, then I may have to have part of my stomach removed and, possibly, have my vagus nerve cut.

But let's get back for a moment to the ideal treatment—simply ordering my vagus nerve to stop its excess activity. I can't do that directly, as I can order my hand to pick up a glass, but if I'm lucky, perhaps I can get the message to my vagus nerve indirectly.

We know from experience that tension and anxiety are what cause the vagus nerve to overreact—taxi drivers and high-powered businessmen are notoriously prone to ulcers—so sometimes, by changing a patient's environment or life style, we can "cure" an ulcer.

However, it's often difficult, sometimes impossible, for a patient to make a radical shift in life style; after all, most of us have to earn a living and it may be difficult to find a new job. Besides, we are what we are, and it's difficult to shift abruptly from being a highly competitive, driving individual to a relaxed "who-cares?" sort of person.

If we can't change our life style, there is another approach that may be used to influence the autonomic nervous system. Sometimes, if a doctor or a healer can persuade a patient to think positively ("I am not going to be so tense"; "I am not going to let my stomach upset me"), then the vagus nerve will stop its excessive activity and the ulcer will heal. The doctor may simply sit and talk with the patient, trying to help him develop more insight into the problem, or he may use more formal hypnotic techniques. The healer may, and probably will, use what the patient believes are supernormal powers. Kathryn Kuhlman, for example, lays on her hands, invokes the power of the Holy Spirit and says, "I rebuke that ulcer"; the patient believes, and the activity of his vagus nerve slows down. Norbu Chen "hits" the patient with his mysterious Tibetan whammy and tells the patient, "Your troubles are over"; the patient believes and his acid production dwindles. For some patients, any or all of these techniques are successful.

The point I'm trying to make is that although we know exactly how we do it, we can sometimes influen autonomic nervous system by suggestion. A person wh forceful character, one who can persuade patients to have faith in him, may, using any of a variety of techniques, cure a symptom or ailment that is caused by a derangement or malfunction of the autonomic nervous system.

I've written at some length about the vagus nerve and duodenal ulcers, but the techniques would apply with equal force to all the other so-called functional ailments— ailments caused by the malfuntion of an organ or system under the control of the autonomic nervous system. I've given a partial list before, but let me repeat and expand on what this might include: alopecia areata (loss of clumps of hair), acne and a multitude of other skin ailments (the skin is notoriously susceptible to derangements of the autonomic nervous system), asthma, irregular heartbeat, heartburn, ulcer, bloating, diarrhea, colitis, impotency, migraine headaches, menstrual disorders and high blood pressure. All these ailments may, without any need for invoking miraculous powers, be cured or relieved by modifying the function of the autonomic nervous system.

Sadly, we don't know yet how to control the autonomic nervous system with predictability; it's a hit-and-miss proposition. Yogis spend years learning by trial and error, to raise and lower their heartbeat and temperature, with some success; but most of us don't want to take the time to do this, and besides, controlling one's heartbeat and temperature have little practical application.

The purpose of all the current research in biofeedback is to try to make personal control of the autonomic nervous system possible and practical. For example, by attaching devices to the body which show the patient a continuing record of his blood pressure, some people can learn to raise or lower their blood pressure at will. Usually it's a matter of thinking angry thoughts or reflecting on a peaceful scene. A patient may even learn to raise and lower the temperature of one part of the body, when the patient can see a recording of what the temperature at any given point and time is. Hopefully, the research in biofeedback may help us cure the functional disorders I've just listed.

We have to remember, however, that it would be terrible if the autonomic nervous system were not autonomous. If we had to decide for ourselves how much to increase our heart rate when we walked upstairs, how much to perspire when we were out in the sun, how rapidly to digest the pizza we've just eaten, we'd be too busy regulating our bodily functions to accomplish anything imaginative or artistic. The autonomic nervous system has to remain largely autonomous, or we'll be in serious trouble.

Let me repeat: a charismatic individual—a healer—can sometimes influence a patient and cure symptoms or a functional disease by suggestion, with or without a laying on of hands. Physicians can do the same thing. These cures are not miraculous; they result from corrections made by the patient in the function of his autonomic system. We don't know yet how to control this system, but we're learning.

Before we leave the autonomic nervous system we ought to at least mention acupuncture, which has been a hot subject in the last few years. No one knows with certainty how it works, and there are a number of imaginative programs being carried out. At the moment it seems probably that the effects of acupuncture are produced through the autonomic nervous system. A number of investigators have noted that when the skin around an acupuncture needle becomes flushed (a sign of activity in the autonomic nervous system), the acupuncture procedure is more likely to be successful than when this effect does not occur.

So far there seems to be solid evidence that in some patients acupuncture can produce anesthesia. The current theory is that the needle stimulates certain elements called "proprioceptors" lodged in tendons and muscles, and these proprioceptors send impulses to the spinal cord. At the spinal cord the impulses create a block; it's as if the acupuncture needle sets off a busy signal in the spinal cord, preventing pain messages from getting through to the brain. For example, a needle in the hand may block pain messages coming from the neck, and permit a surgeon to perform a thyroidectomy. It is not a completely reliable system; it works only on certain patients, and even in China, acupuncture is used as an anesthetic in only about 5 percent of all surgical cases.

Whether acupuncture will actually ever cure a disease remains to be seen. My guess is that if it is ever established that acupuncture will cure diseases, those diseases will be functional. Time will tell.

24

Hypnotism is, essentially, a practice in which certain techniques are used to heighten a patient's susceptibility to suggestion. The hypnotist talks to the patient, perhaps while having the patient stare at a light or a spot on the wall, and persuades him to relax. Then, while the patient's mind is open and receptive, the hypnotist makes suggestions which, hopefully, the patient will follow: "Don't smoke, it's bad for you"; "You don't really like liquor, it always makes you sick"; "You don't want to eat sweets as often as you do, you'd rather have celery or an apple." The more relaxed the patient becomes, the more willing he is to accept and follow suggestions.

I once took a course in hypnotism, and for a while, used it to help a patient, Iris Gloege, to reduce. I'd talk to her in my office until she relaxed: "Sit comfortably in the chair. Now let your feet go loose; let them just lie there; let all the tension go out of them; there, that's just fine." I'd talk to Iris for ten minutes or so and gradually persuade her to relax her entire body. Then I'd talk to her about her eating habits for another fifteen minutes, droning on in a nice quiet monotone.

The only trouble I ran into was that every order to relax that I gave Iris I'd follow myself, and by the time I had Iris in an early stage of hypnotic relaxation, I was as hypnotized as she was. We'd both sit there, I mumbling and she listening, until the twenty-five minutes were up and a nurse interrupted me. It was a very relaxing experience, but I'm afraid it didn't help Iris much.

Hypnosis, or suggestion, will often cure patients whose symptoms are neither functional nor organic but, rather, neurotic or hysterical in origin. Among these patients are many who complain of loss of hearing, loss of vision, or paralysis of one sort or another.

These symptoms usually develop because the patient is unable to cope with some new development in his life. The man who is afraid he is going to lose his job suddenly claims he cannot see out of one eye, the woman whose son has been picked up for possession of marijuana discovers that she can no longer move her right arm. These patients have converted their emotional problems into physical problems, a pattern that is known to physicians as "conversion hysteria."

Louise Flynn is an example of the sort of hysterical patient with whom healers have such great success. When Louise was sixty-three her husband, Kevin, died in an auto accident. Kevin had been drinking at the time and he and Louise had had a fight just before he left the house. Louise, understandably, felt guilty about Kevin's death. Neither her minister nor her friends were able to console her.

About two weeks after Kevin's funeral Louise caught a cold, developed laryngitis and lost her voice. She got over her cold in ten days, but her voice didn't come back. We assured her it would only be a matter of time, that her vocal cords were slow in recovering, but time went by and still Louise talked in a whisper. I referred Louise to an ear, nose and throat specialist; he examined her and said, "Everything's fine. Your vocal cords work just as they should." But Louise still couldn't speak in a normal voice.

Finally I sent Louise to a psychiatrist. After a couple of visits he came to the conclusion that the loss of her voice was hysterical. She was punishing herself for arguing with her husband on the night of his fatal accident. I tried to get this message through to Louise—gently, of course—but she couldn't or wouldn't accept it. For four years she continued to talk in a whisper.

Then Louise developed gall-bladder trouble and I had to remove her gall bladder. After the operation I decided to try something rather unorthodox. "Louise," I said when I visited her the day after surgery, "when we operated on you we had to put a tube into your windpipe to give you the anesthetic. When we did that, I noticed your vocal cords were stuck together just a bit so I spread them apart. I bet that's why you've had to whisper all these years. By tomorrow I think your voice will be back to normal."

Sure enough, when I made rounds the next day Louise was all smiles. She spoke to me in a perfectly normal voice. "It's wonderful, Dr. Nolen," she said. "Spreading those cords did it. Thank you so much."

That was in June 1972, and Louise's voice has remained normal to this day.

I didn't cure her by spreading her cords, but after four years of mourning Louise was ready to forgive herself, and I gave her an excuse for getting her voice back. She didn't think of it this way, of course, but that's the way it worked. The medical literature is full of cures of hysterical symptoms like Louise's.

Patients that go to a Kathryn Kuhlman service, paralyzed from the waist down as the result of injury to the spinal cord, never have been and never will be cured through the ministrations of Miss Kuhlman; Miss Kuhlman cannot cure a paralysis caused by a damaged spinal cord. The patient who suddenly discovers, at a Kuhlman service, that he can now move an arm or a leg that was previously paralyzed had that paralysis as a result of an emotional, not a physical, disturbance. Neurotics and hysterics will frequently be relieved of their symptoms by the suggestions and ministrations of charismatic healers. It is in treating patients of this sort that healers claim their most dramatic triumphs.

There is nothing miraculous about these cures. Psychiatrists, internists, G.P.s, any M.D. who does psychiatric therapy, relieve thousands of such patients of their symptoms every year. Psychotherapy, in which suggestion plays a significant role, is just one of the many tools with which physicians work.

Pseudocyesis (false pregnancy) is an example of the way hysteria can affect not only the menstrual cycle but other organ systems of the body. In *The Making of a Surgeon* I wrote about one such patient, and perhaps the story will bear repeating.

This woman, Roslyn Kaiser, was thirty-five years old. She had been married for twelve years, and despite all sorts of fertility studies and such therapy as was then (1954) available, she had failed to conceive. She was obsessed with a desire to become pregnant and refused to adopt children.

One month she missed her menstrual period and came in to see me about a week after her due date. I was in the Army at the time, at a small hospital in South Dakota. I had had only one year of internship and one year of surgical residency. My only obstetrical training had been in medical school; I'd never even heard of pseudocyesis.

"I suppose it's a false alarm, Dr. Nolen," Roslyn said. "But maybe you could examine me, anyway. I'd like to know."

One week after a missed period is really too soon to tell, by physical examination, if a woman is pregnant, but being young and inexperienced, I thought nothing of it. I examined Roslyn, a rather stocky woman, and couldn't even feel the uterus. But I hated to admit this, so I said, "I can't be sure, Roslyn. It just may be that you are pregnant."

"Oh, my God," Roslyn said. "Do you really think so?"

"I can't be certain," I replied. "Why don't you just come back in another three weeks if you still haven't had a period?"

Roslyn left my office a very excited, hopeful woman. Three weeks later she came back to see me. "Still no period, Dr. Nolen," she said with a big smile. "And now my breasts are getting full and sore. I've been sick every morning. I must be pregnant."

Roslyn convinced me. Because she was so heavy I still couldn't feel her uterus when I did a pelvic examination; but all the other evidence—the swollen breasts, the morning sickness, the continued absence of menstrual periods—supported the diagnosis. I started Roslyn on vitamins and scheduled her for regular monthly checkups.

For seven months I followed Roslyn and her "pregnancy." Except for not being able to feel her uterus, which I continued to attribute to her stocky physique, she had all the usual physiological changes we see in pregnant women. She had an uncomplicated pregnancy.

At eight months, when she came to the hospital for her checkup, I was on vacation. My associate, an experienced G.P., saw her and immediately suspected something was wrong. He ordered an X-ray and, unhappily, found that there was no evidence of a foetus. The diagnosis was pseudocyesis; all of the physical changes that had taken place in Roslyn's body were the result of her emotional stresses, mediated through her autonomic nervous system. Roslyn's was a "hysterical pregnancy," whose long duration was due to the ignorance of her physician—me.

My associate explained to Roslyn, gently, what the true situation was. A few days later she had a menstrual period and in two weeks her breasts were back to normal.

Roslyn adopted a child. Six months after the adoption, her anxiety over pregnancy gone, Roslyn became pregnant—a not uncommon sequence of events.

Separate the mind and the body? Impossible!

Patients who are good subjects can, while under hypnosis, be talked out of symptoms. Aches and pains will disappear promptly, if not permanently, if a forceful person tells the patient that the symptoms will disappear. Mass hypnosis—or mass suggestion, for those who don't like to use the word "hypnosis"—is what Kathryn Kuhlman is using when she persuades patients with backaches to "stand in the aisles and touch your toes; you can do it, you know you can—the Holy Spirit has healed you." Admittedly, the patients who bend and twist at her call are not in a deep stage of hypnosis, but they are in a hyper-suggestible state and that, by definition, is an early stage of hypnosis.

All healers use hypnosis to some extent ("See—your pain is going away. Isn't that wonderful?") and often with success. Making forceful verbal suggestions as one lays on hands or offers prayers works better than the laying on of hands, or prayers used alone.

Doctors use hypnosis, or suggestion, frequently. When I give a patient a pill or a shot, I make a point of saying, "This medicine should make you better in twenty-four or forty-eight hours [or whatever length of time I think is reasonable]. This medicine always works very well." I know that in some cases I'm going to get better results if I suggest to the patient that the medicine will work than I would if I said, "Well, I don't know about this medicine . . . sometimes it works pretty well, sometimes it's not so hot. We'll give it a try and hope for the best." There's a lot to the power of positive thinking, particularly where functional disorders are concerned.

There is a pertinent experiment reported in *Hypnosis Research Developments and Perspectives,* a book edited by Erika Fromm of the University of Chicago and Ronald E. Star of the University of New Hampshire. Thirteen subjects were studied. All were highly allergic to the poisonous leaf of the Japanese wax tree, none were allergic to the nonpoisonous leaves of the chestnut tree.

Five subjects were hypnotized and then blindfolded. They were told that their arm was going to be touched by the nonpoisonous chestnut leaf; in fact, their arms were touched with the poisonous wax-tree leaf. None of the five showed any allergic reaction to the poisonous leaf. They were then told that they would be touched, on the opposite arm, by the poisonous leaf; in fact, they were touched by

277

the nonpoisonous leaf. All five showed a dermatitis as a result of being touched by the nonpoisonous leaf.

We'd probably conclude from this experiment that hypnosis is an amazing phenomenon, except for one thing. The eight remaining patients were blindfolded, and without being hypnotized, the same experiment was carried out. All eight of these patients developed a dermatitis from the touch of the chestnut leaf, and only one of the eight reacted to the poisonous leaf.

If this experiment proves anything—and I think it does—it is that the power of suggestion, with or without hypnotism, can be very effective, particularly in situations, such as skin reactions, where the autonomic nervous system plays an important role.

Suggestion, or hypnotism, can be used in a negative as well as a positive way.

A charismatic person—a healer, for example—might say to a patient, "Unless you pray three times a day for the next week, you will develop a rash over your entire body"; or he might say, "I have received a message from the Lord. He wants you to donate a thousand dollars to my chapel. If you do not donate this sum in the next three days, you are going to be afflicted with severe headaches which will bother you day and night." A patient who believes that the healer has miraculous powers may, indeed, develop these symptoms if he does not follow the healer's instructions. In these instances the healer is using suggestion, or hypnotism, to cause, rather than cure, symptoms.

This negative use of suggestion is prevalent in primitive societies where most of the people have blind faith in the miraculous powers of their witch doctors or healers. The healers lay "curses" on their patients, and the curses work. And just as the healers are the only ones who are authorized by the tradition of the society to inflict curses on the people, so they are the only ones that can take away the curses. "Exorcism" is the label given to the use of suggestion to remove a curse or a "devil."

Even though blind faith in healers is most prevalent in primitive societies, at times we see the same phenomenon in more sophisticated communities. The acceptance of *The Exorcist,* book and film alike, as an authoritative document, shows quite clearly how willing we are to revert to primitive notions. Our society is almost eager to believe in the power of devils and exorcists, even though we know that there is not one shred of evidence that devils exist. The symptoms of every case of possession that has been thoroughly investigated can be rationally explained on the basis of hysteria or some other psychiatric derangement. Indeed, we are not as far removed from primitive society and beliefs as we would like to believe.

Hypnotism is not something with which one should trifle. Relieving symptoms can be dangerous—remember the poor woman whose back pain went away at Kathryn Kuhlman's suggestion, leaving her temporarily free to frolic until her cancerous vertebrae collapsed? Symptoms—pain, nausea, dizziness—may be purely psychological, but they may also be the warning signals of dangerous, possibly life-threatening, organic (as opposed to functional) diseases. To eliminate a symptom without getting at the cause of that symptom can cause delay in treatment which may be serious or even fatal.

25

Now, finally, in our attempt to understand "healing," we must deal with organic diseases—diseases that are caused not simply by dysfunction of an organ but by derangement of the structure of an organ or organs. Infections, heart attacks, gallstones, hernias, slipped discs, cancers of all kinds, broken bones, congenital deformities, lacerations, and multitudes of other diseases and subdivisions of those I've mentioned are included in the organic-disease classification. Some organic diseases are self-limited, i.e., healed by the body itself; the common cold and minor sprains are examples of such ailments. But to cure many organic diseases, the body needs help.

These are the diseases that healers, even the most charismatic, cannot cure. When they attempt to do so—and they all fall into this trap, since they know and care nothing of the differences between functional and organic diseases—they tread on very dangerous ground. When healers treat serious organic diseases they are responsible for untold anguish and unhappiness; this happens because they keep patients away from possibly effective and lifesaving help. The healers become killers.

Search the literature, as I have, and you will find no documented cures by healers of gallstones, heart disease, cancer or any other serious organic disease. Certainly, you'll find patients temporarily relieved of their upset stomachs, their chest pains, their breathing problems; and you will find healers, and believers, who will interpret this interruption of symptoms as evidence that the disease is cured. But when you track the patient down and find out what happened later, you always find the "cure" to have been purely symptomatic and transient. The underlying disease remains.

These organic diseases are the disorders for which M.D.s have something to offer that healers can't match. Usually we can offer help; sometimes we can offer cures.

Take the woman who comes to me with jaundice and pain caused by stones in her gall bladder. Her life is an unhappy one because every time she eats the foods she enjoys, her gall bladder flares up. I operate on her, remove this diseased organ with its stone or stones, and from that time on she is free of her digestive problems. None of the healers can remove a diseased gall bladder for a patient.

Or consider the man who comes to me with diarrhea and hemorrhage caused by a cancer in his bowel. I operate on him, remove the bowel containing the tumor, and his diarrhea and hemorrhage cease. Then years later—perhaps twenty years later—he is alive and healthy, free of the cancer which, untreated, would have killed him. Healers can't cure bowel cancer for their patients.

Take the case of the child who enters the hospital after falling out of a tree. The child is in shock, hemorrhaging massively and rapidly from a ruptured spleen. We rush the child to the operating room, remove the torn and bleeding organ, and tie off the splenic artery and vein that have been pumping blood into the abdominal cavity. Then we transfuse the child with two or three pints of blood, his blood pressure returns to normal levels, and the next day he is up and about, eating, smiling, laughing. Take a child with a ruptured spleen to a healer for treatment and the next day the child will be dead.

Less dramatically, M.D.s use medications to cure patients of serious organic diseases. The man who has had an extensive heart attack goes into heart failure; his internist orders digitalis to strengthen the heartbeat, other drugs to

281

help him eliminate excessive water, and instead of drowning in his own fluids the man lives through his attack and goes on to enjoy a long, comfortable life. In the hands of a healer he would have died.

Take the elderly woman who comes to the hospital hardly able to breathe because of severe pneumonia. Her body has tried to throw off the pneumococcal bacteria that have caused her disease, but the infection has been too overwhelming. So her doctor puts her in an oxygen tent and gives her penicillin, which destroys the pneumonococci. In three days this woman, whose life had been all but snuffed out, is breathing comfortably and is ready to enjoy many more years of comfortable living. Show me the healer who knows anything about the proper cure and management of bacterial infections. If a healer had treated her, this woman would have died.

I could go on and on with these examples, but I think and hope it's unnecessary. The point is simply that medical doctors have the knowledge, training and equipment to treat successfully a multitude of diseases—many of them very dangerous to life and well-being—that healers cannot successfully treat. Of course, some of our patients die—we don't have all the knowledge or skills we'd like to have—but most of them live and get well. The morality in cases of ruptured spleens treated promptly by a surgeon is about 1 percent; the mortality if those cases of ruptured spleens were treated by healers would be 100 percent.

I should point out here that even though cancer is, on the basis of all the evidence now available, an organic disease, it will sometimes, unlike hernia, gallstones, cleft palate, arteriosclerosis and other organic diseases, go away for reasons that are not clear. Occasionally, for example, if a patient with cancer will disappear. We assume that this is because the cancer is caused by a virus and the virus is destroyed by the fever, but as yet we haven't been able to prove that this is the case. When we know more about cancer we should be able to explain, and utilize, whatever it is that causes these spontaneous regressions.

At one time physicians used artificially produced high fevers, induced by injections of Coley's Toxins (an unfiltered mixture of cultures of certain fever-producing bacteria), to treat cancer. The results were unpredictable, only rarely successful, and the treatment was occasionally lethal in itself. In fact, after a period of time it became apparent that the treatment was more dangerous than the disease, and Coley's Toxins are no longer used for cancer treatment.

However, there is hardly a doctor with any sort of extensive practice who has not, at one time or another, either heard of or personally treated a patient with what appeared to be a hopeless case of cancer, only to find after he (the doctor) had given up that the patient had somehow, temporarily or permanently, recovered from that cancer. Drs. Tilden Everson and Warren Cole, the latter a former professor of surgery at the University of Illinois and a former president of the American College of Surgeons, wrote a book in which they reported on 176 documented cases gathered from a review of the world medical literature published between 1900 and 1962. For those who may be interested in reading the book—its title is *Spontaneous Regression of Cancer* and it was published in 1966. (I was certain, after personal inquiry, that spontaneous regression was more common than this book suggested. Most doctors don't report the case, or cases, they see.)

I phoned Dr. Cole, in April of 1974, and asked him if he had any idea, based on his continuing interest in the subject, what the actual incidence of spontaneous regression of cancer might be. Dr. Cole told me, "Excluding those cancers such as leukemia, where it's difficult to differentiate a remission from a regression. I'd estimate that the true incidence of spontaneous regression is somewhere between one in ten thousand and one in a hundred thousand. It's difficult to narrow it down any more than that."

There is another point to make here. Although spontaneous regression has been reported for almost every known type of cancer, it seems to occur most frequently in cases of hypernephroma (kidney cancer), neuroblastoma (a tumor which originates in immature cells found almost exclusively in children), malignant melanoma (a tumor of the pigment cells of the skin or eye) and choriocarcinoma (a tumor of immature cells which grow in the uterus). All of these tumors are probably influenced by hormones, so when we learn more about the effect of hormones on our bodies, we may be able to produce regression in many tumors which are, at the present, beyond our control. To put it another way: we label regression of cancer "spontaneous" because we don't know what causes it. As we learn more about cancer there will probably be fewer "spontaneous regressions" and more induced cures.

I have been a surgeon with a busy practice for fourteen years and in that time I have been lucky enough to treat one patient who falls into the category of spontaneous cures.

In 1964, ten years ago, a general practitioner I'll call Hank Wilbur referred to me a thirty-two-year-old farmer, George Bonham. "George came to me because he'd passed blood in his stool," Hank said. "I got some X-rays and it looks like he has a tumor in the lower sigmoid [the sigmoid is the part of the large bowel just above the rectum]. I'm afraid the damn thing may already have invaded his bladder, since he's got blood in his urine. The radiologist thinks this is a possibility, but he can't be certain."

"Anything in his liver?" I asked.

"I can't feel anything," Hank said. "His liver-function studies are okay."

I examined George, looked at his X-rays, and then called Hank. "I think we'd better explore him," I said. "It certainly looks like cancer. Even if it already has spread to his liver, we ought to try to get it out. Otherwise he'll go on bleeding and I'm sure he'll be obstructed soon. He's almost blocked off now."

After a few days of preparation—low-residue diet, antibiotics to sterilize the bowel, enemas—we operated on

George Bonham. Alas, we had made the correct diagnosis: George had a tumor in the lower sigmoid and it had invaded the bladder. It had also spread to the lymph glands near the blood vessels that ran to the bowel. It was an ugly cancer; not that any cancers are pretty, but I thought I might be able to get it all out, even though I'd have to sacrifice part of his bladder to do so. Hank was assisting me and he agreed we ought to go ahead with the procedure. I ran my hand up over the liver—something surgeons always do after they have entered the abdomen and before they embark on an extensive operation for cancer—and to my great dismay, felt two firm masses, one about three inches, the other two inches in circumference on the left lobe. "Damn," I said, "it's into the liver." This meant we couldn't cure George Bonham with surgery; once a bowel tumor has been spread to the liver, it's impossible to get it all out. The liver cannot be sacrificed.

Hank and I talked the situation over for a couple of minutes and I decided to go ahead with the operation. Death from a bleeding obstructing cancer of the bowel is painful, drawn out, messy—and George, a young man and otherwise robust, might last a long time. Death from tumor in the liver is often relatively painless. We wanted to give George a chance to die in comfort.

The operation was a tedious one. The tumor was stuck to the big blood vessels that deliver blood to the lower extremities and I had to peel it off with great care. I also had to dissect the bowel free from the ureters (the tubes that carry urine from the kidneys to the bladder). Fortunately, everything went smoothly and after an hour and a half I'd removed the bowel containing the cancer, together with a potion of the wall of the bladder into which the tumor had grown. I had also removed the glands near the bowel that had tumor in them. It took me another hour to sew the ends of the bowel together, repair the hole in the bladder and close the incision. Before I closed I took a biopsy—a small piece of tissue—from the larger of the two lumps in the liver. Even though it looked and felt like cancer, we wanted to be as definite as possible when we told George and his wife what the future held for him.

The biopsy was positive: we had left cancer behind in the liver. George made a rapid recovery and ten days after the operation, as he was preparing to go home. I sat down with George and his wife, Carla. I hate these situations, but George, with three young children to think about, had to have all the facts.

"George," I said. "I know you feel well now and I'm delighted. You shouldn't have any more bowel trouble. Unfortunately, as I explained to Carla a few days ago, there was some spread to the liver. We had to leave that behind.

"No one can predict how rapidly that tumor will grow. It may not bother you for two or three years, if we're lucky. Maybe with all the research that's going on we'll come up with a cure before it ever bothers you. No matter how it goes, the best advice I can give you is to take life a day at a time. None of us know what might happen tomorrow."

"Doc," George said, "I appreciate you leveling with me. I wouldn't want it any other way. But I'm going to tell you something—this thing isn't going to kill me. We Bonhams are too damn tough."

Three months after his operation George was back working on his farm when he injured his hand on a piece of barbed wire. George cleaned the wound, put on some iodine and a bandage, and forgot about it until three days later, when he began to run a high fever, could see red streaks running up his arm and feel swollen glands in his armpit. He came to my office and I put him in the hospital. He had infection in his blood—what the layman calls "blood poisoning." I drained an abscess in his hand, started him on antibiotics, and after a week of temperatures running to 103 and 104 degrees, George finally began to get better. By the time he went home, two weeks later, he'd lost twenty pounds. "That was worse than my cancer operation," George told me.

In 1972, eight years after I'd told George he was doomed to die of cancer, George got appendicitis. I operated on him, and since the appendix was only moderately inflamed and I was not concerned about spreading inflammation elsewhere, I stuck my hand up high in the abdomen and felt George's liver: there wasn't a trace of the cancer left.

It's now 1974, ten years since his operation. George's kids are starting college and he's a very successful farmer. He still comes to see me whenever he gets one of the cuts or bruises that are part of a farmer's life, and when he does he always says, "Doc, you're a hell of a good surgeon, but you're sure not much of a fortuneteller." I bet I've heard that line fifty times in the last ten years. It will please me to go on hearing it for the rest of my life.

There are three reasons for this lengthy discussion of cancer.

First, even though we don't yet know all we'd like to know about cancer, we are making strides. We have new drugs, improved operative techniques and sophisticated X-ray equipment that now enable us to cure many patients who, ten years ago, we couldn't help.

For example, three years ago while I was operating on a fifty-four-year-old woman, Florence White, who had been troubled with severe vomiting caused by a tumor that was blocking her small intestine, I found that tumor had already spread to the liver. It had also surrounded some indispensable blood vessels and I couldn't remove it. Instead I used a short-circuiting procedure that would relieve her of vomiting and, temporarily, allow her to eat. I took out a small piece of the tumor from the liver so that the pathologist could make a definite diagnosis, and closed the abdomen.

After the operation I told Mr. White that the outlook was not good. I told him that I'd try treating his wife with 5-fluorouracil, but that the tumor was extensive and I couldn't promise much of a response. If he had asked me how long Mrs. White had to live I'd probably have guessed about six months.

It was fortunate that he didn't ask me because now, after three years on weekly doses of 5-F.U., Mrs. White is still doing very nicely. Every few months I reexamine her and I can still feel the tumor but, if anything, it's smaller now than it was three years ago. The 5-F.U. is, at this time, holding the tumor in check. Ten years ago, before we had this anti-cancer drug, I have little doubt that Mrs. White would have died within six months after her operation.

If research continues as it has, we may in the not too distant future be able to cure or at least control most, possibly all, cancers.

Second, even when we can't promise a cure, even when we think death is inevitable, we may be wrong. Spontaneous regressions do occur now and then, so even if the doctor has nothing to offer, the patient with cancer need never feel completely without hope. Show me the doctor who says with certainty that a patient is doomed, and I'll show you a damn fool.

Now the third point: Don't let one or two isolated cancer regressions mislead you. In the fourteen years I've been in practice I've operated on perhaps 5,600 patients, an average of 400 patients a year. How many of those patients had cancer? I'd have to guess—perhaps 1,400. I've been fortunate enough to see one spontaneous cure; on the other hand, I've cured, by removing their tumors, about 700 out of the 1,400. (If I included skin cancers, I could add perhaps another 200 cancer cases, with 200 cures.)

Now consider Kathryn Kuhlman. In a letter sent to me by Marilyn March, Kathryn Kuhlman's secretary, Ms. March says that Miss Kuhlman conducts "approximately 125 healing services in a years time." Attendance at these services varies; Ms. March mentions that "there are always 7,000 in attendance at the once-a-month services at the Shrine Auditorium [in Los Angeles]"; in Tulsa, Oklahoma, "18,000 people in Mabee Center with 3,000 viewing on closed-circuit TV"; in Atlanta, 8,000; in Ottawa, 16,000. Let's assume that Miss Kuhlman has an opportunity to treat

288

an average of 10,000 patients per service, or 1,250,000 patients a year. We will have to guess, but I think it would be reasonable to say that one third of these patients are cancer victims—about 400,000 cancer victims a year. Miss Kuhlman, therefore, may treat 4,000 times as many cancer patients as I treat in one year, and I have, by national standards, a very busy surgical practice. It would be highly likely that in the approximately 400,000 cancer victims that come to her every year, there might be one patient who would fall into the spontaneous regression category. I know Kathryn Kuhlman (or Norbu Chen, or Tony Agpaoa or any other healer) will never find among the patients she treats a spontaneous cure of a cleft palate, a hernia, gallstones, heart disease, paralysis due to injury, or any of the hundreds of other organic ailments for which patients seek help. What I find most unusual is that there are no well-documented spontaneous cancer cures reported in her books. You'd think, among the millions of cancer patients healers treat, at least one or two would demonstrate a spontaneous regression.

My point, in case I haven't made it clear, is that even if we were to find isolated cases of documented cancer cures in the files of Miss Kuhlman or any other healer, it would prove nothing; isolated spontaneous cures of cancer occur with or without the ministrations of healers. The chances of being cured of cancer by Kathryn Kuhlman or any other healer are the same as the chances of being cured if you do nothing and go to no one at all. To be logical, the cancer patient should go to a healer only if the healer had a cure rate of 50 percent or better—the cure rate physicians can achieve. But cancer patients who go to healers are emotionally distraught and for this reason don't act logically.

Before we end this discussion of organic diseases, I had best make it clear that sometimes diseases have both organic and functional components.

Arthritis is an example. The pain of arthritis—all pain, for that matter—is to a degree functional. Pain is a sensation relayed to the brain by the nervous system and can be relieved by suggestion. But the joint-destruction of arthritis is purely organic.

When I was in California I watched a film that Dr. Edgar Mitchell had made dealing with, among other things, paranormal healing. In it a healer was filmed while treating a woman with the twisted, crippled hands seen frequently in advanced cases of arthritis. The healer stroked the woman's arms, murmuring in a consoling voice, suggesting that the pain would go away. After several strokes the woman looked up, smiling, and said, in effect, "You've done it. There's no more pain. My arthritis is cured."

Later Dr. Mitchell mentioned this scene to me. "We were very lucky, weren't we?" he said. "Imagine catching that scene just as the patient was healed of her arthritis. Wonderful to see, wasn't it?"

I didn't know what to say. I could hardly believe we were talking about the same film. Certainly the woman had said her pain was gone, and I'm sure she had managed to block it out temporarily. But her hands were as twisted and deformed after the healers treatment as they had been before. If Dr. Mitchell actually believed that his film showed a healer curing arthritis—and it was obvious that he did—then he certainly knew very little about arthritis. He was confusing a transient removal of a symptom with the cure of a disease. A lot of believers make this same mistake.

Some diseases which begin as functional disorders become, as they progress, organic.

Consider, again, the duodenal ulcer. In its early stages it can be, and usually is, treated as a functional disorder; the ulcer will heal itself if you can persuade a patient to change his life style. But once a massive hemorrhage begins or a perforation occurs, we are dealing with an organic problem. Changing jobs isn't going to heal the hole in the duodenum or stop the hemorrhage; it's too late for that. Now it's necessary to open the abdomen and put in some stitches or remove part of the stomach.

A dual approach is sometimes necessary in treating diseases which have large elements of both the functional and the organic as their cause. One may try to treat migraine headaches with reassurance and laying on of hands, trying to calm down the nervous system and stop it from triggering the blood vessels into spasms. But if that doesn't work, then we resort to Cafergot, a drug which works directly on the walls of the arteries.

Similarly, it's possible to relieve menstrual pain and irregularity by working on a patient's psyche. The menstrual cycle is particularly susceptible to anxiety, tension, "nerves" in general.

For example, a young unmarried girl came to see me, two weeks overdue, frightened almost to hysteria because she was afraid she was pregnant. I examined her, did a pregnancy test on her urine, and reassured her that she was not pregnant. She cried, she was so relieved, and the next day, her tension gone, her menstrual period began. Every physician has seen dozens of cases of this type.

But when the pain or irregularity in the menstrual cycle doesn't respond to relief of anxiety or tension, then we can resort to hormones. It's nice to correct menstrual irregularity by suggestion, as healers and physicians sometimes do, but it's also nice to know that we have available medicines which, used judiciously, can help those who can't be helped by purely psychological methods.

Healers have neither the knowledge nor the training to administer hormones—or any other medications—effectively and safely. Neither can they perform operations and remove diseased or cancerous organs.

Healers can't cure organic diseases. Physicians can.

26

Volumes have been written about each of the functional and organic diseases, about the interrelationships of the mind and the body, about hypnotism, suggestion, the autonomic nervous system, acupuncture—all the things I've touched on here. It's easy to get carried away by the subject of healing; it's a fascinating phenomenon. But I think I've gone as far in this book as I should, and now it's time to put into focus and perspective the material I've gathered. I think there are some lessons to be learned; I know that in doing the research for this book, I've learned many.

First, I've gotten a better understanding of why intelligent, rational people go to healers. They go to healers because, for one reason or another, the medical profession has let them down.

Sometimes we doctors let our patients down because, quite simply, we have nothing curative to offer. For example, we don't as yet know how to cure multiple sclerosis, widespread cancer or congenital brain disorders. We explain to patients with these diseases that we are truly sorry but we can't help them. No matter how nicely we do this, no matter how logically we explain that no one else, to our knowledge, can help them either, patients sometimes refuse to accept this bad news. So they run off to the healers who never say, "I can't help you." These patients waste their time, their energy and their money, chasing will-o'-the-wisps that don't exist. Sad, but understandable; and there isn't much that anyone can do about it.

A second reason people go to healers—and I hate to admit this, but it's true—is that some healers offer patients more warmth and compassion than physicians do. Sure, we pass out pills and perform operations, but do we really care about the people we treat? The answer, I think is, "Yes, most doctors do care," but too often we get careless and don't show our concern. We're too busy doing other things.

Patients, understandably resent what they interpret as our indifference, and they go to healers like Kathryn Kuhlman or Norbu Chen or David Oligani, who make it a point of showing the compassion that patients want and need. These are the patients doctors shouldn't lose to the healers. Physicians have to be careful not to lose the human touch. The medical profession can take a lesson in compassion from the healers.

A third reason why patients go to healers is that healers do, in fact, help them. Kathryn Kuhlman averts a migraine—Norbu Chen clears up a backache—David Oligani supposedly exorcises a devil and relieves a patient of stomach pains. Patients are pleased with the results the healers achieve; they tell their friends, and the friends, dissatisfied or impatient with their doctors, go to healers too.

We doctors have in the past made the mistake of "putting down" the healers as though they, and those who patronized them, were idiots beneath our contempt. This has been a serious error. The healers are not idiots and neither are those who go to them.

So let us admit that healers do relieve symptoms and may even, as I've already mentioned, cure some functional diseases. They use hypnosis, suggestion if you prefer, just as we M.D.s, to one degree or another, use it. They also encourage patients to think positively and may, by so doing, correct a malfunction of the autonomic nervous system.

I know I've said this before, but it's worth repeating: half the patients who go to the office of a general practitioner have diseases or complaints that are self-limited, e.g., the common cold. No matter what anyone does for these people, they are going to get better. So the healers are going to achieve at least a 50 percent cure rate, even if they do nothing. Add to that 50 percent those patients whom the healers cure of functional disabilities—tension headaches, for example—and they are going to achieve an overall cure rate of 70 percent. We may as well admit this; it's a fact.

What we doctors must do is explain all this to our patients. Tell them we are not miracle men—that nature does a lot more to heal the sick than we do—that, in effect, much of the time patients heal themselves. In the past we've been too busy to tell patients all they have a right to know about their diseases and about healing in general. We've rationalized our point of view by saying, "Without a medical education it's too difficult to understand." And because we've left patients in the dark, they've gone off to healers. In the future we must share our knowledge with our patients.

Finally, we must all realize—and I hope this book may help disseminate that information—that there are certain diseases, many diseases, that physicians and physicians alone can cure. When a patient runs over to the Philippines to have a backache or even multiple sclerosis treated, nothing will be gained except, perhaps, some symptomatic relief, but neither will anything be lost but time and perhaps $3,000. However, if a patient goes to the Philippines, to Kathryn Kuhlman or to any other healer for treatment of a serius organic disease—cancer of the rectum, for example, or a tuberculosis infection of the lung—that patient may well pay for his folly with his life. Tragically, this sort of thing happens every day.

Two years ago I began looking for a healing miracle. When I started my search I hoped to find some evidence that someone, somewhere, had supernatural powers that he or she could employ to cure those patients we doctors, with all our knowledge and training, must still label "incurable."

As I have said before, I have been unable to find any such miracle worker.

So, in a certain sense, I suppose, my two years have been wasted. Yet I hardly feel that's the case.

You see, looking into the healing phenomenon, becoming reacquainted with the interweaving and interdependency of the mind, the nervous system, and the body itself, I have become increasingly aware that all of healing is, in a very real sense of the word, miraculous. God has given us minds, the workings of which we have barely begun to comprehend, and using those minds, we have been able to find the answers to many of the puzzling disorders that afflict us. We have been able to extend our life span and raise the quality of our lives. Admittedly, we've created some new problems and haven't even begun to solve all the old. But we have made a start, and there's every reason to believe that if we persist, we will eventually find cures for many more of the diseases, physical and mental, that still afflict us.

What I've learned, and I hope I've been able to communicate something of this feeling, is that we don't need to seek out miracle workers if we're ill. To do so is, in a way, an insult to God.

Our minds and bodies are miracle enough.

HERE'S TO YOUR HEALTH!

A compendium of useful titles from Fawcett Books.